Defending
Your Faith

Also by Dan Story

Christianity on the Offense:
*Responding to the Beliefs and
Assumptions of Spiritual Seekers*

Engaging the Closed Minded:
Presenting Your Faith to the Confirmed Unbeliever

RELIABLE ANSWERS FOR A
NEW GENERATION OF
SEEKERS AND SKEPTICS

Defending
Your Faith

Dan Story

Kregel
Publications

Defending Your Faith: Reliable Answers for a New Generation of Seekers and Skeptics

Copyright © 1997 by Dan Story

Published by Kregel Publications, a division of Kregel, Inc., P.O. Box 2607, Grand Rapids, MI 49501.

Cover design: John M. Lucas

Library of Congress Cataloging-in-Publication Data
Story, Dan.
  Defending your faith: reliable answers for a new generation of seekers and skeptics / Dan Story.
     p.   cm.
  Originally published: Nashville: Thomas Nelson, © 1992.
  Includes bibliographical references and index.
  1. Apologetics. I. Title.
BT1102.S76   1997   239—dc21   97-30358
                                                 CIP

ISBN 0-8254-3674-5

Printed in the United States of America

1 2 3 4 5 / 07 06 05 04

To my wife, Lisa,
my champion,
my encourager,
my kindest critic

Contents

Acknowledgments

I wish to express my deep appreciation to my daughter, Jody, for her skillful proofreading and her keen eye for typos and wandering commas.

I also want to thank Drs. John Warwick Montgomery, Rod Rosenbladt, R. C. Sproul, and John Weldon, as well as Elliot Miller for taking the time to review my apologetic booklets, the material from which this book is largely derived.

To all of you, may God bless your ministries.

Introduction

A few years ago, I was asked by a Sunday school teacher to visit her class in order to deal with some questions she could not answer. I thought her request was odd. She taught fifth and sixth grade boys and girls. What theological questions could possibly interest ten- and eleven-year-old kids or be too difficult for their teacher to handle?

I agreed to the visit but suggested she have the children write in advance the questions they wanted answered. At their age, I assumed it would be difficult for them to think of relevant questions on the spot. I envisioned them asking such questions as, Were dinosaurs on the ark? How did Jesus walk on water? How old is God? Does God have a beard? Does God eat dinner? When I received their list, I realized how wrong I was.

I saved their questions, and I would like to share with you word-for-word what some of the children asked. It turned out that virtually all of their questions were apologetic in nature. That is, they were concerned with a rational understanding and defense of the Christian faith. For example, they asked "How will we know He [Jesus] is real?" "How do we know that Jesus is the true Son of God, and He died on the cross?" "How will we know that the Bible is real?" "How do we know that God really wrote the Bible?" "Who made God?" "If Adam and Eve did not sin, what would it [the world] be like?" And my favorite, "Who made the maker of the maker of God?"

I was surprised at how sophisticated these questions were and how they parallel the kinds of questions adults usually ask. Later I shared them at a Christian education meeting. The teachers' responses didn't surprise me at all. Most of them remarked, "I would like to know the answers to those questions myself!"

I have discovered over the years that the vast majority of Christians, even theologically literate ones, are virtually ignorant when it comes to understanding and applying the evidences for historic Christianity. Today's average Christian is easily plowed under by the arguments of skeptics, critics, and cultists. This is a dangerous situation. Over the centuries, apologetics has played a crucial role in protecting the church against intellectual attacks and fraudulent religious claims. Every generation has witnessed renewed challenges to the faith, often spawned by prevailing misbeliefs, and every generation has witnessed the Lord raise up faithful apologists to defend orthodoxy.

In our time the average Christian has access to an amazing amount of diverse information. Knowledge and claims to truth wash upon us through education, newspapers, television, movies, magazines, radio, and other forms of communication. Sometimes these sources convey truth and support Christianity. But more often they are used to propagate false theologies. These beliefs are frequently dressed in appealing—if not deceptive—garb; many of them claim to be kindred souls of Christianity, the very world view they undermine while appealing to it to give themselves credibility.

It would take superhuman effort on the part of local churches to confront every spurious religion or philosophy that comes down the pike and to warn believers of their dangers. Consequently, at no time in church history has there been such a need for you and I—ordinary Christians—to rally to the defense of Christianity. We are confronted by a host of counterfeit religions and anti-Christian philosophies, which demand that each of us be prepared to "contend earnestly for the faith which was once for all delivered to the saints" (Jude 3).

The vast array and spread of information is not the only factor which has led to an unprecedented proliferation of non-Christian ideologies and anti-Christian attacks. The other critical factor is the intellectual orientation of our society. We no longer live in a society that filters deviant world views through the sieve of Christianity. We live today in what many historians refer to as a "pluralistic" and "post-Christian" world. What they mean is that Christianity has ceased to be the dominant force controlling Western culture's religious beliefs and practices, moral standards, and other social norms. A host of other religions and philosophies are vying for the position Christianity once held.

As a result, more and more nonbelievers (and even believers) are questioning Christianity's authenticity and demanding proof of its truthfulness. They want to know why we believe Jesus Christ is God and what evidence we have for the biblical plan of salvation. They want to understand the Trinity, know why evil exists, and know what happens to people who have never heard of Jesus when they die. If Christians are not prepared to answer these and other questions, non-Christians will assume we don't have the answers. Unfortunately, most of us are unprepared to answer such questions. In fact, we want answers to the very same questions!

So I have written this book for two reasons. First, I want to help Christians such as yourself to see that Christianity is a reasonable and intelligent faith grounded on objective, verifiable evidence. I pray the Holy Spirit will use the contents of this book to reaffirm and strengthen your faith, to remove any doubts you may have about the authenticity of Christianity. In this way apologetics can spur you on to spiritual maturity.

Second, I have written this book as a tool for evangelism. Its information is designed to be shared with family members, friends, and co-workers who are critical of Christianity or who simply want honest, reliable answers to their questions about the truthfulness of our faith. If you feel uncomfortable or unequipped to "give a defense" (1 Pet. 3:15) of Christianity but have a heart to share and defend our Lord Jesus Christ, this book can help you.

What lies ahead in the following chapters is not exhaustive; every answer to every challenge against Christianity is not laid out here. However, you will find good, reasonable, honest answers to the questions and issues most often raised. If you strive to master this material, you will be prepared to defend your faith against the vast majority of criticisms you'll ever hear. So let's press ahead. A dying world needs answers, and we have the answers she needs.

1

Why Does God Want Our Defense?

I am a Christian apologist. When people discover that, they often make the joke, "Do you *apologize* for being a Christian?" Or, the runner up, "What are you *apologizing* for?" Although said in jest, their comments reveal the fact that the word *apologetics* and its role in the Christian life are foreign to many believers. In fact, after I explain that an apologist defends Christianity against objections, some people respond, "Why does God need our defense? He has the Holy Spirit to convict and convince unbelievers; He doesn't need 'evidences.'"

Before we go any further, we need to understand one thing: God doesn't *need* anything from us, much less a defense. The Bible is very clear about this. God "gives to all life, breath, and all things" (Acts 17:25). We need Him, even to keep breathing moment by moment, since He sustains all of creation in existence (Col. 1:17). But there's nothing we have that He needs.

So let's rephrase the question. Does God *want* our defense? Does He want us to exert time and energy offering evidence to support the validity of Christianity?

If not, apologetics is at best a waste of time and at worse interferes with the ministry of the Holy Spirit. On the other hand, if the Holy Spirit uses apologetics to convict and convince people of the truth, it is vital that we arm ourselves from the apologetic arsenal accumulated by the church over the past two millenniums.

Our first task, then, is to discover what apologetics is and what an apologist does, so we can answer the question, "Does God want our defense and, if so, why?"

COMING TO TERMS

The term *apologetics* is derived from the Greek word *apologia*, which is found seven times in the New Testament (Acts 22:1; 25:16; 1 Cor. 9:3; Phil. 1:7, 16; 2 Tim. 4:16; 1 Pet. 3:15). The English equivalent of *apologia* is *defense* (literally, "a speech for the defense"), and it's translated that way in 1 Peter 3:15 in the New American Standard and New King James versions of the Bible. In the original Greek language, *apologia* had a definite legal connotation. It was a technical term in ancient Greek law.[1] When *apologia* is used in the New Testament, it describes a public defense of the gospel, as illustrated in Acts 22:1. Sometimes, in fact, this defense was carried out in a court of law (Acts 25:16; 2 Tim. 4:16).

Of course, apologetics didn't die out in the first century when the apostles left the scene. Christianity came under attack from numerous sources, so many believers took up the challenges and answered them with all the intellectual resources available. As a result of their courageous efforts, Christianity finally won political acceptance in the fourth century—a victory that allowed Christianity to spread throughout the world until even our own day.[2]

Over the centuries, the apologetic discipline has been understood in a variety of ways. But perhaps one of the best definitions in our time flowed from the mind of the late Edward John Carnell, former Professor of Apologetics at Fuller Theological Seminary. According to Carnell, apologetics "is that branch of Christian theology which answers the question, Is Christianity rationally defensible?"[3] In other words, can Christianity be defended (and therefore substantiated) by using the same procedures reasonable people everywhere use to determine the truthfulness of anything—whether it be a scientific, historical, legal, philosophical, or religious question? For example, can Christians defend the authenticity and authority of the Bible? Can they demonstrate that the Bible contains accurate and truthful information and does not contradict itself? Can Christians defend their claim that Jesus Christ is God incarnate (that He took on bodily form) and that Jesus "died for our sins . . . and that He was buried, and that He rose again the third day according to the Scriptures" (1 Cor. 15: 3–4)? Can Christianity stand the test of critical scrutiny?

Although believers have answered yes to these questions, they have offered different arguments with differing assumptions. In part this has been the consequence of two broad and opposing approaches to apologetics. The differences between these approaches are very important. As we'll see, they impact what we defend, how we defend it, and why. The two approaches are presuppositional and evidential.

PRESUPPOSITIONAL APOLOGETICS

The presuppositional approach to apologetics says that any defense of Christianity must begin with the assumption that God exists and that the Bible is His authentic and authoritative Word. A presuppositionalist will not attempt to demonstrate these two truths; instead he will assume their validity and build on them without ever accepting any challenges against them. Why? Because of his view of humanity and the effects of sin.

The presuppositionalist argues this way: Human rebellion against God caused a fundamental rift to occur between God and man. This rift was so traumatic and devastating that it rendered human beings incapable of responding to and thinking clearly about their Creator. The only way these terrible consequences can be overcome is by God reaching out to us, redeeming and restoring us to our right minds and a right relationship with Him. Until He does that, however, we are not capable of accepting or even understanding Christianity, much less accurately considering whether its claims to truth are really valid or not. Consequently, the presuppositionalist contends that any attempt to present evidence supporting the truth-value of the gospel is wrong and actually muddies the water of good dialogue between Christians and non-Christians. You don't present evidences supporting Christianity until *after* the non-Christian has accepted the existence of God and the authority of Scripture and possibly even Jesus as Lord and Savior. Put another way, apologetics for the presuppositionalist is preaching to non-Christians and discipling to Christians. Evidences for the faith fall on deaf ears with nonbelievers, so you should simply share the gospel message with them while you draw on the faith's facts to strengthen the belief of believers.

EVIDENTIAL APOLOGETICS

Evidential apologists strongly disagree with the presupposition-alist approach. They insist that non-Christians deserve to hear and can understand the case for Christianity. And when nonbelievers voice intellectual objections (real or imagined), they should receive concrete, verifiable answers that support the authenticity and authority of Christianity. We live in a world with many contradicting beliefs and claims. If we don't provide answers to the non-Christian's objections, he will assume we don't have any answers, so he'll seek religious truth elsewhere. Too much is at stake to allow this to happen, especially when we have the evidential resources to provide adequate answers to honest questions.

Presuppositional vs. Evidential Apologetics

Presuppositional	Evidential
Subjective	Objective
Assumes God exists	Offers evidence for the existence of God
Assumes Bible true	Offers evidence for the reliability of the Bible
Holy Spirit convicts and convinces people of the truth *only* through the Bible and personal testimony	Holy Spirit *also* convicts and convinces people of the truth through extra-biblical evidences
Evangelizes by appealing *only* to the Bible; does not attempt to overcome objections to Christianity	Evangelizes by *also* appealing to extra-biblical evidences; seeks to overcome objections to convince nonbelievers of gospel's truthfulness

WHICH APPROACH IS BEST?

You can probably already tell which approach I side with. Though one can find dedicated, thoughtful Christians on each side of this debate, the evidentialist approach has a much longer track record in church history, and I think it has several advantages over the presuppositional approach. Indeed, I have found the evidential approach much more dependable and most likely to bear fruit in witnessing situations. Let me explain.

The presuppositional view takes the steam out of evangelism. If non-Christians really are unwilling or even unable to understand revealed truth, then when they ask us questions, we should say, "Sorry, I cannot answer your questions. You just have to accept Christianity on 'faith,' and later, if God wishes, you will just know in your heart that it is true. Even if I gave you an answer now, you will still not believe the truth of Christianity." A consistent presuppositionalist must respond this way. Put yourself in the place of the non-Christian who already doubts the authenticity of Christianity. How would you respond to the presuppositionalist? Would you find his answer satisfactory? Not likely. And why should you? If someone told you to accept a view different from Christianity and to embrace it on faith with no evidence, would you? Christianity would see few converts on the presuppositionalist approach.

Another problem with this position is that it assumes the Holy Spirit is unable to minister and convict through Christian evidences. It limits God to working only subjectively in the lives of unbelievers. This is absurd, unbiblical, and contrary to reality. Many Christians contribute their ultimate acceptance of Jesus as Lord and Savior to objective means such as unpleasant circumstances in their lives, Christian literature other than the Bible, the testimonies of others, and even the presentation of confirming factual evidence.[4] Moreover, the writers of Scripture commonly used evidential apologetic methods with non-Christians, as we will soon see. Although we'll look in detail at the role of the Holy Spirit in apologetics shortly, it seems clear enough that He uses a vast variety of means to bring people to salvation, and that variety mix includes objective evidence.

One other serious problem with presuppositionalism is that it can be turned against itself. If I presuppose God exists, and I ask you to presuppose that too, what's to keep you from saying, "Well I presuppose that God does *not* exist, and I think you should presuppose that also. In fact, I think Christianity is a man-made religion and the Bible is a mythical book. Why should I—or, for that matter, you—presuppose differently?" That's a great question. And if I was a presuppositionalist, I could give no reason against accepting your position. You see, simply because you or I claim something is true doesn't make it so. Presuppositions don't justify or authenticate themselves anymore than you can lift yourself into the air without outside help. Presuppositions need outside help too and that must come in the form of supporting evidence—reasons to accept them as true. Without such help, we have no way to determine which presuppositions are correct. Let me put this another way.

Because we live in a world that embraces a profusion of opposing world views, people have an incredible smorgasbord of options. When religious convictions clash—when contradicting beliefs all declare to reflect divine truth—logic says that only one side can be right. But which set of beliefs should someone accept? Without any clear, objective way of choosing, we might throw up our arms in despair and reject all religions, believing that there is no way to intelligently discern which, if any, really is true. Or we might arbitrarily choose one, or even sample several options to try and discover what we like best. But then truth would be abandoned in favor of personal preference. Our only real hope is to have some way of examining the qualifications of the various contenders to determine which religion can validate its claims. Presuppositionalism can't provide that criteria, but evidentialism can.

Finally, because apologetics is directed to *unbelievers,* it must start where they are. Unbelievers reject Christianity for any number of reasons, but presuppositional apologetics demands they accept the truth of the Bible *before* communication can begin. Evidential apologetics, on the other hand, meets non-Christians where they are and seeks to meet their challenges to Christianity. The evidentialist opens the door for dialogue, whereas the presuppositional shouts through a closed door, telling all who knock that the door will remain shut and locked until they accept the validity of the very beliefs they question. Which invitation would you accept?

So which apologetic approach is best? The evidentialist one, and that is the approach I'll take throughout this book.

A JOB DESCRIPTION

The task of apologetics, then, is to give a reasoned defense of historic, biblical Christianity. As R. C. Sproul explains, apologetics demonstrates "why Christians are Christians and why non-Christians should be Christians."[5] In order to do this, we need to learn what an unbeliever believes and what obstacles are preventing him from seriously considering Christianity. Once we identify these obstacles, we can attempt to overcome them through the appropriate means. Intellectual objections require intellectual answers; emotional problems require emotional support and sensitivity. The apologetic job description is no mystery: communicate Christian truths to non-Christians in such a way that they will listen; the goal is always evangelistic—to lead non-Christians to a saving relationship with Jesus Christ. Apologetics is not preaching. But apologetics does clear the way for the proclamation of the Christian message. You might say, if Jesus is the message, apologetics is the John the Baptist to Jesus; it rids the path of obstacles to the Savior as it points to Him as the one and only way.

I will expand on this job description as we move ahead, but I want to emphasize here that the responsibility of giving a reasoned defense of Christianity is *not* the job of a select few theologians who specialize in apologetics. The Bible makes it clear that the job of defending Christianity belongs to every Christian and that all of us should be prepared to do this at any time. In 1 Peter 3:15, the apostle Peter instructs us to always be "ready to give a defense (*apologia*) to everyone who asks you a reason for the hope that is in you." Just as all Christians are called to evangelize, so all are called to defend their faith.

Jude supports Peter's exhortation and expands on it too. He tells us to "contend earnestly for the faith which was once for all delivered to the saints" (Jude 3). In his letter, Jude instructs his readers to defend

Christianity against the false teachings that were arising in the church. So not only are we to defend Christianity against the attacks of those who distance themselves from Christianity (such as atheists and skeptics), but we are to defend it against those who call themselves friends of the faith while undermining its historic, orthodox teachings (two examples would be Mormons and Jehovah's Witnesses).

WHY THE EFFORT?

This may sound like a lot of effort. And frankly, it is. So why do it? Don't we have enough to do already? Trying to understand our spouse, raising our kids, hacking our way through school, maintaining our sanity on the job, paying the bills, finding time to pray and study the Bible. . . . And now you want to add one more responsibility? I'm afraid so. But please note this, and this is extremely important: *God* commands you and I to defend the faith; it's not my idea. The passages cited above from 1 Peter and Jude are enough to confirm that.

"Okay," you might say. "Granted God tells me to give reasons for my faith and answer challenges to it. If I do that, what's the payoff? What will it accomplish?" More than you or I could ever imagine, but let me give you a taste.

GLORIFIES GOD

The foremost purpose of apologetics is to bring glory to God by honoring and serving His Son, Jesus Christ. The apostle Paul tells us that "whatever you do, do all to the glory of God" (1 Cor. 10:31). Elsewhere he adds, "whatever you do in word or deed, do all in the name of the Lord Jesus, giving thanks through Him to God the Father" (Col. 3:17, NASV). By defending the truths of God, we defend His honor and name.

EXONERATES CHRISTIANITY

Challenges to the faith may come in the form of a false religion claiming to supersede Christianity as the one true religion. They may come from secular humanism or atheistic evolution, which claim God doesn't exist and all religions are human creations. They may come from Mormons or Jehovah's Witnesses canvassing the neighborhood. Or they may flow from your next-door neighbor in the form of objections to the Jesus of the Gospels. No matter what form challenges take, when apologetics confronts them effectively, it exonerates Christianity.

STRENGTHENS BELIEVERS

Many Christians are comfortable in their faith and don't feel a need to corroborate it with evidence. This is certainly admirable. Jesus Himself said to doubting Thomas, who demanded "proof" that Jesus rose from the grave: "because you have seen Me, you have believed. Blessed are those who have not seen and yet have believed" (John 20:29). But even Jesus provided Thomas with the evidence he desired (vv. 24–27).

Likewise, many of us desire the affirmation of apologetics to strengthen our faith. Much of the world rejects Jesus Christ as God and all the other major tenets of the Christian faith. Believers are confronted with non-Christian ideologies that contradict or attempt to refute our sacred beliefs. God can and does use apologetics to help believers whose faith is wavering and to ease the suffering caused by doubt. Apologetics can be especially reassuring to new believers seeking to rationally justify their step of faith. It is a wonderful and joyful experience to discover that our faith is firmly grounded on objective truths that are confirmed by sensible, verifiable evidence.

MAKES CHRISTIANITY RELEVANT

Although many of the current attacks against Christianity are the same as those that confronted the early church, nevertheless, each generation has its own set of particular objections. And Christians of each generation have a responsibility to address those objections.

Cultures and societies change, so we shouldn't expect the problems of this generation to be the same as the former one or the next. For example, second-century apologists debated pagans who accused Christians of atheism, incest, and cannibalism (because believers claimed to "eat" the body of Christ). Obviously, second-century unbelievers either misunderstood or purposely perverted the true meaning of certain Christian beliefs and practices. Today, these accusations against Christians are nonexistent.

On the other hand, twentieth-century apologists deal with issues that didn't plague the second-century church. Today's unique apologetic challenges include philosophical naturalism (the belief that nothing exists outside the material world, including the supernatural) and the various New Age philosophies that have evolved out of Eastern pantheism. We also have to confront the thoroughly unchurched, non-religious individuals who have little outward concern for spiritual things and no interest at all in Christianity. At the other extreme, we find militant secular humanists—people out to rid society of any remnant of Christianity. We even have to deal with a host of heretical cults that try to appear Christian while subverting the orthodox understanding of the faith.

We certainly have much to handle, but apologetics provides the resources we need to meet these challenges head-on.

EVANGELIZES THE LOST

The final purpose I'll touch on is what apologetics does for evangelism.

Christianity has a lot of competitors. Many millions of people worldwide are bypassing Christianity and sampling as well as aligning themselves with cults and other false religions. Bouncing from one unhealthy and unfulfilling ideology to another, Christianity is just another item on the menu of available religions. So tempting is the smorgasbord of religious beliefs that even many Christians are tasting these religious flavors. Some Christians bring these erroneous ideas into the church, while others abandon the faith altogether. Sadly, many of those who join the cults come from the Christian church.

In light of this, the purpose of apologetics is to lay a factual foundation for faith so non-Christians searching for spiritual truth will find good reasons to believe. We must do more than try to "out shine" other beliefs. We must, on the one hand, give convincing reasons why other religions are fraudulent, and, on the other hand, give convincing reasons why Christianity is authentic. Apologetics involves not only defending Christianity against skeptics and critics but also challenging the truth-claims of other world views and religions.

If we do our job well, we will present such compelling evidence for Christianity that if one chooses to reject Jesus Christ, he will know why he is doing so. He will not be able to cite intellectual reasons because the overwhelming preponderance of evidence endorses Christianity. He will realize, however, that his rejection of the faith is based on his unwillingness to make the sacrifices that a commitment to Christ will ultimately convict him to do. His unbelief is ultimately moral and willful, not intellectual. Once he sees this, we have done our job as an apologist. And, hopefully, the unbeliever will be ready to listen to why he needs Jesus Christ and how Jesus will change his life if he will only let Him.

WHAT DOES THE BIBLE SAY?

Now that we know what apologetics is, why the evidential approach is best, and what apologetics can do, let's make sure it has a firm foundation in the Christian's most important book—the Bible.

Apologetics played an essential part in the spread and life of the early church, we can see that in the Scriptures. In fact, much of the New Testament was written as an apologetic response to challenges to Christianity. We can see this in the evangelistic endeavors of the apostles and even in the ministry of Jesus. Let's take a look, beginning with Jesus.

JESUS AS AN APOLOGIST

Unlike many Christians today, who think their only responsibility in evangelism is to give the plan of salvation along with their personal testimony, Jesus spent much of His time answering questions and rebuking the religious leaders for their distortion of God's Word. When Jesus was questioned by the Pharisees, Sadducees, Herodians, and others who wanted to discredit Him, He never hesitated to argue for the truth of Scripture. Throughout His ministry, Jesus endorsed His divine credentials with "proofs" (signs and wonders; see John 5:36; 20:30–31). For example, Jesus proved His divine right to forgive sins by healing a paralytic (Luke 5:17–24).

The most explicit example of Jesus' offering evidence to support His claim to deity is His response to doubting Thomas. In John 20, Jesus first appears to the other disciples before He appears to Thomas (vv. 19–24). When the disciples tell Thomas they have seen the Lord alive, Thomas responds, "Unless I see in His hands the print of the nails, and put my finger into the print of the nails, and put my hand into His side, I will not believe" (v. 25). In a word, Thomas would not accept the good news of the risen Christ unless he had empirical proof.

How did Jesus respond? Did He ignore Thomas and turn away from him because he wanted evidence for belief? Did He say that Thomas's desire for proof was a sign of spiritual immaturity? Not at all. Instead, our Lord gave Thomas exactly the kind of evidence he requested; He responded specifically to Thomas's particular obstacle to faith. He appeared to Thomas and invited him to examine the signs of His crucifixion. Thomas was immediately convinced and pronounced the very words that Jesus calls all unbelievers to utter: "My Lord and my God!" Afterwards, Jesus reminded Thomas that he should have accepted the testimony of the other disciples, but Jesus first gave Thomas the evidence he needed to encourage a step of faith.

THE APOSTLES AS APOLOGISTS

Like Jesus, the apostles actively used apologetics in their evangelism. They gave their personal testimonies, not to evangelize or defend Christianity, but to *confirm* their message. In the Book of Acts, the apostle Paul furnishes the most explicit examples of this.

Paul's custom was to "reason" with the Jews in the synagogues of the various cities he visited. In Acts 19:8, for example, Paul "went into the synagogue and spoke boldly for three months, *reasoning* and *persuading* concerning the things of the kingdom of God" (emphasis mine). In Acts 26:1, Paul stood before Agrippa and "proceeded to make his defense" (NASV; see Phil. 1:16). Perhaps the best example of New Testament apologetics is Paul's defense of Jesus' resurrection before the Greek philosophers at the Areopagus (Acts 17:16–31). Paul builds his case for Christ by appealing to the Greeks' sense of reasoning, to empirical evidences, and even to their own poets (v. 28).

The apostles used many other apologetic techniques as well to make their case. They referred to eyewitness accounts (1 John 1:1), well-known historical data (Luke 3:1–2), the common knowledge of their audience (Acts 26:26), fulfilled Old Testament prophecy (v. 22), and legal reasoning (25:16). The apostles also instructed their followers to defend the gospel as they did (see 2 Tim. 2:24–26; 4:2–5; Titus 1:9–14).

IS APOLOGETICS NECESSARY?

In spite of all this support for doing apologetics, many Christians hold on to the belief that apologetics is anti-faith and anti-Holy Spirit. These Christians think apologetics is unnecessary because they claim that (1) non-Christians don't need it as a foundation for a step of faith, and (2) in evangelism the Holy Spirit works only as an agent of conviction when one gives his personal testimony and shares the plan of salvation right from Scripture.

These claims disturb me. They reveal a lack of understanding of apologetics' role in evangelism and the Holy Spirit's work in the lives of unbelievers. This is such an important issue that I want to spend some time commenting on it. Here's why I reject this.

Consider the first objection, that apologetics plays no important role in an unbeliever's step of faith. Underlying this is a confusion between faith and reason. The argument goes something like this: A person becomes a Christian by accepting Jesus Christ as Lord and Savior only by faith. If reason is involved, the faith element is missing. Consequently, any attempt to reason a person into accepting Jesus is at best a useless endeavor and at worst is unspiritual—it usurps the power and authority of the Holy Spirit. A person cannot be argued into the kingdom.

I do not deny that people are ultimately saved by a step of faith. Nor do I question the fact that innumerable people have become Christians without ever questioning the truth of Christianity. I'll even admit that the most sophisticated and thorough apologetic arguments provide probable, not air-tight, evidence for Christianity's truth-claims. On the other hand, I side with Clark Pinnock when he says, "The notion that nobody is ever converted to Christ by argument is a foolish platitude."[6] The fact is, reason and faith are inseparable—you cannot have one without the other. Let me explain what I mean.

First, Christianity affirms that we were created with a free will, the ability to choose. Therefore, any of us can refuse to accept evidences for Christianity no matter how compelling they are. Furthermore, if a person insists on having absolute proof that Jesus is Lord and Savior, he will never get it. Absolute proof, in the sense that most critics mean it, would necessitate Jesus Himself physically confronting every unsaved person face-to-face and demonstrating, as He did to Thomas, that He really is the risen Lord. That just doesn't happen. So somewhere along the pilgrimage to salvation, a person must accept Christ on faith—she must trust in Him with the evidence available.

However, God is the author of human reason just as He is the author of our faith. Although because of the Fall, human sin has weakened our ability to reason (see Eph. 4:18), this faculty is not so impaired that we cannot make rational decisions or discern truth from error. Otherwise, any attempt God would have made to communicate to us would have been in vain, for none of us would ever have been able to understand Him. But Scripture reveals that shortly after the Fall, God looked for Adam in the Garden. In spite of Adam's recent separation from God through sin, he still heard God call him and understood precisely what God was saying. The Fall "did not render Adam incapable of comprehending a word from God. Had it done so, subsequent divine revelation would have been impossible in principle."[7]

The foremost commandment, according to Jesus, is to "love the LORD your God with all your heart, with all your soul, with all your *mind,* and with all your strength" (Mark 12:30, emphasis mine; see Deut. 6:5). Our minds are an important part of our love and acceptance of the Lord. God created us as rational creatures capable of processing and understanding data. In fact, by virtue of being created in God's image, our ability to think is a God-given attribute that separates human beings from all other creatures. This is why things need to make sense to us if we are to accept them. We violate our created human nature when we embrace something that our mind rejects as irrational. This is one source of nagging doubts.

Am I saying that faith is dependent on reason? No. But I am saying that faith is impossible without knowledge, and knowledge comes through our ability to reason. Faith and knowledge are bedfellows; they are not enemies. Is it possible to become a Christian without understanding what Christianity is all about? The apostle Paul didn't think so: "How then shall they call upon Him in whom they have not believed? And how shall they believe in Him whom they have not heard? And how shall they hear without a preacher? . . . So faith comes from hearing, and hearing by the word of Christ" (Rom. 10: 14, 17, NASV).

The Bible clearly teaches that knowledge is needed prior to salvation. Historically, the church has never separated knowledge from belief. The goal of Christian apologetics (indeed, the goal of all evangelism) is not to coerce a person into accepting Christ on blind faith but to lead him to make an *informed* decision for the Lord. The kind of faith believers receive from the Holy Spirit is an intelligent faith. Our apologetic job is to help unbelievers arrive at saving faith by appealing to their God-given capacity to reason. When one takes the step from intellectual evidences to emotional certainty, he has taken a step of faith. Not blind faith, but faith resting on a foundation of facts.

FAITH	REASON
God the Source	God the Source
Act of Will	Act of Mind
Believes Truth	Knows Truth
Involves Trust	Involves Logic and Evidence
Founded on Fact	Deals with Facts
Rejects Contradictions	Exposes Contradictions
Consistent with Reason	Consistent with Faith
End of Reason	Beginning of Faith
Guides Reason	Affirms Faith

Now let's consider the second and closely related objection: the Holy Spirit acts as an agent of conviction only when one shares his testimony and witnesses directly from Scripture. There are no biblical grounds for this belief, and it flies in the face of what we observe in the ordinary world. As I already pointed out, an untold number of Christians can testify to the work of the Holy Spirit in their lives through unpleasant circumstances and other life experiences, through Christian literature other than the Bible, through observing the lifestyles of Christians, and through a variety of other methods. In other words, the Holy Spirit convicts anyway He deems best for the individual He is calling.

Christians, then, need to understand that the Holy Spirit can also work just as effectively and actively through the medium of apologetics as He can through the "Four Spiritual Laws" or any other structured presentation of the biblical plan of salvation. As Edward Carnell puts it, "when one defends his faith, he is not in competition with the Holy Spirit. The Spirit of God draws men *through* the convicting power of evidences."[8]

What a preacher or an apologist says doesn't bring a person to saving faith or cause a sinner to repent, no matter what a fine orator one is or how trained in theology or the art of evangelism one happens to be (see John 16:7–15). The Holy Spirit is the agent of salvation, and He can just as easily use a well-presented apologetic defense to overcome an obstacle to faith as the most eloquent sermon. The words of a preacher or an apologist are only as good as the degree to which the Holy Spirit has prepared a person to receive them (see Acts 16:14). Consequently, the claim that apologetics is void of the Holy Spirit is simply theologically naive. It puts God in a box by limiting the ability of the Holy Spirit to work through any circumstance or message He chooses. Our responsibility is to create an environment in which the Holy Spirit is set free to work in the lives of non-Christians regardless of the obstacles that separate them from accepting the love of Jesus Christ. We must convey saving truth to them. The Holy Spirit's responsibility is to open their hearts and minds so they will be willing to receive it.

THE BOTTOM LINE

Christianity is not a *mystical* religion, such as many Eastern religions and their New Age clones. Neither is it a *mythical* religion with idols and man-made gods. Nor is Christianity a *misinformed* religion, such as the various cults. Rather, Christianity is an historic religion, and its truth-claims are grounded on objective, historical facts.

When God came to earth as the incarnate Son, Jesus, He did so in a discernible way. It was a space/time advent perceptible by ordinary senses. Jesus was a physical man, and His deeds, including His resurrection, were witnessed by ordinary people (see 1 Cor. 15:6). His coming was not an esoteric event seen by a privileged few. His advent and the documents that record and comment on it can be checked out by the normal methods of investigation.

This book is written to do just that. In the remaining chapters, I will present historical, legal, scientific, and other concrete, verifiable evidences for the central claims of Christianity. And you will be able to take these evidences into the marketplace of religious ideas and philosophical assumptions and use them to defend the faith and the hope that lies in each of us who believe.

2

How Do We Know
God Exists?

Only a small fraction of the world's population question the existence of a deity. In fact, the belief in supernatural beings is a universal ingredient in all human cultures, whether they are highly technical like the United States or primitive like the Australian aborigines. For most people, the issue isn't whether a God exists but what deity is like. Is God one or many? Personal or impersonal? Good and fair or harsh and capricious? Is He the God of the Judeo-Christian religion or the God of some other religion?

Because there is a small—but extremely vocal—faction who denies there is a God at all, we will focus here on the issue of God's existence. The nature and character of God will be treated in later chapters.

THE ATHEIST'S DILEMMA

An atheist is a person who denies the existence of a God. A little reflection, however, reveals that the atheist's position is indefensible. The only way anyone can prove no God exists is to be a God himself. Let me explain.

The total amount of knowledge any single human possesses is infinitesimal compared to the vastness of the universe and the immeasurable amount of information it contains. A person would have to be omnipresent (present everywhere at once) and omniscient (have all awareness and understanding) in order to have enough information to know that no deity exists. And these are the very attributes that are a part of most concepts of God! Hence, no finite human being can prove God does not exist because God may very well exist beyond one's comprehension or experience.

Of course, this fact stops few atheists from arguing against the existence of God. Rather than admitting (or even recognizing) the irrationality of their own position, many atheists attempt to remove the rationality of the Christian position. They often put Christians on the defensive by insisting believers in God are obligated to prove He exists, rather than atheists bearing the burden of proving God does not exist. These atheists argue that because they don't believe in God, because their belief is negative, they don't have to martial any arguments in their favor. So states George Smith:

> Proof is applicable only in the case of a positive belief. To demand proof of the atheist, the religionist must represent atheism as a positive belief requiring substantiation. When the atheist is seen as a person who lacks belief in a god, it becomes clear that he is not obligated to "prove" anything. The atheist *qua* atheist does not believe anything requiring demonstration; the designation of "atheist" tells us, not what he believes to be true, but what he does *not* believe to be true. If others wish for him to accept the existence of a god, it is their responsibility to argue for the truth of theism—but the atheist is not similarly required to argue for the truth of atheism.[1]

Consequently, in the atheism versus Christianity debate, atheists claim that the "burden of proof" is on the Christian.

Although it is generally true that the burden of proof is on the person who asserts something, the atheist is wrong for at least two reasons. First, as we'll see, Christians have given ample evidence for the existence of the Judeo-Christian God. In light of this, if atheists claim God does not exist, they must be prepared to explain why. When Christians state that God exists and offer evidences to support this claim, they have moved the debate into a new arena—an arena in which atheists must prove that the Christian *evidences* are erroneous.

Generally, the person who claims that he does not have to defend his position normally does so because he has no evidence to support his view. The fact is, atheists cannot refute Christian evidences for the existence of God. Science writer Isaac Asimov, who signed the *Humanist Manifesto II*, is being intellectually honest when he states: "Emotionally I am an atheist. I don't have the evidence to prove that God doesn't exist, but I so strongly suspect he doesn't that I don't want to waste my time."[2]

The second reason the atheistic "burden of proof" argument is fallacious is this: Christians have a document (the Bible) that testifies to the existence of God. It is always up to the person contesting a document to prove it is false. In other words, a document is innocent until proven guilty. For example, in court cases involving a will, in order to win a judgment, the person contesting the will has the responsibility to prove the will is bogus. In the debate over the existence of God, Christians have a historical document that reveals God exists. If atheists wish to challenge the existence of God, they must prove this document is spurious. Hence, the burden of proof rests on atheists. They do not have to prove the nonexistence of God, but they do have to disprove the objective evidence offered for His existence. If they can't, then Christian theism is true and atheism is false.

THE CHRISTIAN'S CASE

That the Bible *is* divine revelation (and thus a true testimony to the existence of God) will be demonstrated in the next chapter. There I'll show that, by using the same methods of investigation used to determine the authenticity of any ancient document, the Bible is truthful in all areas open to investigation. It is not only philosophically consistent, but its prophetic, historical, geographical, and scientific claims have been verified to be factual. If the Bible is reliable in all areas in which historical and other forms of investigation can be applied, it is logical to assume that, in areas of religious truth (such as God's existence), it will be equally reliable and truthful. So, based on the objective, verifiable testimony of the Bible, the Judeo-Christian God exists.

Now, just because the Bible is true in testable areas does not automatically make it true in nontestable areas. Arguments for the existence of God do not end with mathematical certainties. They are based on probability evidences, the same kind of evidences relied upon by science, history, and law in their search for truth. If someone rejects the preponderance of evidence supporting God's existence because it is not absolutely certain, then, to be logically consistent, he must also reject all other truths from the other disciplines that reach no higher than probability conclusions. For example, no one is alive today who witnessed the assassination of Abraham Lincoln. However, we can be certain (though less than absolutely so) that the event occurred because of the vast amount of historical evidence that confirms it. The probability that Lincoln was assassinated is overwhelming. In a similar way, scientific theories are a product of experimentation and observation (evidences). However, there is always the chance that future experiments and observations may disprove an existing theory. Thus scientific theories are the product of probability evidence.

Christians insist that the burden of proof is on the atheist when dealing with the existence of God so she will have to confront Scripture. The testimony of Scripture is the most important and potent weapon in the Christian's arsenal. Why? Because the Bible offers objective, testable evidence for God's existence, not just philosophical arguments. Moreover, the Bible does double duty: it brings the atheist face to face with the fact that God exists, and it reveals the true nature of God in the person of Jesus Christ. It's one thing to prove God exists, but quite another to prove He is the God revealed in the Bible. By arguing for His existence from Scripture, both goals are achieved.

At first blush, this may sound like a presuppositional approach to apologetics, but it isn't. The atheist doesn't have to accept the Bible as true apart from any evidence. Rather, we first confront her with the Bible's authenticity through the use of objective evidences, then we let these facts corroborate the truth-claims of Scripture.

Unfortunately, atheists reject the Bible because they reject the existence of God. So they will not accept the Bible as evidence for God's existence. For atheists to consider the testimony of Scripture, the Bible usually has to be set aside so they can be met on their own turf. This involves presenting philosophical evidence for God's existence.

And these are supported by historical and empirical (observable) facts. Let's consider some of these arguments.

IN THE BEGINNING . . .

It doesn't take much reflection for us to realize that we exist, and we did not create ourselves. And since that's true, it's easy to figure out that something or someone besides ourselves brought us to be. And with a little more reflection, we can also see that the entire universe came to be in one of three possible ways: (1) it created itself; (2) it has always existed, and therefore had no Creator; or (3) it was created by something or someone outside of itself. Let's take a close look at each option.

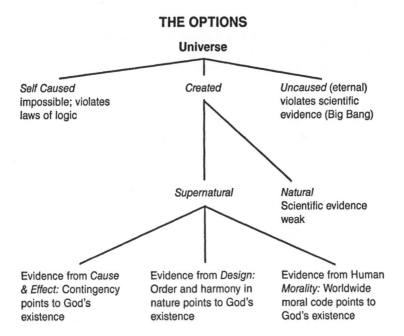

THE OPTIONS

Universe

Self Caused
impossible; violates laws of logic

Created

Uncaused (eternal) violates scientific evidence (Big Bang)

Supernatural

Natural
Scientific evidence weak

Evidence from *Cause & Effect:* Contingency points to God's existence

Evidence from *Design:* Order and harmony in nature points to God's existence

Evidence from Human *Morality:* Worldwide moral code points to God's existence

The Universe Created Itself

This view can be quickly eliminated because it violates a basic law of logic known as the law of non-contradiction. This law states that a proposition cannot be true and not true at the same time and in the same relationship. For the universe to have created itself, it must have both existed and not existed at the same time. In other words, in order for the universe to have caused itself to be, it could not have existed prior to itself. Yet, in order for it to have created itself, it must have had to have already existed. So, on this view, the universe existed and did not exist at the same time. Sounds too complicated to understand? It does so for a good reason: It amounts to a contradiction. It's like saying circles are square or bachelors are married. It makes no sense because it's nonsensical, absurd, contradictory. Nothing can exist prior to itself to bring itself to be. That's logically absurd, hence impossible.

The Universe Is Eternal

Although this view once had scientific respectability, it has fallen on hard times. Most scientists agree with theists that the universe had a very specific beginning. In recent decades, discoveries in astronomy have provided an abundance of evidence that the universe came into existence abruptly (the big bang theory). This theory is supported by the fact that all the galaxies are moving away from one another at tremendous speeds. By tracing these movements backwards, scientists believe that, at some point in time, a tremendous explosion occurred that ejected all matter outward from a central point of high density compression. This, scientists say, marks the birth of the universe.

Further evidence that the universe had a beginning lies in the fact that it is aging. The second law of thermodynamics, one of the most important laws of physics that has no known exceptions, states that the amount of usable energy in the universe is decreasing due to continuing heat loss. In other words, the universe is running out of usable fuel; it is slowly dying a heat death. If the universe is running down, then there must have been a starting point in which it was wound up with a maximum amount of energy. Again, scientific evidence is in agreement with the Bible that the universe is not eternal.

Another piece of evidence is the principle of contingency, which states that everything in the physical universe is dependent upon something else for its existence. Thus, for the universe itself to exist, there must be a cause for its existence. Logically, the universe cannot be eternal if something else caused it to come to be.

Of course, many theists disagree with modern science on the age of the universe and its originating cause, but theologians and scientists agree that the universe had a beginning—it is not eternal.

For many scientists, this conclusion has come as quite a shock. Robert Jastrow, an internationally known astronomer and founder and director of NASA's Goddard Institute for Space Studies, has detailed this difficult and surprising search in his book *God and the Astronomers*. His concluding comments speak volumes:

> For the scientist who has lived by his faith in the power of reason, the story ends like a bad dream. He has scaled the mountains of ignorance; he is about to conquer the highest peak; as he pulls himself over the final rock, he is greeted by a band of theologians who have been sitting there for centuries.[3]

The Universe Was Created by Something or Someone Else

We are now left with the third possibility, which the Bible confirms: Something or someone outside of the universe caused it to come into being. Creation out of nothing is the only plausible explanation for the existence of the universe. If this is so, then we have proved the existence of God in the broadest sense. Only God, a Being who is Himself uncaused, eternal, and all-powerful, could by definition be a Creator.

At this juncture, an objection is often raised: If it makes no sense to argue that the universe brought itself into being out of nothing, then what sense does it make to claim that the universe was created out of nothing? Out of nothing, nothing can come, right? This objection raises a good point, which requires an important clarification.

As I demonstrated, it is logically contradictory to argue that the universe is self-caused. It could not create itself without existing prior to itself, which is impossible. It's also true that nothing—total nonbeing—can cause something to be. Nothing cannot cause anything because there's no cause present to create an effect. So where does that leave the Christian view of creation out of nothing?

The Bible affirms that something, namely God, created the universe out of nothing. God didn't happen upon some matter and energy and fashion the universe out of it. God spoke, and the universe came to be (Gen. 1). There was no preexistent stuff out of which God created the world. Is that contradictory? No. Something (God) caused something else (the universe) to exist. That satisfies the law of causality and doesn't violate the law of noncontradiction.

Therefore, if this philosophical case for God's existence is valid and sound, which it is, then there should be empirical (observable) evidence to support it, which there is. We have already seen some of this evidence—the big bang theory, the second law of thermodynamics, and the law of contingency. Now let's look further.

GOD REVEALS HIMSELF

The only way we can know for sure that God exists is if He reveals Himself. If God wanted to, He could certainly withhold evidence of His presence if He chooses, but we've already seen some evidence that He is there. That we can even know this much implies He has revealed this information. It also shows that He has made Himself known in ways we can recognize.

When we search for revelational evidence of God's existence, we discover He has revealed Himself in two specific ways: general revelation and special revelation.

Special revelation is found in the Bible. Scripture not only confirms God's existence, but it also includes very specific information about the nature of God. For example, the Bible states that God is holy, eternal, omniscient, omnipresent, omnipotent, and omnibenevolent. It tells us that God is triune—Father, Son, and Holy Spirit. However, because many people reject the Bible, they don't accept special revelation. Consequently, we will continue to focus on evidence found in general revelation.

General revelation is information about God found outside of the Bible. So it is accessible and understandable by *all* people at all times throughout history. It is a perpetual or continuous revelation of God. It shows that God exists, and it unveils some of His attributes, but it does not provide all the information the Bible does about God, such as details about His triune nature. General revelation occurs primarily through nature (Rom. 1:20; Ps. 19:1; Acts 14:16–17) and an intuitive moral consciousness God placed in all human beings (Rom. 2:14–15).[4] From these sources, several arguments for God's existence can be developed.[5] We'll focus on three.

The Cosmological Case

The cosmological argument is from cause and effect. It states that because the universe exists, there must be an explanation—a cause—for its existence. And since no effect can be greater than its cause, whatever caused the universe must be greater than the universe itself. That greater cause must be God. He is the first cause.

At this point, skeptics often ask, "Who caused God?" This question must be answered if the cosmological argument is to be valid. So let me explain the argument in more detail.

It is an observable and undeniable fact that every effect has a cause in the physical universe. Nothing in the universe exists that is not contingent (dependent) on something else. A tree's existence is contingent on seed from another tree. It is also contingent on water, minerals, and sunshine. Rivers need rainfall. In the human realm, every tool serving humanity has a cause for its existence. Someone made it. In a word, nothing in the universe is able to explain its own existence.

Unless a first cause (i.e., God) exists, the universe would have to be eternal because there would be an infinite series of causes and effects that would never lead to a first cause or starting point. But, as we have already seen, the universe is not eternal. Therefore, an infinite series of causes and effects are impossible. At some point there must have been a first cause or nothing subsequent would exist. Moreover, because no contingent being (one whose existence is dependent on another) can cause itself to exist, the first cause must be uncaused or self-existent and thus must transcend the contingent universe. This uncaused, self-existent being would really be the *first* cause, and all contingent beings would ultimately depend on this cause for their existence.

In short, to explain the existence of a contingent, noneternal universe, there has to be a noncontingent being (Creator) who is absolutely independent of the physical universe. This is the theistic God, and He is identical to the Christian God. According to the Bible, God is self-existent (uncaused—see Exod. 3:14; John 5:26) and eternal (has no beginning and no end—see Deut. 33:27; Rev. 4:10). Thus, He could not have been created. He is not subject to the law of cause and effect in any way. On the other hand, the fact that the universe *is* subject to the law of cause and effect demands (proves) the existence of God.

The Design Case

Closely related to the cosmological argument is the teleological argument, which centers on the order and design we see in nature. In recent decades, the ecologic crisis has focused our attention on the delicate balance of nature. Everywhere we look, we see interdependence, harmony, order, and purpose. The teleological argument points out that such design and order cannot be the product of random processes and chance. Rather, these characteristics indicate an intelligent being caused them.

By analogy, we easily distinguish an arrowhead lying among countless other pebbles because it obviously had an intelligent creator. When we look at a painting, we know it's the product of a thoughtful artist. Neither do we see computers as chance accidents of nonintelligent causes. In like manner, the design and order in the universe can only be the result of an intelligent creator, God.

Without realizing it, many atheists acknowledge the concept of an intelligence behind nature when they use the term *Mother Nature*. It plainly carries the idea of a creator who designed and maintains the natural world.

Now some atheists argue against teleology by claiming that given enough time, the apparent design in the universe could occur by accidental random processes. However, there is no convincing evidence to support this claim, as we'll see in Chapter 11.

The Moral Case

The cosmological and teleological arguments outlined above represent general revelation in nature. The third evidence for the existence of God also comes from general revelation, but more specifically through human moral consciousness.

The most serious (and common) argument used by atheists to disprove the existence of God is called the problem of evil. In its many forms, it boils down to this: because there is suffering and evil in the world, God must not exist. If He did exist, He would not allow suffering and evil. So either God does not exist, or if He does, He is not the loving, sovereign, all-powerful God described in the Bible. A fuller answer to this argument is found in Chapter 13, but it deserves a short response here.

There is a fundamental contradiction in the claim that evil precludes the existence of God. The moral standard used to determine what evil is can only have its source in God. Hence, by identifying what is evil, atheists implicitly acknowledge that God is. Let me explain.

We could not know what evil is, in any universal sense, unless a moral standard exists outside of us. Without a moral absolute—namely—independent of human consciousness, there would be no criteria to determine what is right or wrong, whether what is wrong today will be wrong tomorrow, whether what is wrong for me is also wrong for you, and whether what is wrong in my culture is also wrong in yours. In short, I could not justify telling you what you ought to do unless there was an absolute standard of moral behavior independent of individual persons and cultures. But such a standard does exist.

Comparative studies in anthropology and sociology reveal a universal standard of behavior in all people, regardless of their culture, religion, or their period in history. Not only Western culture, but also Eastern societies of Hindus and Buddhists and Egyptians have had a similar concept of right and wrong. Even primitive cultures have exhibited this universal awareness of what is evil, this innate sense of right and wrong that helps people everywhere judge the injustice of others and themselves.

This generic moral code is manifested worldwide in prohibitions against murder, stealing, lying, rape, cheating, and so on.[6] Interestingly, this moral standard was written in the Bible some thirty-five centuries ago and summarized in the Ten Commandments (Ex. 20:1–17). Although God revealed these commandments to a small culture, living at the time in a foreign land, they were just as applicable to every culture on earth then as they are today. The Ten Commandments represent a worldwide, universal standard for moral behavior.

Since a universal moral code exists, where did it originate? It must have come from a standard outside of man if it is to judge the actions of man. History has consistently shown that when we follow our own standards of behavior, our natural tendency is to do evil, not good. So if morality is relative—if it is determined by whatever culture we happen to reside in or by whatever beliefs we happen to agree with—there would be no worldwide moral continuity. A universal moral code would be nonexistent. The only reasonable and satisfactory explanation for a universal standard of moral behavior is that it is derived from a moral absolute independent of human thoughts and feelings. And this absolute could only be God.

By nature, God is perfect in love, wisdom, goodness, and righteousness. Thus only God is able to judge perfectly what is right and wrong. God's eternal, unchanging nature guarantees unchanging, universal, and permanent moral standards not subject to human capriciousness. Only God can be considered the source of moral ideals. Therefore even human moral codes point to the existence of God—the moral lawgiver.

THE BEST IS YET TO COME

We've surveyed enough evidence to know that the facts overwhelmingly weigh in favor of the existence of God. But the best proof—the Bible—still remains to be explored. For if God has spoken to us in Scripture, then we can be certain that He is.

This brings us to Jesus Christ—where all apologetics ultimately lead. As Christians, we know God exists because the Bible teaches that He came to earth in the Son, Jesus Christ, and lived among us (John 1:1, 14). Jesus is the "exact representation" of God's nature (Heb. 1:3, NASV), and in Him "all the fulness of Deity dwells in bodily form" (Col. 2:9, NASV). If one wants to know if God exists and what He is like, all he has to do is read the Bible and there meet Jesus Christ (John 1:18). No further search is necessary. Nor does one have to debate philosophical proofs. God has taken the initiative and revealed Himself to us: in nature, in our moral conscience, in Scripture, and in Jesus Christ.

3

Why Should We Trust the Bible?

When I was in graduate school, I took a course entitled "Biblical Criticism and Authenticity." Its purpose was to examine the accuracy and reliability of the Bible. Thirty-five percent of my course grade depended on how well I wrote an apologetic brief and how well I defended it orally before a moot jury. My jury consisted of Dr. John Warwick Montgomery and John Stewart—both well-known and very knowledgeable Christian apologists.

The rules were simple. I had fifteen minutes to argue my case, and the jury was free, in the style of appellate advocacy, to interrupt at any time and to fire critical questions during my presentation. The topic I chose was "Should the Bible be read in public schools?"—not a dull subject, to say the least. With Montgomery and Stewart playing the devil's advocates, it was a lively debate.

My argument went like this: The Bible is an historical document of demonstrated accuracy and reliability. In every area in which it can be checked-out—historically, culturally, geographically, scientifically, and so on—it has been verified as factual by extra-biblical sources. It is full of information on the history of the Jews and other ancient civilizations, as well as early Christianity. It presents unique and invaluable information on the customs, languages, cultures, ethics, and religion of what is the foundation of all Western civilization. Because of this, and in spite of the Bible's religious significance, I argued it should be used as a resource for historical information in public schools.

What follows in this chapter forms the meat and potatoes of my moot-court argument. If Christians can demonstrate that the Bible is truthful in all areas in which it can be validated, we have before us the most powerful and compelling evidence for the truthfulness of Christianity. Every apologetic argument rests on the reliability of the Bible, including the deity and resurrection of Jesus Christ.

All religions in the world claim to possess divine truth and make emphatic statements about the nature of God, the question of sin, the destiny of man, and other critical issues. If one approaches all religions in the same fashion—if one accepts or rejects them based solely on the evidence—he will soon discover that the Bible alone can sustain its truth-claims. This is vital if Christianity is to attract skeptics and advocates of other religions. There has to be some kind of objective and testable evidence to verify religious truth-claims, or there would be no way to determine which religion, if any, among the hundreds of contenders actually expresses divine revelation.

Let me carry this a step further, and this is the crux of the apologetic argument in this chapter. If the Bible alone *can* sustain its truth-claims in areas in which it can be investigated, then it is reasonable to trust it in spiritual matters. We have a solid foundation from which to assert that what the Bible says about Jesus as Lord and Savior, sin and its consequences, and the path to salvation must be correct. And if what the Bible says is true, contrary religious claims must be false.

THE RELIABILITY OF THE OLD TESTAMENT

We'll begin with the Old Testament. Three categories of evidence lead to the conclusion that the Old Testament is reliable. These categories are the Old Testament's transmission, its archaeological record, and its fulfilled prophecy.

TRANSMISSION

Before printing presses and photocopiers, duplicate books, letters, and other forms of written communication were reproduced by hand. During the development of the Old Testament, during the two millennia prior to Jesus' birth, this reproduction process was carried out by Jewish scribes.

The original Bible manuscripts (called autographs) were written on material such as papyrus, which deteriorated quickly. Consequently, scribes were needed to copy and recopy the Old Testament books letter by letter. These copyists knew they were duplicating God's Word, so they went to incredible lengths to prevent error from creeping into their work. The whole process of recopying the Bible was controlled by strict religious rituals, and the scribes carefully counted every line, word, syllable, and letter to ensure accuracy.

As a result of their diligence, the Old Testament in our Bible today is virtually identical to the autographs. Bible scholars have demonstrated this by comparing ancient copies of the Bible with more recent copies. For example, prior to the discovery of the Dead Sea Scroll manuscripts in 1947, the oldest existing (extant) Old Testament manuscript was the Massoretic Text, dated around A.D 900. But with the discovery of the Dead Sea Scrolls, fragments of almost every book in the Old Testament were found, many of them dating back to around 150 B.C., a thousand years earlier. One of the most important manuscript discoveries was two copies of Isaiah. So far they are the oldest known copies of any complete book of the Bible.

What did textual critics discover when they compared the Dead Sea manuscripts of Isaiah with the Isaiah preserved in the Massoretic Text dated a thousand years later? Old Testament scholar Gleason Archer provides the answer: "Even though the two copies of Isaiah discovered in Qumran Cave 1 near the Dead Sea in 1947 were a thousand years earlier than the oldest dated manuscript previously known (A.D. 980), they proved to be word for word identical with our standard Hebrew Bible in more than 95 percent of the text. The 5 percent of variation consisted chiefly of obvious slips of the pen and variations in spelling."[1]

From manuscript discoveries like the Dead Sea Scrolls, Christians have undeniable evidence that today's Old Testament Scripture, for all practical purposes, is exactly the same as it was when originally inspired by God and recorded in the Bible.

ARCHAEOLOGY

Over the past one hundred years, the archaeologist's spade has verified numerous events, customs, cities, and nations mentioned in the Old Testament. At one time many scholars dismissed some of the Old Testament as mythical because they had no outside confirmation of the people, places, or events in doubt. But archaeology has changed all that, demonstrating the Old Testament's reliability on literally hundreds of historical facts. Here are a few examples:[2]

- The Ebla Tablets. Since 1974, archaeologists have unearthed seventeen thousand tablets at Tell Mardikh in northern Syria. These tablets contain a record of laws, customs, and events from the same area Moses and the patriarchs lived. This discovery helped to disprove the Documentary hypothesis which, in part, claimed that Moses lived before the invention of written language and therefore could not have composed the first five books of the Old Testament (the Pentateuch). Thus, Bible critics claimed that the Old Testament was written much later (and by many unknown authors) than traditionally thought. However, the Ebla Tablets prove that written language existed at least a thousand years before Moses, which once again vindicated Moses as the most likely author of the Pentateuch.
- Archaeology has proven that Israel derives its ancestry from Mesopotamia, as the Bible teaches (Gen. 11:27–12:4).
- Archaeology suggests that the world's languages likely arose from a common origin, as Genesis 11 implies.
- Jericho, and several other cities mentioned in the Old Testament, previously thought to be legendary by skeptics, have now been discovered by archaeologists.
- Bible critics used to claim that the Hittite civilization mentioned in Genesis did not exist at the time of Abraham because there was no record of it apart from the Old Testament. However, archaeology has discovered that it not only existed but it lasted more than 1,200 years. Now you can even get a doctorate in Hittite studies from the University of Chicago.
- Social customs and stories in the Old Testament credited to the time of the patriarchs (Abraham, Jacob, and Isaac) are in harmony with archaeological discoveries, casting additional light on the historical accuracy of the biblical record.

Nelson Glueck, a scholar who specialized in ancient documents such as the Bible, remarked, "it can be stated categorically that no archaeological discovery has ever controverted a Biblical reference."[3] In other words, in every instance where the Bible could be checked-out historically against extra-biblical sources, the Bible has always been found accurate in what it reports.

FULFILLED PROPHECY

Fulfilled prophecies give clear attestation to the hand of God in human history and are some of the most important evidences for the historical reliability and truthfulness of the Old Testament. The Bible is the only religious document in existence that provides more than two thousand prophecies that validate its historical claims. These prophecies deal with Jesus Christ, the nation of Israel, other nations (e.g., Babylon, Persia, Greece, and Rome), cities (e.g., Tyre and Babylon), and even people (e.g., Nebuchadnezzar and Cyrus). Of course, some other religions make prophetic claims, however, in no other religion in the world has prophecy been fulfilled so completely and so accurately as that recorded in the Bible.

In Deuteronomy 13:1–5 and 18:20–22, God issued strong decrees concerning the use and misuse of prophecy and the identification of true and false prophets. God instructed Israel to put to death anyone who prophesied on any authority other than God's—even if his prophecy came true. Furthermore, if a prophecy did not come to pass, even if it was spoken in the name of the Lord, that person was to be put to death as a false prophet.

False prophets abound in our society, even in established religions such as Jehovah's Witnesses and Mormonism. But their unfulfilled prophecies expose them for what they are. On the other hand, all biblical prophecies concerning events up to the present time have come to pass—without exception.

THE RELIABILITY OF THE NEW TESTAMENT

The New Testament is about Jesus Christ. So much of what follows deals with Him, not just with the New Testament documents. In other words, we will consider evidence that establishes the historicity of Jesus as well as the historical reliability of the New Testament. The first grouping of evidence is bibliographical.

BIBLIOGRAPHICAL EVIDENCE

We do not possess any of the autographs of the New Testament. Like the Old Testament, the New Testament books were originally written on materials that quickly wore out and therefore had to be copied and recopied by hand for centuries before the invention of the printing press. So we need to determine how closely the extant copies represent the autographs. That is, how do we know that the New Testament we have today is close enough to the original writings as to be equally reliable? The bibliographical evidence is concerned with answering this question. And here we find three primary areas of evidence that demonstrate our present New Testament documents are virtually identical to their original writings.

Copies Galore

The first area of evidence has to do with the available number of New Testament manuscripts. What we discover is that there are more extant New Testament manuscripts than any other document from antiquity. More than 24,000 partial and complete copies of the New Testament are in existence today. By comparison, the ancient document second in number of available copies is the *Iliad*, which has only 643 surviving manuscripts. And this number is extremely high compared to other ancient documents. For example, the *History of Thucydides*, the *History of Herodotus*, Caesar's *Gallic War*, Tacitus' *Histories* and *Annals*, and many other ancient documents have fewer than two dozen surviving copies.[4]

In addition to New Testament manuscripts, there are over 86,000 early patristic (church fathers') quotations from the New Testament and several thousand Lectionaries (early church-service books containing selected Scripture readings) dating to the early centuries of the church. In fact, there are enough quotations from the early church fathers that even if we did not have a single copy of the Bible, scholars could still reconstruct all but 11 verses of the entire New

Testament from material written within 150 to 200 years from the time of Christ.[5]

AUTHOR	When Written	Earliest Copy	Time Span	No. of Copies
Caesar	100–44 B.C.	A.D. 900	1,000 yrs.	10
Livy	59 B.C.–A.D. 17			20
Plato (Tetralogies)	427–347 B.C.	A.D. 900	1,200 yrs.	7
Tacitus (Annals)	A.D. 100	A.D. 1100	1,000 yrs.	20 (–)
also minor works	A.D. 100	A.D. 1000	900 yrs.	1
Pliny the Younger (History)	A.D. 61–113	A.D. 850	750 yrs.	7
Thucydides (History)	460–400 B.C.	A.D. 900	1,300 yrs.	8
Suetonius (De Vita Caesarum)	A.D. 75–169	A.D. 950	800 yrs.	8
Herodotus (History)	480–425 B.C.	A.D. 900	1,300 yrs.	8
Horace			900 yrs.	
Sophocles	496–406 B.C.	A.D. 1000	1,400 yrs.	193
Lucretius	Died 55 or 53 B.C.		1,100 yrs.	2
Catullus	54 B.C.	A.D. 1550	1,600 yrs.	3
Euripides	480–406 B.C.	A.D. 1100	1,500 yrs.	9
Demosthenes	383–322 B.C.	A.D. 1100	1,300 yrs.	200*
Aristotle	384–322 B.C.	A.D. 1100	1,400 yrs.	49†
Aristophanes	450–385 B.C.	A.D. 900	1,200 yrs.	10

*All from one copy.
†Of any one work.
From Josh McDowell, *Evidence That Demands a Verdict,* rev. ed. (San Bernardino, CA: Here's Life, 1979), 42.

Shorter Is Best

The second area of bibliographical evidence concerns the short time span between when events recorded in the New Testament actually happened and when they were first written down. The time span is shorter for the New Testament than for any other document from antiquity. There is strong evidence that the gospels of Matthew, Mark, and Luke were written within thirty years of Jesus' death, and the gospel of John before the end of the first century. A. T. Robinson, a scholar who once assumed that all the New Testament books were written between the late first century and second century, later changed his mind radically after examining the evidence. In his book *Redating the New Testament,* he went against the Bible critics he once agreed with and argued that all the New Testament books were written before the destruction of Jerusalem in A.D. 70, only thirty or so years after the death of Christ.[6]

When we compare these facts with the writings of the vast majority of other world religions, we find an incredible contrast. Many other religious documents have tremendous time spans between when they were transmitted orally and when they were eventually written down. For example, the sayings of Buddha were not recorded until five hundred years after his death.

Moreover, no other ancient document can boast as short a time span between its autographs and presently existing copies. The John Rylands fragment of the gospel of John may date to within twenty-five years of its original writing. There are numerous other manuscripts, some containing most of the entire New Testament, dating from early in the second century. And from the early fourth century (ca. A.D. 325–350), complete New Testament manuscripts are available. In short, Bible scholars have in their hands copies of New Testament manuscripts dating to within a generation of their original writings, which is absolutely incredible for works of antiquity.

By comparison, the *Iliad* has a time span of five hundred years between its original writings and the oldest existing manuscripts. Many other ancient documents have an even greater time span. The ancient works mentioned above all have a time span of one thousand years or greater between their autographs and existing copies.

WORK	When Written	Earliest Copy	Time Span	No. of Copies
Homer *(Iliad)*	900 B.C.	400 B.C.	500 yrs.	643
New Testament	A.D. 40–100	A.D. 125	25 yrs.	24,000†

From Josh McDowell, Ibid., 43.

What is significant about all this? Simply this: In the case of the New Testament Gospels, unlike other ancient works, whether secular or religious, not enough time elapsed between when Jesus spoke and when His words were recorded to allow for misrepresentation or the development of legendary material about Him. Nor has enough time elapsed between the autographs and existing translations to allow significant transmission errors or tampering. We can be certain, therefore, that the New Testament Gospels accurately record the sayings of Jesus and the events in His life.

Practically Perfect

The final area of bibliographical evidence concerns the lack of textual corruption in the New Testament. A comparison of the copies of New Testament with other ancient manuscripts shows that the New Testament possesses a smaller percentage of textual errors than any other ancient document. Textual critics estimate that only one half of one percent (.5 percent) of the New Testament is in doubt. And of this one-half percent, no doctrinal or historical truth is left in question. The *Iliad,* on the other hand, has suffered about 5 percent corruption. Other ancient manuscripts have suffered even more corruption. For example, the national epic of India, the *Mahabharata,* has about 10 percent of its text in doubt.

Experts in the field of textual criticism (the science of establishing the accuracy of ancient texts) agree that the New Testament we have today is unquestionably a near perfect offspring of the autographs. Sir Frederick Kenyon, past director and principle librarian of the British Museum and probably the greatest textual critic of the twentieth century, states:

> The interval between the dates of original composition [of the New Testament] and the earliest extant evidence becomes so small as to be in fact negligible, and the last foundation for any doubt that the Scriptures have come down to us substantially as they were written has now been removed. Both the authenticity and general integrity of the books of the New Testament may be regarded as finally established.[7]

INTERNAL EVIDENCE

With the bibliographical evidence before us, we're now ready to move on to the internal evidence, which looks at the internal reliability and consistency of the New Testament. We'll focus on two important areas of internal evidence.

The Law Rules

The first area has to do with what law professor and historian John Warwick Montgomery calls "the fundamental principles of the law of evidence." He applies four of these rules to the Bible. Each one is used in our legal system to determine a document's acceptability.[8]

The ancient documents rule

In evaluating ancient documents, it is customary to assume that a document is truthful unless the author disqualifies himself by contradictions or by provable inaccuracies, unless, of course, there is internal evidence of text tampering. In the law area, when a document is in dispute, the burden of proof is always on the accuser. In addition, unsolved problems or unclear material in a document do not automatically lend credence to the conclusion of error or unreliability. Biblical textual criticism, for instance, has seen historical research resolve numerous so-called problem passages in favor of the Bible's reliability. So the Bible has proven itself and should be trusted.[9]

The parol evidence rule

"External, oral testimony or tradition will not be received in evidence to add to, subtract from, vary, or contradict an executed written instrument such as a will. Applied to the Bible documents, which expressly claim to be 'executed' and complete (Rev. 22:18–19), this rule insists that the Scripture be allowed to 'interpret itself' and not be twisted to external, extra-biblical data."[10] In other words, as we would with any document, we give Scripture a fair hearing. We do not interpret the Bible in light of our own—or others'—preconceived assumptions. For example, some Bible critics seek to short-circuit the reliability of Scripture by off-handedly denying miracles. They simply accept the prevailing scientific view that miracles are impossible, so their minds are made up before they ever examine the biblical evidence.

The hearsay rule

"A witness must testify 'of his own knowledge,' not on the basis of what has come to him indirectly from others [hearsay]. Applied to the New Testament documents, this demand for primary-source evidence is fully vindicated by the constant"[11] assertion of the New Testament authors that they were eyewitnesses of the events they recorded (e.g., 1 John 1:1).

The cross-examination principle

The more a witness is subjected to "close and searching cross-examination," the more confidence we can place on his testimony. We see this applied especially in the eyewitness testimonies of Jesus' resurrection (the historic foundation of our faith). Witnesses called to account for their faith by confirming the resurrection story did so "in the very teeth of opposition, among hostile cross-examiners who would certainly have destroyed the case of Christianity had"[12] the early Christians' testimony been contradicted by the facts.

If we put the New Testament documents through the rigors of these four principles from our legal system, they would be unequivocally pronounced valid and reliable as evidence for the life, ministry, and resurrection of Jesus Christ. They tell "the whole truth and nothing but the truth."

The Best Sources

The second internal evidence supporting the reliability of the New Testament is its *primary source value*. The New Testament Gospels were written either by eyewitnesses to the events in Christ's life (Matthew and John) or by men who knew and interviewed eyewitnesses (Mark and Luke). The authors of the New Testament were careful to note this first-hand, eyewitness testimony as verification of their authenticity (e.g., Luke 1:1–3; John 19:35; 20:30–31; 21:24; Acts 10:39–42; 1 Cor. 15:6–8; 1 Pet. 5:1; 2 Pet. 1:16; 1 John 1:1–3). Moreover, the New Testament authors appealed not only to their own observations but also to those of their readers and listeners—even when the witnesses were hostile (see Acts 2:22; 26:24–28).

Why did the writers appeal to eyewitness testimony? The reason was that many people who knew Jesus or had observed His miracles were still alive when the New Testament was written. Since many of these people were hostile to Christianity, they had every opportunity to publicly refute the apostles' accounts. And yet, in the case of the birth, ministry, death, and resurrection of Jesus, not a single piece of contrary historical evidence surfaced during the first century to claim these events were false. The enemies of Christianity could not refute the Gospels' accounts, which is convincing attestation that the New Testament documents are historically reliable.

It is also worth noting that the New Testament authors didn't hesitate to report events that cast themselves in an unfavorable light. So you'll find Peter denying Jesus and the disciples arguing over which of them will be the greatest in the kingdom and their abandoning Jesus during His arrest. Also, these writers made no attempt to soften the harsh words Jesus spoke or to cover-up the inflammatory accusations thrown at Him, such as the claim that His power was derived from Satan. The New Testament authors recorded Jesus' anger and bitterness, His despair on the cross, and other less than complimentary incidents. If the gospel accounts were fiction or written merely to implement a new religious movement instead of recording historical facts, why would its leaders record so many "negative" elements? That they did is compelling evidence for the authenticity and integrity of their writings and witness.

And finally, as J. P. Moreland points out, the New Testament authors had nothing to gain and all to lose if they were writing a spurious religious document:

> It seems clear that the New Testament writers were able and willing to tell the truth. They had very little to gain and much to lose for their efforts. For one thing, they were mostly Jewish theists. To change the religion of Israel with its observance of the Mosaic law, Sabbath keeping, sacrifices, and clear-cut non-Trinitarian monotheism would be to risk the damnation of their own souls to hell. A modern atheist may not worry about such a thing, but members of the early church surely did.[13]

EXTERNAL EVIDENCE

Now let's consider four significant areas of external evidence. By "external evidence," I mean evidence derived from sources other than the New Testament authors or documents.

Christian Sources

Corroborating information comes from Christian writers who lived close to the time of the New Testament authors.[14]

Papias (Bishop of Hierapolis) and Irenaeus (Bishop of Lyons) together confirm the authorship of the four Gospels. Papias was a friend of the apostle John, and Irenaeus was a student of Polycarp, who was a disciple of John. They report that John not only wrote his gospel but told them that the gospel of Mark was written by Mark, the companion and interpreter of Peter, that Matthew's gospel was published "among the Hebrews [the Jews] in their own tongue," and that Luke wrote his gospel as it was "preached by his teacher," Paul. This evidence counters the claim that the authors of the Gospels were other than those whom the Bible names.[15]

Non-Christian Sources

Several non-Christian writers living close to the time of Christ further support the New Testament record. Although these individuals are not as explicit as Papias, Irenaeus, and other early Christian writers, they nevertheless give additional credibility to the historicity of the New Testament.[16]

Jewish historian Flavius Josephus wrote about John the Baptist and mentioned Jesus by referring to James "the [half] brother of Jesus, the so-called Christ." In another, although controversial passage, it appears that Josephus may even have referred to Jesus as "a wise man" condemned to die on the cross by Pilate.[17]

Roman historian Cornelius Tacitus alluded to Jesus' death and the existence of Christians in Rome. He wrote of "Christus," who "was put to death by Pontius Pilate, Procurator of Judea in the reign of Tiberius."[18]

Pliny the Younger wrote a letter to Emperor Trajan about A.D. 112

asking his advice on how to deal with "the troublesome sect of Christians."[19] It seems that Pliny, as governor of Bithynia in Asia Minor, had been killing innumerable Christians, but their numbers were still "embarrassingly" high. He didn't know whether to continue killing as many as he found or to be more selective![20]

Suetonius, in his *Lives of the Twelve Caesars: Vita Claudius,* mentions that the Jews were expelled from Rome because of disturbances over "Chrestus" (Christ).[21]

In addition to these references, other Roman and Jewish sources, such as the Talmud and the Mishnah (authoritative Jewish writings), make numerous literary references to Jesus of Nazareth, and many of them were written in the first century. All this evidence confirms that Jesus really lived, and the New Testament record of His life is accurate. As New Testament scholar F. F. Bruce makes clear:

> Whatever else may be thought of the evidence from early Jewish and Gentile writers . . . it does at least establish for those who refuse the witness of Christian writings, the historical character of Jesus Himself. Some writers may toy with the fancy of a "Christ-myth," but they do not do so on the ground of historical evidence. The historicity of Christ is as axiomatic for an unbiased historian as the historicity of Julius Caesar.[22]

Fulfilled Prophecy

As I mentioned earlier, the Bible is the only religious document in existence that presents an enormous number of prophecies that validate its historical claims. Of the over two thousand prophecies in the Bible, several hundred of them apply specifically to events in the life of Jesus Christ, such as His place of birth, tribe and lineage, ministry, betrayal by Judas, suffering, crucifixion, and resurrection. These prophecies touch all areas of Jesus' life, and they were uttered centuries before His birth.

All attempts to debunk these fulfilled Old Testament prophecies have failed. Even when critics have rejected the traditional 450 B.C. date for the completion of the Old Testament, they have never been able to get around the fact that the Greek Septuagint, a translation of the Hebrew Scriptures, was completed around 250 B.C., proving that the prophecies about Jesus could not have been written after the events they foretell.

Archaeology

The fourth area of external evidence is archaeology. Over the past hundred years, archaeology has verified the factuality of literally hundreds of events, customs, cities, geographic features, and nations described in the Old Testament. Many of these facts were previously thought to be legendary because there was no record of them anywhere other than in the Bible.

We see this same kind of validation for the New Testament. Archaeology has substantiated numerous customs, places, names, and events mentioned in the New Testament. For example, archaeology has verified the existence of the city of Nazareth, where Jesus was raised, as well as most of the ancient cities mentioned in Acts. Archaeology has documented the accuracy of Luke's account of Paul's missionary journeys and has confirmed the periodic Roman censuses that caused Joseph and Mary to be in Bethlehem at the time of Jesus' birth. Archaeology has also authenticated the historicity of Pontius Pilate, who sentenced Jesus to die by crucifixion.

But the most important contribution to the truthfulness and reliability of the New Testament lies in the discovery of the many thousands of New Testament manuscripts, patristic quotations, and lectionaries now in the hands of scholars. Their availability has allowed the enormous success of textual critics in verifying the New Testament's reliability.

THE GREATEST TRUTH

All this evidence proves that the Bible is clearly the most trustworthy historical document from antiquity. A comparison with other ancient manuscripts demonstrates that the Bible is far more factual, accurate, and truthful than any other religious document.

If the Bible is thrown out as unreliable and the critics' standards remain consistent when evaluating the truth-claims of other ancient books, then virtually all other books from antiquity must be discarded as unreliable. Apologist Josh McDowell says it well:

There is more evidence for the reliability of the text of the New Testament as an accurate reflection of what was initially written [the autographs] than there is for any ten pieces of classical literature put together. . . .

[The Bible is] also in better textual shape than the thirty-seven plays of William Shakespeare written in the seventeenth century, after the invention of printing.[23]

The evidence also demands that the Bible be accepted as God's chosen medium for revealing spiritual truth. If the Bible is truthful in areas where investigation can be applied, it is legitimate to believe that, in the area of religious truth, the Bible is equally reliable. The wise person searching for truth will do well to take seriously the claims of Scripture. And when this is done, he will come face to face with the greatest truth of all: Jesus not only really lived but He was who He claimed to be—the One and only God, the creator, sustainer, and Savior of all. Jesus claimed that He was "the way, the truth, and the life," and that "no one comes to the Father" but through Him (John 14:6). Just as He asked Peter centuries ago, so He asks us today: "Who do you say that I am?" (Mark 8:29). Without a doubt, our eternal destiny rests in who we believe Jesus is and in how we respond to Him. But more on that later.

4

Why Interpret the Bible Literally?

Have you ever heard comments like these?

- "Accept the story about Adam and Eve and a talking snake? You've got to be kidding! That's a nice children's tale, but no one really believes it actually happened."
- "If you think the world was created in six twenty-four-hour days, you might as well join the Flat Earth Society too. Neither theory has any scientific credibility."
- "The story about Jonah is a whale-of-a-tale if I ever heard one. That anyone could survive three days in the belly of a whale is so incredible that it's impossible."
- "Right . . . God told Noah to build an ark, load it up with animals, then shut the ship's doors so God could drown the rest of the world with a heavenly downpour. Children shouldn't even be taught such a cruel story, much less told it's true."
- "You don't take the Bible *literally* do you? Everyone knows that the Bible is mostly myth and that most of its stories are scientifically and historically inaccurate."

All these comments have one thing in common: they challenge the *inerrancy* of the Bible; they question whether the Bible is without error not only in matters of faith and practice (spiritual and moral

49

truths) but also in its historical, geological, and scientific information.

They undermine how the Bible should be interpreted by assuming it's not entirely true because some of its stories don't fit with a modern mindset that tends to reject the supernatural. People who make such comments don't believe the Bible should be taken literally. "The ancients," so they say, "had a more primitive view of the world. They readily accepted the unusual and fantastic because they were not as scientifically astute and highly educated as we are. Today we know better. We know much of what they believed was really myth, with perhaps vague resemblances to what actually happened. There wasn't a worldwide flood, but maybe a local one that did a lot of damage and killed scores of people. The Adam-and-Eve myth was created to explain how the presence of evil can be reconciled with belief in an all-good God." And so the explanations go.

Are these people right? Is the Bible pockmarked by myth? Are there good reasons to interpret it less than literally?

The first step in dealing with these questions of inerrancy is to clarify what a literal interpretation of the Scriptures really means.

As we've seen, the original manuscripts of the Bible are unavailable to us, but the science of textual criticism has proven beyond doubt that the copies we currently possess are nearly 100 percent accurate to the autographs. Although this in itself does not prove that the Bible is inerrant, it does guarantee that the Bible contains few errors due to textual transmission.

Christians believe that the Bible is the *inspired* word of God. This means that the Holy Spirit, working in the hearts and minds of chosen men, authored the Bible so that what God wanted recorded was recorded. However, this doesn't mean that God acted as a divine stenographer, dictating the Bible word for word. Rather, God superintended the writing of Scripture, retaining the authors' own writing styles and personalities, so that the end product was God's.

Taking the Bible literally, then, like believing it is inerrant, does not mean that every word or phrase denotes only its exact literal meaning. The human authors of Scripture used the same literary techniques as other authors. Figures of speech in the Bible should be treated the same as figures of speech found in any other piece of literature. In John 16:25, 29–30, for example, Jesus states that He speaks in "figurative language" (NASV). When Jesus says "I am the door," common sense and normal language usage tells us He is not literally calling Himself a door. When Peter calls Satan a "roaring lion, seeking someone to devour," we know from other passages that Satan is not really a lion and that he doesn't really eat people. People do not always communicate to each other in an exact literal fashion, and we shouldn't expect God to speak to us differently. God used normal modes of language in the Bible. He spoke to us as we speak to each other.

Actually, it is common sense that God would inspire the authors of the Bible to use normal language. To claim otherwise is to question the ability of God to communicate truthfully and accurately. God created man to love and to have fellowship with Him. This requires communication between them. If God wishes to convey to us important truths (e.g., how to receive eternal life), He would unquestionably do so in a way we could easily understand. He would use normal human language. Thus, figures of speech used in Scripture, such as metaphors and personifications, would be easily recognized and understood, which is what we find to be true.

The Bible is also a historical document because God chose to reveal Himself within a historical context. It would be inconsistent with revelation if the Bible contained inaccurate historical information.

Inerrancy, then, simply means that the Bible contains truthful information revealed through normal methods of communication, and what it relates is without error. This applies not only to spiritual truths, such as salvation through Jesus Christ, but to historical, geological, and scientific matters (e.g., the fall of Adam is a true historical account of sin entering humanity; the Noahic flood resulted in catastrophic changes seen in the geological record; creation was by divine mandate rather than naturalistic evolution).

But why should biblical inerrancy be accepted as true? I could cite numerous reasons, but I'll simply focus on six here. Although all of these would not convince every skeptic, they do show the extreme importance of inerrancy to the Christian faith.

THE CASE FOR BIBLICAL INERRANCY

INERRANCY PRESERVES THE BIBLE'S AUTHORITY

Christians claim the Bible is God's written Word, and as such, it is their primary source of authority. Why? Because God is the Bible's ultimate author (2 Tim. 3:16; 2 Pet. 1:21), and in it He has revealed Himself and His plan for mankind.

The reason inerrancy is so vital to the Bible's authority is that without inerrancy, this authority is baseless. For example, if the Bible contains error, how do we know that the gospel message (salvation through Jesus) is true? Perhaps some of the errors in the Bible are found in the teachings ascribed to Jesus. You can't have any assurance that an inerrant gospel appears in an errant Bible.

Moreover, if the Bible contains error, who determines where the error lies? The answer has to be human beings. Therefore man becomes an authority over Scripture because it is up to him to decide what's true and what's false. Man, not God, becomes the determining factor of what is divine revelation. But because man is fallible and makes mistakes, he might judge wrongly. He might even interpret the Bible heretically. In fact, church history stands as a witness that this has sometimes happened.

So if man becomes the authority over Scripture, the Bible loses its authority and we lose our moorings. We end up adrift in a dangerous sea of fluctuating opinions, ulterior motives, and half-truths.

Another problem arises if inerrancy is rejected. The Jehovah's Witnesses and other false religions make the same claim as Christianity, that they are the only true religion. But the truth of Christianity does not rest on the subjective, personal experience of men independent of objective (testable) revelation. Christianity is a historical religion grounded on objective, verifiable facts. No other religion or cult in the world can make this claim and then substantiate it. For this reason, Christianity stands elevated above all other religions as the one true faith. But if we admit to error and allow human beings to become the determining factor of what is truth in Scripture, we reduce Christianity to the same level as all other religions. Its authority becomes human subjectivity and opinion. On the other hand, if the Bible is God's inerrant Word, we have an objective and absolute standard for judging and rejecting the claims of false religions and their false prophets.

INERRANCY RESTS ON THE BIBLE'S HISTORICAL RELIABILITY

The historical reliability of the Bible is the foundation for the inerrancy of Scripture. The Bible claims to be inerrant, as we'll see in a few moments. However, no matter what the Bible claims about itself, if it is not reliable, we could not trust what it says in any area, including inerrancy. On the other hand, if the Bible is a reliable, trustworthy document, then what it says about itself can be trusted. And we saw this fact verified in Chapter 3.

Therefore, since we found the Bible inerrant in all areas in which it can be checked out, we are logically consistent to insist that problem passages (i.e., passages that appear to contain historical or scientific error due to the current unavailability of extra-biblical verification) will eventually be settled in favor of inerrancy. Over the past hundred years, scores of so-called problem passages have been resolved in favor of Scripture. Clark Pinnock reports that "in 1800 the French Institute in Paris issued a list of 82 errors in the Bible which they believed would destroy Christianity. Today none of these 'errors' remain! With further reflection and new discoveries, these 'errors' were cleared away."[1] So it's perfectly reasonable to believe that as additional evidence surfaces, those remaining problem texts will also be validated by nonbiblical sources.

INERRANCY IS TAUGHT IN SCRIPTURE OVERALL

In 2 Timothy 3:16 and 2 Peter 1:21, we're told that what the biblical authors wrote did not flow from their own opinion or theology. Rather, "all Scripture" is inspired by God—it did not ultimately come from a human mind. It is absurd to think that all Scripture is divinely inspired and valuable for teaching and spiritual growth yet can give faulty information. God would not breathe out (which is what *inspire* literally means) error.

Revelation 22:18–19 and Deuteronomy 4:2 come at the inerrancy issue from a different angle. They teach that God's Word should not be added to or subtracted from. Take note that this command occurs in both the Old and New Testaments. Also observe that Deuteronomy is the concluding book of the Old Testament Law, and Revelation is the last book of the New Testament as well as of the entire Bible. There is little doubt that this injunction covers the entire Bible. Unless God's Word is without error, a command not to add to or subtract from Scripture loses its significance.

Consider Psalm 119:105, 130, which teaches that Scripture is designed to give understanding even to the "simple." It would be contradictory to claim that something containing error can lead to understanding. Similarly, in 2 Timothy 3:15, God's Word is said to give wisdom, which would be impossible if it contained mistakes.

Many other passages (such as Isa. 55:10–11; John 17:17; Titus 1:2; Heb. 4:12; 6:18) say that God cannot lie; He inspired the writing of Scripture through the Holy Spirit; Scripture was written clearly and contains specific, truthful information; it should not be changed in any way; and it is adequate for guidance in all matters of Christian living. These claims are totally inconsistent with an errant Bible, but they do support inerrancy.

INERRANCY IS EMBEDDED IN THE OLD TESTAMENT

When we turn to examine the Old Testament, we find inerrancy supported throughout. Texts such as Exodus 4:10–15, Deuteronomy 18:18, 2 Samuel 23:2, and Jeremiah 1:9 tell us that God selected certain individuals, called "prophets," to speak His Word. Some were selected even before they were born (see Jer. 1:5; Luke 1:11–15, John the Baptist is considered the last of the Old Testament prophets). These men were God's mouthpieces. What they spoke was what God wanted communicated. The prophets themselves recognized that they conveyed God's words, not their own (e.g., Jer. 30:2). As God's mouthpieces, they must have spoken inerrantly because God would not have allowed them to speak error in His name.

Not only did God select His spokespersons, but, to ensure that His words were passed on to future generations accurately, He commanded His prophets to record them (Exod. 34:27–28; Isa. 8:1; Jer. 30:2). Now why would God select His own mouthpieces and command them to write His words, then allow them to record error?

God instructed these same prophets to preserve the recorded Word and pass it on as an everlasting testimony (Exod. 17:14; 40:20; Deut. 10:5; 31:24–26; Isa. 30:8; Hab. 2:2). In Romans 15:4, the apostle Paul states that "whatever was written in earlier times was written for our instruction, that through perseverance and the encouragement of the Scriptures we might have hope" (NASV). If God insisted that the Old Testament be recorded and preserved for future instruction, we can be certain that God would have prevented the contamination of error.

Or consider Psalms 105 and 106. In these and other passages, the human authors recall historical events from Israel's past. These texts are examples of the Old Testament validating its own historicity. The Old Testament was written over a thousand-year time span. When newer books in the Old Testament acknowledge historical events in older books, it shows that the later authors believed in the historical inerrancy of the older books. The Psalms noted above were written hundreds of years after the events they acknowledge occurred. The psalmists praise God for the plagues on Egypt that resulted in their people's release from bondage and for parting the Red Sea during their exodus. Obviously, the Israelites alive at the time Psalms 105 and 106 were written did not consider these events as myths or legends. If the Old Testament writers did not believe in the inerrancy of the Old Testament (their Bible), it would be meaningless for them to recount historical data as factual.

It's beyond doubt, then, that the Old Testament claims to be inerrant, and the Israelites accepted it as so. It was written by individuals personally selected by God and instructed in what to write, how to record it, and how to preserve it. It contains not only spiritual truths (matters of faith) and moral truths (matters of practice) but also trustworthy historical facts.

INERRANCY IS EMBRACED IN THE
NEW TESTAMENT

Passages such as 2 Timothy 3:15, 2 Peter 1:21, and 1 Thessa-
lonians 2:13 echo what the Old Testament teaches: all of Scripture is
inspired by God, the Holy Spirit superintended the writing of Scripture, and the Bible contains the words of God, not of men. These texts
also lay a foundation for other New Testament passages that teach
biblical inerrancy.

The apostles acknowledged that the Old Testament authors wrote
under the authority of the Holy Spirit (Acts 1:16; 4:24–25). The New
Testament writers also acknowledged that what they wrote originated with God, not with them (1 Cor. 14:37; 2 Pet. 1:21).

The New Testament authors frequently demonstrated their belief
in the truthfulness of the Old Testament by referring to fulfilled
prophecy (John 12:37–41; Acts 1:16; Rom. 3:1–2). This is nowhere
more evident than in their many references to the prophetic passages
concerning Christ's coming ministry (see Matt. 1:22; 2:5, 15, 23;
13:35; 21:4; 27:9). It's unlikely that the apostles would place such a
heavy emphasis on Old Testament prophecy if they thought it was
less than truthful.

A compelling evidence demonstrating that the New Testament
writers considered the Bible to be inerrant is that they referred to Old
Testament characters and events as fully historical, with no hint that
they were legendary (Luke 3:38; Rom. 5:12–21; 1 Tim. 2:13–14; Heb.
11:4–11; 2 Pet. 3:6). If the New Testament writers considered the Old
Testament as anything other than inerrant historically, it would make
no sense for them to refer to it in such a fashion. There are many
passages throughout the New Testament that refer to events in the
Old Testament as literal history. People and events in Genesis are
mentioned or quoted at least 160 times by the New Testament
writers—and more than 100 of these pertain to the most controversial passages. For example, in the above passages, Peter refers to the
Noahic flood, and Paul refers to Adam and Eve. In Romans 5:12–21,
Paul uses the historical event of the Fall as the reference point for his
teaching on Christ's work of redemption. He states that just as sin

entered the world due to the single act of one man (Adam), so too is the effect of this sin undone by the one act of righteousness when Jesus died on the cross. It is impossible to sustain the parallel between the work of Adam and the work of Christ if Adam was not a historical person and if the fall was not a historical event.

Altogether, such passages demonstrate that the New Testament writers believed their Bible (the Old Testament) was inerrant. They staked their lives on it. Believing Jesus Christ was the prophesied Messiah, many of them died under religious persecution. Like the Old Testament prophets, the New Testament authors recognized they wrote under the inspiration and guidance of the Holy Spirit. To them, all of the Bible was God's inerrant Word

INERRANCY WAS TAUGHT BY JESUS

The most compelling evidence supporting the inerrancy of the Bible is the testimony of Jesus Christ. To all Christians, Jesus is God and the final and supreme authority in all things. If this is true, then His opinion on the inerrancy of Scripture must be accepted as truth. Jesus believed and taught that the Hebrew Bible was inerrant, not only in matters of faith and practice, but in its prophetic, historical, geographical, and scientific data. Jesus also predicted the writing of the New Testament under the power of the Holy Spirit, therefore putting a stamp of approval on its inerrancy. The following is a summary of Jesus' teaching on the Bible's inerrancy.

Now some people may argue that because Jesus' teaching on inerrancy is recorded in the Bible, it's circular reasoning to use the Bible to prove Jesus' view of inerrancy and then use Jesus to prove the inerrancy of the Bible. However, this is not what we're doing here. In Chapter 3, we established the historical reliability of the Bible *independently* of Jesus' testimony by relying on nonbiblical evidences. So we are not guilty of the fallacy of circular reasoning.

Jesus on the Scriptures

Matthew 4:4

In this and many other passages, Jesus either quotes or refers to the Old Testament (His Bible) to teach religious truth or resolve is-

sues. Jesus considered the Hebrew Old Testament completely authoritative; He never questioned its truthfulness. He taught that whatever
the Old Testament pronounced was the last word on the subject at
hand, and He used it to rebuke the Jewish leaders when they misap-
plied Scripture (see Matt. 22:29). For Him to use Scripture in this manner would be meaningless unless He considered it inerrant.

Luke 24:27, 44; John 5:39

Jesus knew He was the Son of God and the Messiah. He also knew
the Old Testament was a witness to Him. Thus, in His communication
with both His disciples and the Jewish people, He referred to Scripture to validate who He was. If Scripture was not accurate and truthful, this would have been a futile exercise. Jesus would have been a
hypocrite and worse if He knew that the Old Testament was false and
yet tried to use it to validate His claims. Clearly, Jesus believed the
Hebrew Scriptures spoke inerrantly of Him.

John 14:26; 16:12–13

In these passages, Jesus certifies the inerrancy of the New Testament by predicting it will be written and that the Holy Spirit will
superintend its authorship. By this He confirmed the inerrancy of the
soon-to-be-written New Testament just as convincingly as He confirmed the divine authorship of the Old Testament.

Matthew 5:17–19

Jesus implied in this text that every letter and word in the Old
Testament Law was put there for a purpose. What the Bible claims as
truth is truth, and what the Bible says will happen will happen. The
only way Jesus could guarantee that everything recorded in the Old
Testament will come to pass is if He knew that it was inerrant.

John 10:35

Again, referring to His Bible, Jesus stated that "Scripture cannot
be broken," confirming its reliability and authority. If Scripture is reliable and authoritative, it must be inerrant. A reliable and authoritative Bible would not contain error.

Jesus on the Old Testament as History

The most compelling evidence that Jesus considered the Old Testament to be inerrant was His reference to Old Testament passages in a historical sense. Although the Scriptures use figurative language to illustrate spiritual truths (e.g., John 10:1–6), it is easy to identify those instances as figurative. To use an earlier example, saying that Satan goes around like a roaring lion seeking someone to devour (1 Pet. 5:8) is an accurate figurative description of Satan's desire to destroy people, but it is obviously not saying Satan is a real lion that eats people. But Jesus did not refer to Old Testament people and events as allegories or myths. He took them literally and historically and thereby clearly endorsed their inerrancy. The following passages illustrate this.

Matthew 19:3–6 (see Genesis 1:27; 2:24)

In this passage, Jesus authenticates the literal creation of Adam and Eve and confirms their historicity in His teaching on divorce. If Adam and Eve were not real people, Jesus' instruction would be hollow. The divorce issue was raised by the Pharisees, and Jesus stated His position by referring to the historical event on which His doctrinal stand rests.

Matthew 12:38–41 (see Jonah 1:17)

In Jesus' mind, Jonah was a real person who really spent three days in the belly of a "great fish" (the Hebrew word used here can be applied to any large creature, including an animal specifically created by God for the purpose it served). It is impossible to draw any other conclusion than that Jesus regarded the experience of Jonah as an historical parallel to His own forthcoming experience between His death and resurrection. If these events in Jesus' life are factual, so too must Jonah's experience, or the comparison would be meaningless. A myth cannot be used to validate a fact. The historicity of this event is further reinforced in Matthew 12:41, where Jesus claims that the people of Nineveh repented at the preaching of Jonah. They would not have done so if Jonah never lived. Thus Jesus aligned the historical events surrounding His resurrection with the historical events in Nineveh and the historical person of Jonah.

Luke 17:26–30 (see Genesis 6, 19)

Here Jesus refers to Noah, the worldwide flood, Lot, and the city of Sodom—all within an historical framework. Although many people have rejected the Noahic flood as scientifically unacceptable, Jesus obviously accepted it as fact. His prediction of a future historical event (His second coming) rests on the literal occurrence of a past event (the Noahic flood). If the flood was myth, then Jesus' prediction would be absurd.

John 6:49 (see Exodus 16)

Skeptics scorn the Exodus account of the supernatural feeding of about two million Israelites during their forty years of wandering in the wilderness. But once again, this passage illustrates that Jesus accepted Old Testament history as completely truthful and accurate.

Luke 20:37–38 (see Exodus 3:1–6)

In this passage, Jesus acknowledges the historical reality of Abraham, Isaac, Jacob, and Moses. He also defends the doctrine of the resurrection. But even more controversial, Jesus speaks of these people in connection with the burning bush, a supernatural occurrence rejected by Bible critics. It is irrational to think that Jesus would refer to historical people, an historical event (the resurrection), and another historical event (the burning bush) all in the same sentence if part of what He was talking about was factual and part (e.g., the burning bush) was not. The entire statement would lose its credibility.

THE LITERAL TRUTH

Jesus accepted and taught the inerrancy of Scripture. The authors of the Old and New Testaments believed the same. The early church fathers accepted the Bible as the inerrant Word of God and treated it as such in their sermons and writings. Augustine, Thomas Aquinas, Martin Luther, John Calvin, and countless other theologians and scholars from other disciplines have embraced the inerrancy of Scripture. For two thousand years, the church has accepted the Bible, as originally inspired and recorded, to be free from error in all that it says. God condemns hypocrisy and false testimony on all fronts. It is unthinkable that a sovereign and holy God would allow error to infiltrate the Bible.

Since the Bible is God's inerrant record of what He wants us to know and do, what it says about moral standards, the human condition, the remedy for sin, the path to salvation and eternal life, the way to a more abundant life here . . . everything it affirms, we should accept as true. What the Bible says, God says. And when God speaks, we better listen.

The Bible Is Inerrant

Old Testament	New Testament
God selects men as prophets to speak His Word (Deut. 18:18)	God inspired all Scripture (2 Tim. 3:16)
God instructed the prophets to record His Word (Isa. 8:1)	The NT authors claim they wrote the words of God (1 Cor. 14:37)
God instructed the prophets to preserve His Word (Isa. 30:8)	The NT authors acknowledge the truthfulness of OT prophecy (Acts 1:16)
The Israelites saw Scripture as historical information (Ps. 105, 106)	The NT authors accepted OT prophecy concerning Jesus Christ (Matt. 1:22–23)
	The NT authors accepted OT people and events as factual (1 Tim. 2:13)

Jesus

Jesus uses the OT to resolve issues (Matt. 4:4)	Jesus says that all OT prophecy will come to pass (Matt. 5:17–18)
Jesus taught that the OT prophesied of Him (Luke 24:27)	Jesus says that Scripture cannot be broken (John 10:35)
Jesus certifies the inerrancy of the soon-to-be-written NT (John 14:26; 16:13)	Jesus referred to OT events and people as factual history (Matt. 12:38–41; Luke 17:26–30)

Conclusion:

The Israelites accepted the OT as the inerrant Word of God; Jesus and the authors of the NT accepted the OT (their Bible) as the inerrant Word of God; Jesus announced the soon-to-be-written NT, thereby certifying its inerrancy. The Bible claims to be the inerrant Word of God. It contains truthful information, and what it relates is without error.

5

Why Should We Reject Religious Writings Other Than the Bible?

Islam, Hinduism, Mormonism, Jehovah's Witnesses, the New Age movement, Christian Science, the Unification Church. What do these religious movements, as well as countless others, have in common? They all believe their writings are superior to the Bible. They may sometimes include the Bible in their list of acceptable religious books, but they will hold on to their belief that their writings significantly expand on, if not correct, what the Bible teaches.

Are they right? Is it possible that the writings of non-Christian religions are inspired by God and thus equal in authority to the Bible?

Some of these same religious groups, including some Christian ones, also argue that some God-inspired writings have been lost or that those in the Protestant Bible are only a partial listing of the extant books God inspired. Are they right?

All these claims are common, and if any of them are true, some of what I've argued may have to be rejected or at least modified. Let's carefully consider each one.

ARE OTHER RELIGIOUS WRITINGS EQUAL OR SUPERIOR TO THE BIBLE?

One of the common denominators of non-Christian religions is that the Bible is not God's final revelation. Many groups teach that their particular prophets have been inspired by God to write new revelation that supersedes Scripture. The Christian response to this claim takes four steps: (1) define the qualifications of a prophet, (2) determine the source of a prophet's revelation, (3) examine what the Bible says about "new" revelation, and (4) compare the Jesus of Scripture with the Jesus promoted by other prophets.

A PROPHET'S QUALIFICATIONS

We have already established that the Bible is God's written revelation and is completely inerrant. So we can turn to Scripture to see what it says about the qualifications of a prophet, then we can take that list and match it against those who are held up as prophets. If these prophets don't meet the qualifications, then they are false prophets and anything they teach contrary to Scripture is also false. In other words, if Joseph Smith of the Mormons, Charles Taze Russell of the Jehovah's Witnesses, Mary Baker Eddy of Christian Science, Muhammad of Islam, or any other self-proclaimed prophet fails the biblical test, then their so-called revelations are a lie and their followers are being duped into believing a false religion.

In Deuteronomy 13:1–5 and 18:20–22, God reveals what counts as the use and misuse of prophecy and who shall prophesy. A false prophet could make true predictions but still not be appointed by God. If a prophecy ever failed to come true, even if it was prophesied in the name of the Lord, then the one who uttered it was considered a fraud.

All non-Christian prophets have failed the second test and thereby demonstrated that God was not inspiring them. For example, in *Doctrine and Covenants* 84:1–5, 31, September 1832, Joseph Smith claimed that "Mount Zion, which shall be the city of New Jerusalem . . . shall be built, beginning at the temple lot, which is appointed by the finger of the Lord, in the western boundaries of the State of Missouri, and dedicated by the hand of Joseph Smith, Jun., and others with whom the Lord was well pleased. . . . which temple shall be reared in this generation."

Likewise, the official writings of the Jehovah's Witnesses proclaim numerous unfulfilled prophecies. One well-known example is their prediction that the battle of Armageddon would occur between 1874 and

1914: "In view of this strong Bible evidence concerning the Times of the Gentiles, we consider it an established truth that the final end of the kingdoms of this world, and the full establishment of the Kingdom of God, will be accomplished at the end of A.D. 1914."[1]

A more recent example of false prophecies concerns "Moses" David Berg, founder of the Children of God, also known as the Family of Love. In 1973, he prophesied that the coming of the comet Kahoutek would result in the destruction of the United States unless America repented: "I believe God means what he says in this shocking revelation above! You in the U.S. have only until January to get out of the States before some kind of disaster, destruction or judgment of God is to fall because of America's wickedness!"[2] Thus, the religious writings of these false prophets and all other "prophets" who have failed prophecies are disqualified as revelations from God.

On the other hand, all biblical prophecies concerning events up to this point in history have come to pass. As we saw in Chapter 3, numerous Old Testament prophecies have been confirmed by archaeology, including not only those pertaining to the Jewish nation and the Messiah but also those dealing with other nations and peoples. Even if we ignored all the Bible's prophecies except for those more than three hundred concerning the Messiah and recorded in the Old Testament, we would be as assured as possible that God had spoken to us through His chosen prophets. Why? Because the possibility of these prophecies being fulfilled in one person by sheer chance is a tiny fraction of one percent—namely, one over eighty-four followed by 123 zeros.[3] Those are odds only God could fulfill!

Another criterion that disqualifies many so-called prophets is the use of objects of divination. Many New Age prophets use crystal balls, mediums, tarot cards, and other "mystically empowered" objects to communicate with spiritual forces. But God plainly warns in Deuteronomy 18:10–12 that no one should use divination, practice witchcraft, interpret omens, or use a sorcerer, medium, or spiritualist. Yet this is exactly what many modern-day prophets do. For example, Joseph Smith used a divining stone and carried an occult Jupiter Talisman around his neck.[4] On these grounds alone, many "prophets" could be dismissed as false.

A third test for prophethood revolves around the biblical injunction not to add to or take away from Scripture (Deut. 4:2; Rev. 22:18–19). In other words, the Bible is God's complete and final revelation, so any other religious writings claiming to have the same or greater authority as Scripture is a false revelation—it is not from God. Again, the message is plain: Any so-called holy book, whether it claims to be additional revelation to Scripture (e.g., the Book of Mormon) or claims to contain spiritual truths contrary to the Bible (e.g., New Age philosophies) must be rejected as divine revelation.

A final test to determine if a prophet is from God is to compare his revelation of Jesus with the Jesus described in Scripture. The cults portray a much different Jesus than the one revealed in the Bible. If God inspired other prophets to write about Jesus, He certainly would not contradict His revelation of Christ in the New Testament. This is the case in Scripture. The Jesus of the New Testament fits perfectly with the Jesus prophesied by various Old Testament prophets. In a similar way, if Jesus revealed Himself in other writings, He would be the same Jesus we find in the Bible.

However, in every case, none of the cults bear witness to the Jesus of Scripture. They all reject Him as part of the triune Godhead—one in essence, power, and authority with the Father and the Holy Spirit. The apostle John warns in 1 John 4:1–2 that many false prophets will go out into the world, but he assures us that we can know if they come from God because they will confess "that Jesus Christ has come in the flesh." In other words, Jesus is God incarnate (in bodily form). Any alleged prophet who claims to speak new revelation from God but teaches a false Jesus is *not* from God.

DO OTHER ANCIENT WRITINGS BELONG IN THE BIBLE?

The second question to answer is a little more difficult: How do we know that the books presently in the Bible are the only ones that belong there? This question has to do with the canon, the sixty-six books (thirty-nine in the Old Testament and twenty-seven in the New) officially accepted by the Protestant church as God's inspired and complete revelation. How do we know there should be just sixty-six books?

Although the Old Testament canon was established by about 400 B.C., the New Testament was not firmly established for nearly three hundred years after the last book (Revelation) was written. Nor, in some people's minds is the matter settled yet. For instance, in 1945, forty-nine ancient religious books were discovered near Nag Hammadi in upper Egypt. Many people claim that these books, and other ancient writings, contain additional words and deeds of Jesus. Should they be added to the Bible?

The problem of possible missing books becomes even muddier when we read in 1 Corinthians 5:9 about a letter Paul wrote to the Corinthians that is not found in Scripture—a letter that some people think belongs in the Bible but was lost. In Colossians 4:16 Paul mentions a second letter written to the church at Laodicea, which we also don't have. Even the Old Testament mentions some documents not included in the biblical canon (Num. 21:14; Josh. 10:13). How do we explain the absence of documents written by the authors of Scripture? Why are some books considered canonical while others, perhaps even written by the same authors, are not?

One of the dangers of apologetics is that we can get so involved seeking objective evidence to validate biblical claims that we overlook the faith element. We must never lose sight of the fact that nothing in proclamation (preaching), teaching, or apologetics is done independently of the Holy Spirit. Christianity has a subjective element, and it's there that truth is vindicated by no other power than that of the Spirit of God. Even if we didn't have all the objective evidence currently available, the Bible would still be validated by the inner witness of the Holy Spirit (see Rom. 8:16; 1 Cor. 2:6–14).

Furthermore, God has not given clear answers to all of the questions asked by Christians and non-Christians. The information Scripture gives is designed to persuade us to trust Jesus Christ for our salvation (see John 20:30–31; 21:25). The author of Hebrews reminds us that "faith is the substance of things hoped for, the evidence of things *not seen*" (11:1). We are perfectly justified to accept the Bible strictly on faith.

The question of what books belong in Scripture falls largely into the faith category. Ultimately, canonicity is not based on human rationality but on divine inspiration (2 Tim. 3:16). In other words, God determined canonicity by inspiring the writing of certain books, and man discovered through the power of the Holy Spirit which of these writings (books) are canonical or authoritative and which are not.

With this in mind, I can now point you to certain tests the Holy Spirit allowed the church fathers to use in discovering which books belong in the Bible. Two scholars, Norman Geisler and William Nix, list five questions that acted as guides in discovering which books were truly inspired.[5]

"*Is it* authoritative?"

Throughout the Old Testament, introductory phrases such as "Thus says the Lord," "The Lord spoke," and "The Word of the Lord came to me" are used more than two thousand times. The Old Testament authors never claimed authority for themselves, but they did acknowledge the Scripture's authority. While Jesus, of course, spoke with His own authority ("Truly, I say . . ."), the authors of the New Testament also maintained that what they wrote came from God. Their words were His words, and vice versa (1 Cor. 14:37; 2 Pet. 1:21).

By comparison, other books were not accepted into canon because they either made no claim to convey God's spoken word or their claim of divine inspiration faltered when their contents were examined. In many cases, noncanonical books are full of fanciful and magical events that obviously lack the earmarks of historicity.

"*Is it* prophetic?"

Perhaps the most important evidence for the canonicity of the books of the Bible is that they were written either by a prophet, as in the case of the Old Testament, or by an apostle or the companion of an apostle, as in the case of the New Testament. The apostles Matthew, John, and Peter wrote their own books. Mark was an associate of Peter, and Luke was a fellow worker with Paul. Paul was an apostle appointed by Jesus (Gal. 1:1). Tradition claims that James and Jude were half brothers of Jesus. The author of Hebrews puts himself in apostolic company when he says that the gospel was "confirmed to *us* by those who heard" (Heb. 2:3, emphasis mine).

The importance of apostolic authority is reinforced by the selection of a replacement for Judas. When Judas died, the two qualifications noted for becoming an apostle were being an eyewitness of Jesus from the beginning of His ministry at His baptism by John and being a witness to His resurrection (Acts 1:21–22).

The importance of apostolic authority in the authorship of the New Testament cannot be underestimated. If only an apostle, or a companion of one, writing from an apostle's personal account, could write a book and have it accepted as canonical, no writings could gain such acceptance if they were composed after the death of the twelve apostles. This automatically renders the Book of Mormon and other cultic writings as noncanonical.

"Is it authentic?"

The Bible is the most historically reliable document from antiquity. In every area in which it could be checked out, it has proven itself to contain truthful information. Moreover, the Bible is consistent throughout. The New Testament is in complete harmony with the Old Testament on its views about God, salvation, sin, and all other major doctrines.

But many of the writings that were turned down as canonical are totally out of harmony with Scripture. Some contain moral incongruities, blatantly heretical teachings, and false prophecies. They could never fit with the rest of the Bible.

For example, in the apocryphal book Ecclesiasticus 33:25–28, we read quite a different attitude toward slavery as found in Philemon:

> Make your slave work, if you want rest for yourself;
>   if you leave him idle, he will be looking for his liberty.
> The ox is tamed by yoke and harness,
>   the bad servant by racks and tortures.
> Put him to work to keep him from being idle,
>   for idleness is a great teacher of mischief.
> Set him to work, for that is what he is for,
>   and if he disobeys you, load him with fetters.

In The Prayer of Manasses (vv. 8–9), we read that Abraham, Isaac, and Jacob never sinned against God—quite a different picture from the Genesis accounts.

Other apocryphal books teach false doctrines, such as prayer for the dead (2 Macc. 12:44–45), and give fanciful, unbelievable accounts of alleged historical events (2 Macc. 14:41–46).

"Is it dynamic?"

A book was not accepted as Scripture if it lacked the power to change people's lives (see 2 Tim. 3:16–17; Heb. 4:12). God's Word moves people away from sin and toward lives of holiness. The Bible contains the perfect recipe for an abundant life (John 10:10). It holds the secret (the love and power of Jesus) for healing broken, wounded lives (Matt. 11:28–30). Throughout the past two thousand years, these promises have been borne out in the experiences of many millions of Christians. No other book in the world can, or has, affected so many lives in such a dramatic and positive fashion as the Bible. The fact that biblical principles have been the guiding moral light of Western civilization for centuries further testifies to its dynamic power.

"Was it received?"

Perhaps the major reason the Bible was not fully canonized in its present form until the fourth century is because communication was slow in ancient times. There were no telephones and fax machines, and travel was ponderous and dangerous. The church was scattered throughout most of the known world, and many of the church fathers lived hundreds of miles apart. It was impossible for councils to meet frequently to discuss the scores of books vying for canonicity. Hence, it took nearly three hundred years for the sixty-six books of the Bible to be approved by the church fathers and for them to study and reject contending books. However, in spite of this, all of the books in the Bible were commonly accepted by most of the church fathers long before they were formally approved as canonical.

Aside from these five tests, there are internal validations in Scripture. For example, in Luke 24:44, Jesus said that everything concerning Him in the "Law of Moses and the Prophets and the Psalms" had to be fulfilled. The Law, the Prophets, and the Psalms marked the threefold division of the Hebrew Scriptures. So in this passage, Jesus displayed His acceptance of the entire Old Testament as canonical, as God-inspired. Jesus also referred to many Old Testament books, many times quoting from them—another indication of His belief in their inspiration.

Likewise, the authors of the New Testament quoted and referred to most of the Old Testament books. In fact, of the twenty-two books numbered in the Hebrew Bible (the same books which Christians have divided into 39 books), eighteen are cited by the New Testament authors.

In a similar way, Jesus and the New Testament authors verified the canon of the New Testament. In John 14:26 and 16:13, Jesus prophesied that the New Testament would be revealed through the power of the Holy Spirit. And in 2 Peter 3:16, Peter confirmed that Paul's letters were part of the "Scriptures."

DOES THE APOCRYPHA BELONG IN THE BIBLE?

Now we need to deal with an issue that divides Christians. It concerns the apocrypha—the fourteen or fifteen books written between 200 B.C. and A.D. 100 (after the completion of the Old Testament canon and before the establishment of the New Testament canon) that are considered canonical by the Roman Catholic church. When we apply the tests listed above to the apocrypha, we find that these books don't pass. I'd like to summarize the reasons Protestantism has rejected the apocrypha as Scripture. Together these reasons represent a formidable case.

First, the apocrypha was never included in the Hebrew Bible, and it was not even formally included in the Catholic Bible until the Council of Trent in A.D. 1546. The Catholic church embraced the apocrypha to counter the attacks of Martin Luther and other Reformers who discovered that several aspects of Catholic theology came from the apocrypha, not from the sixty-six books of the Bible. Some of these doctrines concerned mass for the dead, merits acquired through good works, purgatory, penance, and indulgences. In short, the Catholic Church added the apocrypha to Scripture after the fact to give divine authority to already existing doctrines.

Second, neither Jesus nor the New Testament writers quoted from the apocrypha as Scripture, even though they cited passages from the

Old Testament nearly three hundred times. Jude quotes the noncanonical book of Enoch, but the prophecy he cites was originally uttered by the Enoch mentioned in the Bible (Gen. 5:19–24). In any event, it is fallacious to assume that just because the Bible quotes a noncanonical book that that implies it is inspired. Paul quotes pagan poets in Acts 17:28. Certainly we should not conclude from this that these poets or their writings were inspired by the Holy Spirit.

The Old Testament Apocrypha

Type of Book	Revised Standard Version	Douay
Didactic	1. The Wisdom of Solomon (c. 30 B.C.)	Book of Wisdom
	2. Ecclesiasticus (Sirach) (132 B.C.)	Ecclesiastes
Religious Romance	3. Tobit (c. 20 B.C.)	Tobias
	4. Judith (c. 150 B.C.)	Judith
Historic	5. I Esdras (c. 150–100 B.C.)	III Esdras*
	6. I Maccabees (c. 110 B.C.)	I Machabees
	7. II Maccabees (c. 170–110 B.C.)	II Machabees
Prophetic	8. Baruch (c. 150–50 B.C.)	Baruch Chaps. 1–5
	9. Letter of Jeremiah (c. 300–100 B.C.)	Baruch Chap. 6
	10. II Esdras (c. A.D. 100)	IV Esdras*
Legendary	11. Additions to Esther (140–130 B.C.)	Esther 10:4–16; 24
	12. Prayer of Azariah (second or first century B.C.) (Song of Three Young Men)	Daniel 3:24–90
	13. Susanna (second or first century B.C.)	Daniel 13
	14. Bel and the Dragon (c. 100 B.C.)	Daniel 14
	15. Prayer of Manasseh (second or first century B.C.)	Prayer of Manasseh*

*Books not accepted as canonical at the Council of Trent, 1546.
From Norman L. Geisler and William Nix, *A General Introduction to the Bible* (Chicago, IL: Moody, 1983), 169.

In Luke 11:51, Jesus accuses the scribes of slaying all the prophets God had sent to Israel from the time of Abel to the time of Zechariah.

Abel died in Genesis, and Zachariah's death is recorded in 2 Chronicles 24:20–21, the last book in the Hebrew Bible (Malachi is the last book in our English Bible). In making this statement, Jesus expresses the extent of the Old Testament canon, omitting completely any of the apocryphal books.

Third, most of the leading church fathers recognized a distinction between the canonical Hebrew Bible and the noncanonical apocryphal books, and many, such as Origen and Athanasius, spoke out against the apocrypha. Moreover, no local synod or canonical listing included the apocryphal books for almost the first four hundred years of the church's existence.

Fourth, even Jerome, who first translated the Bible from Greek into Latin (the Vulgate—which is the official translation of the Roman Catholic church) rejected the apocrypha as part of canon.

Fifth, while the apocrypha includes some valuable historical information, it contains numerous nonbiblical, fanciful, and heretical doctrines. It also relates numerous historical, geographical, and chronological errors that are totally inconsistent with the inerrancy of canonical Scripture.

Sixth, the apocrypha doesn't claim to be the inspired Word of God, and it was written well past the era of the Old Testament prophets.

THE BIBLE SUPREME

We can conclude that the church today has the complete, full, and final revelation of God in sixty-six books. Therefore it's virtually inconceivable that an alleged lost book would be discovered that belongs in the Bible. Nor is there any reason to suspect that any new revelation will come for inclusion in Scripture. God would not inspire a written revelation, guide the church by its mandates for nearly two thousand years, then suddenly reveal additional truths that expand on or contradict His previous revelation. Yet this is exactly the kind of revelation groups such as the Mormons and Jehovah's Witnesses claim to possess. God is a God of truth, not of confusion (1 Cor. 14:33). He has spoken completely, finally, and supremely in the sixty-six books rightfully called Holy Scripture.

6

Is Jesus a Legend, Lunatic, Liar, or Lord?

The most critical issue of the Christian faith is the identity of Jesus of Nazareth. Christianity stands or falls on who Jesus Christ is. What He said, did, or taught are important, but they are not foundational. Jesus' identity is. He is more than just the founder of Christianity; He *is* Christianity. If you substitute anyone else for Jesus—the greatest Christian theologian or the most beloved pastor or the wisest teacher, take your pick—Christianity would collapse.

Jesus asked His disciples, "Who do you say that I am?" (Matt. 16:15). This same question rings down through the centuries. Who is Jesus Christ? Is He just a man? Is He a religious prophet? Is He a great moral teacher? Or, as Christians claim, is He really God in the flesh? When Peter answered this question, he replied for all Christians throughout the ages: "You are the Christ, the Son of the living God" (v. 16). If Peter is right, if there is even the remotest possibility that Jesus Christ is God, then it is crucial that everyone investigate this matter. For if Jesus is God, then what He says about sin, salvation, judgment, how to live an abundant, joyful life . . . indeed, everything He said must be true. Our eternal destiny rests on our answer to the question, Is Jesus really God?

In this chapter, I will show that what the Bible says about Jesus and what Jesus says about Himself will provide the evidence we need to affirm Jesus' deity. But you should take note that the validity of this evidence rests on the reliability of the Bible. If the Bible doesn't contain truthful information, we can discount what it says about Jesus. But, as we determined in previous chapters, the Bible is not only reliable historically, but it's totally inerrant because it's God's written revelation. So what it states—even about Jesus—must be true.

THE BIBLE'S WITNESS

JESUS REALLY LIVED

We have already seen that the Bible was written by men who personally knew Jesus or His apostles and therefore recorded the facts of Christ's life based on first-hand testimony. Moreover, extra-biblical sources, such as Roman historian Cornelius Tacitus and Jewish historian Flavius Josephus, also confirmed Jesus' existence and the movement He began. The evidence for Jesus' historicity is so great hardly any scholar ever questions it. Even Jewish and atheistic critics agree that Jesus Christ really existed.

What the critics do reject, however, is the Christian claim that Jesus is more than a mere man, that He is also God. But this is inconsistent. The same evidence that demonstrates Jesus was a historical person also demonstrates that He was truly God incarnate. So the only rational way to reject the evidence for His deity is to reject the evidence for His historicity, which virtually no one does anymore. In fact, those few remaining hard-core critics who try to dismiss the abundance of facts proving Jesus' historicity, to be consistent, would have to do the same with about everyone else in recorded history. If all the evidence pointing to Jesus is wrong, then so is the evidence pointing to Socrates, Caesar Augustus, Galileo . . . name your person. No one's historical reality is as well substantiated as Jesus'.[1] If He goes, we might as well close down history classes and departments. They won't have much to teach anymore.

JESUS HAD DIVINE ATTRIBUTES

The Bible reveals that Jesus possesses attributes only God could possess. For example, Jesus is omnipresent—everywhere present at the same time (see John 14:16, 26; 16:7, 13 with Matt. 18:20; 28:20).

He is omniscient—has infinite knowledge (Matt. 24:24–25; John 16:30; 21:17; Luke 6:8; 11:17). Jesus is also omnipotent—all-powerful. He created the universe (Col. 1:16), exercises power over death and gives eternal life (John 5:25–29; 6:39), controls nature (Mark 4:4; Matt. 21:19), overpowers demons (Mark 5:11–15), and heals diseases (Luke 4:38–41). He performs miracles too (John 5:36; 10:25, 37–38; 20:30–31). Moreover, Jesus is eternal; He pre-existed with the Father from all eternity (John 1:1–2). Jesus' life reveals other characteristics reserved only for God: He accepts worship (Matt. 14:33), forgives sins (Matt. 9:2), and commits no wrong (John 8:46). So Jesus' behavior and character exhibits deity.

Although some of the marks of deity (performing miracles, knowing the future, etc.) ascribed to Jesus can also be seen among His apostles and some Old Testament prophets such as Moses and Elijah, in all cases their power to perform these feats had its source in God (see 1:18). Jesus, on the other hand, is His own source of power and authority by virtue of divine mandate (see Matt. 28:18; Mark 2:10; 3:15; John 10:18).

The Deity of Christ

Attribute	Scripture
Omnipresent	Matt. 28:20
Omniscient	John 16:30; Matt. 24:24–25; John 13:21–26; Matt. 12:25
Omnipotent	Matt. 28:18; John 1:3; John 5:25–29; Mark 4:41; Mark 5:11–15; Luke 4:38–40
Eternal	John 1:1–2
Performed Miracles	John 10:37–38
Accepted Worship	Matt. 14:33
Forgave Sins	Matt. 9:2
Sinless	John 8:46
Holy	John 6:69

In addition to this, Jesus is referred to by the Old Testament name for God. In the Hebrew Bible, the sacred name for God was YHWH, likely pronounced Yahweh. When the Hebrew Scriptures were translated into the Greek around the middle of the second century B.C., Yahweh was translated into the Greek word *kyrios* (Lord). In Romans 10:9 and 13, 1 Corinthians 12:3, Philippians 2:11, and other passages, the word *Lord,* when applied to Jesus, refers to Yahweh, the sacred Hebrew name for God.

Furthermore, Jesus is called *God* by the New Testament writers and apostles, including John (John 1:1, 14), Paul (Col. 2:9; Titus 2:13), the author of Hebrews (Heb. 1:3, 8), Peter (Acts 2:34–39; 2 Pet. 1:1), and Thomas (John 20:28).

JESUS FULFILLED MESSIANIC PROPHECY

One of the major evidences for the deity of Jesus is fulfilled prophecy. The apostles often appealed to fulfilled prophecy as proof that Jesus was the Messiah prophesied in the Old Testament. Jesus knew that He fulfilled these futuristic utterances and used this knowledge to confirm His own claims to be the Messiah (the Son of God incarnate). He referred to the teachings of Scripture to reveal Himself to His disciples (Luke 24:25–27) and taught that prophecy about Himself must be fulfilled (Matt. 26:54, 56). He claimed that the entire Bible bore witness to Him (Luke 24:27; John 5:39).

The Bible contains several hundred prophecies relating to the birth, life, ministry, death, resurrection, and future return of Jesus Christ. Almost thirty of them were literally fulfilled in one twenty-four-hour period just prior to His death (e.g., those relating to His betrayal, trial, crucifixion, and burial). Some of the most important prophecies about Christ accurately predicted His birthplace (Mic. 5:2), flight to Egypt (Hos. 11:1), the identity of His forerunner (Mal. 3:1), His entering Jerusalem on a donkey (Zech. 9:9), betrayal for thirty pieces of silver (Zech. 11:12), humiliation and beating (Isa. 50:6), crucifixion with other prisoners (Isa. 53:12), hand and feet wounds (Ps. 22:16), side wound (Zech. 12:10), soldiers gambling for His clothing (Ps. 22:18), His burial in a rich man's tomb (Isa. 53:9), resurrection (Pss. 16:10; 49:15), and second coming (Ps. 50:3–6; Isa. 9:6–7; Dan. 7:13–14; Zech. 14:4–8).

Important Old Testament Prophecies About Jesus

OT Prophecy & Scripture	NT Fulfillment
Born of a virgin (Isa. 7:14)	Matt. 1:22–23
Born in Bethlehem (Mic. 5:2)	Luke 2:4–7
Preceded by a forerunner (Mal. 3:1)	Matt. 11:10
Entered Jerusalem on a donkey (Zech. 9:9)	Matt. 21:4–5
Betrayed for 30 pieces of silver (Zech. 11:12)	Matt. 26:14–15
Spat on and struck (Isa. 50:6)	Matt. 26:67
Crucified with other prisoners (Isa. 53:12)	Luke 22:37
Pierced through hands and feet (Ps. 22:16)	John 20:25–27
Pierced through His side (Zech. 12:10)	John 19:34–37
Soldiers gambled for clothing (Ps. 22:18)	Matt. 27:35
Buried in a rich man's tomb (Isa. 53:9)	Matt: 27:57–60
Would be resurrected (Ps. 16:10)	Matt. 28:5–7
Would return a second time (Dan. 7:13–14)	Rev. 19

Jesus could not have accidentally or deliberately fulfilled these prophecies. Obviously, events such as His birthplace and lineage, method of execution, soldiers casting lots for His garments, or being pierced in the side are events beyond Jesus' control. Peter Stoner and Robert Newman, in their book *Science Speaks,* demonstrate the statistical improbability of any one man, accidentally or deliberately, from the day of these prophecies down to the present time, fulfilling just eight of the hundreds of prophecies Jesus fulfilled. They demonstrate that the chance of this happening is 1 in 10^{17} power. Stoner gives an illustration that helps visualize the magnitude of such odds:

Suppose that we take 10^{17} silver dollars and lay them on the face of Texas. They will cover all of the state two feet deep. Now mark one of these silver dollars and stir the whole mass thoroughly, all over the state. Blindfold a man and tell him that he can travel as far as he wishes, but he must pick up one silver dollar and say that this is the right one. What chance would he have of getting the right one? Just the same chance that the prophets would have had of writing these eight prophecies and having them all come true in any one man, from their day to the present time, providing they wrote using their own wisdom.[2]

It is mathematically absurd to claim that Jesus accidentally or deliberately fulfilled Old Testament prophecy. Obviously, this evidence stands as a powerful demonstration of Jesus' messiahship.

JESUS PERFORMED MIRACLES

Still another way in which Jesus demonstrated His deity is through miraculous acts. Jesus told His followers that if they do not believe His words, they should believe His miraculous works (John 10:37–38). The New Testament authors also recognized the value of miracles to validate Christ's claims (see Acts 2:22).

Jesus performed countless miracles: He healed the sick, made the blind see, changed water into wine, quieted the sea, cast out demons, walked on water, raised Lazarus and others from the dead, and fed five thousand men (plus women and children—Matt. 14:21) with only five loaves of bread and two fish. These miracles were not done clandestinely. All were performed before believers and unbelievers and under a variety of circumstances. As with other events in Jesus' life, His miracles were recorded in the Bible by eyewitnesses.

It's significant that the question of miracles was not a controversy in Jesus' day, or, for that matter, throughout most of church history. In John 11:45–48, after Jesus raised Lazarus from the dead, the chief priests and the Pharisees convened a council to decide what to do about Jesus' growing popularity. The issue they discussed was not whether He actually performed miracles, but rather how to stop Him from performing more so His popularity would wane. The Jewish authorities didn't deny He performed miracles. Instead, they claimed that He got His power to perform miracles from Satan (Matt. 9:34; 12:24; Mark 3:22). They couldn't refute what they and many hundreds of people saw.

Miracles are dramatic and clear evidence that Jesus is the Son of God, and they were used by Christ to validate this claim to the world.

JESUS ROSE FROM THE DEAD

The most important evidence for the deity of Jesus Christ is His resurrection (Rom. 1:4). The resurrection sets Jesus apart from all other religious leaders and unquestionably shows Him to be God. Because evidence supporting this historic event is so essential and enormous, we'll take the entire next chapter to deal with it. So now we'll move on to what Jesus claimed about Himself.

AFFIRMATIONS

It's one thing to show from Scripture that Jesus possesses divine attributes; it's still another to demonstrate that Jesus actually claimed to be God. If Jesus never affirmed His deity, then the evidence presented so far would be suspect. Christians could be charged with misinterpreting Scripture, and the New Testament authors with misunderstanding Jesus' identity and mission. On the other hand, if Jesus did claim to be God, and if the Bible supports this claim by demonstrating He possesses attributes of deity, then surely we have sufficient evidence that Jesus is God.

Once again, our evidence rests on the proven historical reliability of the Bible, which supports the Bible's claim that it's divinely inspired and inerrant. If the Bible is God's Word, then not only what the authors of Scripture say about Jesus must be true, but what Jesus Himself says must also be true. And Jesus does claim divine status in numerous ways.

Jesus makes several explicit statements concerning His deity: "I and My Father are one" (John 10:30); "If you had known Me, you would have known My Father also; and from now on you know Him and have seen Him. . . . He who has seen Me has seen the Father" (John 14:7, 9).

In Mark 14:60–64 (see Matt. 26:63–66), Jesus is questioned by Caiaphas, the high priest. In response to Caiaphas's question as to whether Jesus was the "Christ, the Son of the Blessed," Jesus acknowledged His deity by stating "I am." Caiaphas had no doubt that Jesus was making such a claim. He referred to it as blasphemy, and the rest of the religious leaders agreed by condemning Jesus to death. Caiaphas even ripped his clothes, a customary reaction upon hearing blasphemy, which Jesus' claim to be equal with the Father was to the high priest. According to Jewish law, blasphemy was a capital offense punishable by stoning. In fact, this charge provided the Jews with their only legal excuse to have Jesus crucified. (Compare this with John 5:16–18, where the Jews were seeking to kill Jesus because He was "making Himself equal with God.")

Still another direct claim to deity is found in John 8:56–58. Speaking to the Jews, Jesus said, "Your father Abraham rejoiced to see My day, and he saw it and was glad. . . . before Abraham was, I AM." If we compare this passage with Exodus 3:13–15, we see that the phrase "I AM" in John 8:58 is a claim by Christ to be the Yahweh of the Old Testament. In Exodus 3:14, "I AM" is the divine name Yahweh, by which God revealed Himself to Moses at the burning bush. It emphasizes God's eternal self-existence. Thus in John 8:58, Jesus is saying more than the fact that He existed prior to Abraham. It is a distinct claim to be God, the one and only. Once again, it is evident that the Jews understood this claim. In verse 59, we read that they picked up stones to throw at Him for what they considered to be His blasphemous self-affirmation.

In many other direct ways, Jesus claimed to be God. He said He was "Lord even of the Sabbath" (Matt. 12:8). Who but God could be this? He tells a paralyzed man that his "sins are forgiven" (Mark 2:5). Who but God can forgive sins? Jesus said to the multitudes in His famous Sermon on the Mount, "You have heard that the ancients were told . . . but *I say* to you . . ." (Matt. 5:21, 27, 31, 33, 38, 43, 44, NASV). Who but God could speak with such finality, with such authority? In Matthew 23:34, Jesus says, "I am sending you prophets and wise men" (NASV). Who but God can do this?

In addition to these claims to deity, there is other evidence to consider. For instance, Jesus claimed to have God's authority. Whereas other religious leaders pointed men away from themselves and to their respective gods, referring to themselves as mere spokesmen, Jesus referred to Himself as the very source of authority and truth (Matt. 28:18; John 14:6).

Jesus also equated people's attitudes about Himself with their attitudes toward God. He said that to know Him is to know God (John 8:19), to see Him is to see God (John 12:45), to believe in Him is to believe in God (John 12:44), and to hate Him is to hate God (John 15:23).

The titles "Son of Man" and "Son of God," which indicate deity, were taken by Jesus as applying to Him. "Son of Man" frequently occurs in the Old Testament (see Dan. 7:13–14). By the time of Christ, it had tremendous messianic significance. And the Messiah was believed to be divine, as Isaiah 9:6 makes clear, where we read that the Messiah is called "Wonderful Counselor" (referring to the Messiah as a supernatural counselor) and "Mighty God" (designating Yahweh). By taking the title "Son of Man" for Himself, Jesus declared His deity, as the Jews recognized (see Matt. 26:64–65; Luke 22:69–71).

Although, in the Old Testament, the title "Son of God" is applied to angels, Adam, and the Hebrew nation, it denotes deity in the New Testament. In Matthew 26:63–65, Jesus accepted the title when the high priest applied it to Him in a messianic sense. Once again, the Jewish reaction to His claim demonstrates that they understood Jesus to be calling Himself God.

Jesus also used the "Son of God" title to underscore His special union with God the Father (John 3:16). Moreover, the repeated use of *Son* with *Father* may be alluding to Jesus' equality with the Father in the Godhead. Since Jesus the Son is part of the triune Godhead, "Son of God" likely means that Jesus is a part of the Godhead.

THE TRILEMMA ARGUMENT

So far three important truths have been established: (1) Jesus is an historical person, (2) He possesses the attributes of God, and (3) He claimed to be God. Since the Bible is God's Word, this is sufficient to establish beyond doubt that Jesus is who He claims to be—God.

Unfortunately, many non-Christians will not take the time to evaluate this evidence. And although the historicity of Jesus is seldom doubted, most non-Christians believe that Jesus is simply a great moral teacher or religious philosopher. They do not accept Him as God.

For such people, there remains a simple, rational exercise to determine whether Jesus is deity. It's called the trilemma argument. It poses three options for Jesus: (1) Jesus says He is God, but He knows that's not true, so He's a deceiver (a liar); (2) Jesus really thinks He is God, but He isn't, so He's a madman (lunatic); (3) Jesus claims to be God because He really is God (Lord). If we accept the fact that Jesus is an historical person who claimed to be God, then these are the only rational options. Notice that moral teacher and religious philosopher are not included. He could not be either if He was a liar or a lunatic. And certainly if He is God, He is infinitely greater than either one. C. S. Lewis makes the point clearly and forcefully:

> I'm trying here to prevent anyone from saying the really silly thing that people often say about Him: "I'm ready to accept Jesus as a great moral teacher, but I don't accept His claim to be God." That's the one thing we mustn't say. A man who was merely a man and said the sort of things Jesus said wouldn't be a great moral teacher. He'd either be a lunatic—on a level with the man who says he's a poached egg—or else he'd be the Devil of Hell. You must make your choice. Either this man was, and is, the Son of God: or else a madman or something worse. You can shut Him up for a fool, you can spit at Him and kill Him as a demon; or you can fall at His feet and call Him Lord and God. But don't let us come with any patronizing nonsense about His being a great human teacher. He hasn't left that open to us. He didn't intend to.[3]

WAS JESUS A LIAR?

If Jesus claimed to be God and yet knew He was not, He was lying. In fact, He was a liar of the worse kind because He tricked people into following a religion that, if not true, would inevitably lead them away from the true God and into eternal damnation. But given what the Bible reveals about Jesus' teachings and the life He lived, He could not have been a deceiver. Nor is it likely that a liar would have had the profound and lasting influence He has had. No other person in history has been considered as morally righteous and honest as Jesus has. He taught His followers to be truthful at all costs, to give sacrificially to others, and to share unconditionally. Jesus not only taught these things but lived them. His was not the character of a liar.

Besides, even supposing Jesus knew He was leading people astray regarding His deity claims, it seems ludicrous that He would suffer brutal torture and the excruciating execution by crucifixion just to maintain a lie. Someone may die for something he thinks is true, but certainly not for something he knows is false. It is hard to imagine that Jesus would have lived such a monumental lie when it brought

JESUS CLAIMS TO BE GOD

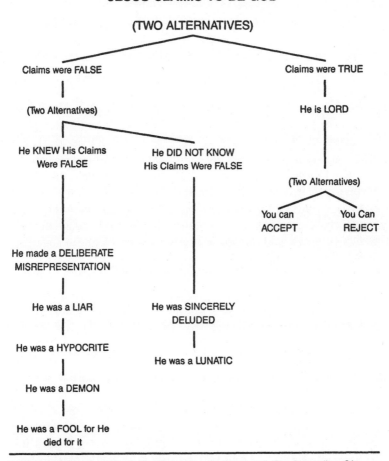

From Josh McDowell, *Evidence That Demands a Verdict,* rev. ed. (San Bernardino, CA: Here's Life, 1979), 104.

Him no material gain, no immediate fame, and eventually led to a horrible death.

WAS JESUS A LUNATIC?

Is it possible Jesus actually thought He was God but was self-deluded? Many people have claimed divine status, but their madness was virtually always obvious. Does what we know about Jesus fit this image? Not in the slightest.

Neither the Bible record nor the testimony of history gives the barest hint that Jesus was a lunatic. He showed none of the symptoms of madness common to people suffering from mental disorders or hallucinations. His teachings were not the ravings of a madman. He never exhibited signs of paranoia or schizophrenia. He was never rash or impulsive. Under all circumstances, even when suffering the anguish of the cross, Jesus appeared self-assured and in complete possession of His senses. Regardless on what subject He spoke, His advice was always profound, insightful, intelligible, and reliable. His instructions in all areas of human relationships (religious, moral, political, psychological, social) were so reliable that they have molded and shaped Western civilization for nearly twenty centuries. Jesus has set countless thousands of people free from the bondage of mental illness, drugs, and alcohol. There is not a shred of evidence that Jesus Christ was anything less than fully sane.

IS JESUS LORD?

Logic and the preponderance of evidence force us to eliminate liar and lunatic choices. And there's only one option left—Lord. If anyone made a decision for Christ based on no other evidence than probability and common sense, he would be driven to conclude that Jesus Christ is who He claimed to be: God in bodily form, the Savior of all who trust in Him by faith.

The significance of this is, literally, a matter of life and death. If Jesus Christ is God, which He is, then what He teaches about sin and salvation is not merely the speculation of a great moral teacher but the very words of God. Jesus said that He is the only way to achieve eternal life (John 14:6). In light of the evidence, it would be foolhardy to reject His claim.

7

Is the Resurrection a Fraud, Fantasy, or Fact?

The resurrection of Jesus Christ is the climax of the New Testament. If it really happened, it is a historic event of such magnitude that it affects every person on the face of the earth. Why? Because it powerfully demonstrates that Jesus is God (Rom. 1:4). Who else could overcome death by rising bodily from the dead? Furthermore, Jesus promised that we too can be resurrected to eternal life by accepting Him as Lord and by believing in His resurrection (10:9). Thus our salvation rests on the authenticity of His resurrection. In 1 Corinthians 15:17–19, the apostle Paul explains: "if Christ has not been raised, your faith is worthless; you are still in your sins. Then those also who have fallen asleep in Christ [died as Christians] have perished. If we have only hoped in Christ in this life, we are of all men most to be pitied" (NASV).

In short, the resurrection of Jesus Christ not only offers the most dramatic and explicit evidence for His deity, but it also guarantees our own eternal salvation. His rising from the dead is the culmination, the capstone of all other Christian evidences.

But how do we know it really happened? Let's consider the evidence.

THE EVIDENCE

THE PROPHETIC WITNESS

The New Testament writers taught that Jesus' coming was prophesied in the Old Testament and that His resurrection proved His deity.

The apostle Paul stated that the gospel of God (the good news of Jesus) was "promised before through His prophets in the Holy Scriptures" (Rom. 1:2). He then adds that Jesus "was declared to be the Son of God with power . . . by the resurrection from the dead" (v. 4).

In 1 Corinthians 15:1–19, Paul presents the essence of the entire gospel in capsule form. And his primary message is: (1) Jesus died according to the prophecy of Scripture; (2) His resurrection was observed by eyewitnesses (in fact, many were still alive when Paul wrote 1 Corinthians and could have easily refuted his claim were it not true); and (3) without His resurrection, there is no Christianity, no Savior, and believers are lost in their sins, still unsaved.

In Acts 2:27, Peter quotes Psalm 16:10 where David writes, "Thou wilt not abandon my soul to Hades, nor allow thy Holy One to undergo decay" (NASV). David refers to his own future resurrection, but his words are also prophetic because they refer to the resurrection of a future Messiah. Peter argues that the "Holy One" who will not be abandoned to hades nor have His flesh suffer decay is Jesus, the Messiah (v. 36). David is dead, buried, and still in his tomb. Thus, Peter says, David's words look "ahead and [speak] of the resurrection of the Christ" (v. 31, NASV). Peter uses Jesus' resurrection as the focal point for his argument that Jesus is the "Holy One" of God, the divine Messiah.

When we turn to the four Gospels, we find that all of them record Jesus predicting His death and resurrection from the dead in three days (Matt. 16:21; Mark 8:31; Luke 9:22; John 2:19–21). Moreover, He claimed that He would raise Himself from the grave— an obvious claim to be God because only God can resurrect the dead. And when the scribes and Pharisees asked Him for a "sign," for proof of His identity, He prophesied His coming resurrection (Matt. 12:38–40). It takes little reflection to realize that if Jesus did not know who He was (the Son of God) and that He would die and raise Himself again in three days, He would not have risked destroying His new religious movement with false prophecy, especially in a Jewish context which placed a high premium on accurate predictions.

SOME LEGAL CRITERIA

John Warwick Montgomery suggests some direct parallels between the "law of evidence" as it is used in our legal system and how it can be used in defending historic Christianity. Montgomery explains that this law supports the Bible's contention that Jesus' deity can be substantiated by His resurrection. Montgomery gives three specific evidential rules that show this.[1]

First, the factuality of an event is determined by the probability of the evidence supporting it. Thus, Christians are "precisely on the right track when they defend their position in terms of the weight of factual evidence for Christ's deity." Moreover, this probability evidence is considered independently on its own weight. Says Montgomery, "the non-Christian will be prevented from arguing against Christ's resurrection on the ground that regular events in general [e.g., natural laws] make a particular miracle [such as the resurrection] too 'improbable' to consider." In other words, just because no one has witnessed a person rise from the dead since Jesus does not lessen the factuality of Christ's resurrection, so long as the evidence supporting it is sufficient, which it is.

Second, evidence must be derived from "the most reliable sources of information." This means that statements from eyewitnesses are the most trustworthy and carry the most weight. The New Testament is "primary source" information because it was written by those who personally knew Jesus or who were close associates of His apostles. The resurrection of Jesus was recorded in the Bible by eyewitnesses to Jesus' post-resurrection appearances. Moreover, because the Bible is primary source information, the burden of proof in any attempt to disqualify the authenticity of the resurrection rests on the critic.

Third, in cases where no direct eyewitnesses are available, the law allows circumstantial evidence to be determinative. In the case of the resurrection, no one was actually there the moment Jesus arose from the dead. However, as Montgomery explains, eyewitnesses testified that Jesus was put to death by crucifixion, placed in a tomb, disappeared from that tomb unaided, and later made numerous post-resurrection appearances over a forty-day period. This is more than enough circumstantial evidence to establish the authenticity of His resurrection.

In summary, then, the resurrection of Jesus Christ was observed by eyewitnesses to the event, recorded by them in a document of proven historical reliability (the Bible), and no shred of historical, archaeological, scientific, or contrary circumstantial evidence has ever been presented to disprove it.

HISTORY'S CONTRIBUTION

Since the Bible is historically reliable and it records Jesus' resurrection, that's enough to conclude that it actually happened. However, some additional historical insights will make this truth even plainer.

When the resurrection event was recorded in Scripture, a sufficient number of people were still alive to verify its actuality. For example, in 1 Corinthians 15:5-6, Paul states that, after Jesus' resurrection, Christ appeared to the eleven apostles (Judas was already dead) and to "over five hundred brethren at once, of whom the greater part remain to the present" (i.e., were still alive at the time he wrote).

Jesus' post-resurrection appearances were numerous, widespread, and occurred under a variety of circumstances. The Bible states that Jesus made fifteen different appearances in His resurrected body. Luke writes in Acts 1:3 that Jesus "presented Himself alive after His suffering [death on the cross] by many infallible proofs, being seen by them [the apostles] during forty days." In His post-resurrection appearances, Jesus walked and talked with His disciples, ate in their homes, fished and had breakfast with them, and taught them about the kingdom of God (John 21:1-14; Luke 24:28-30). He appeared in a garden near His tomb, in an upper room, on the road from Jerusalem to Emmaus, and in faraway Galilee. Jesus even made several appearances to Paul, Stephen, and the apostle John after His ascension into heaven (Acts 7:55; 9:3-5; Rev. 1:9-13).

The New Testament writers carefully documented their accounts of Jesus' life, including His resurrection. Wrote Luke, "Inasmuch as many have undertaken to compile an account of the things accomplished among us, just as those who from the beginning were eyewitnesses and servants of the Word have handed them down to us, it seemed fitting for me as well, having investigated everything carefully from the beginning, to write it out for you in consecutive order" (Luke 1:1-4, NASV). Peter added, "For we did not follow cleverly devised tales when we made known to you the power and coming of our Lord Jesus Christ, but we were eyewitnesses of His majesty" (2 Pet. 1:16, NASV). Elsewhere Peter showed that he recognized the value of eyewitness testimony when he reminded his critics that they too were witnesses to the miracles Jesus performed among them (Acts 2:22). And the apostle John penned, "What was from the beginning, what we have *heard,* what we have *seen* with our eyes, what we *beheld* and our hands *handled,* concerning the Word of Life [Jesus]" (1 John 1:1, NASV, emphasis mine).

The most sensational evidence found in history for the validity of Christ's resurrection is the changed lives of the apostles. Matthew 26:56 reports that after Jesus was arrested by the Jewish leaders, "all the disciples forsook Him and fled." John 20:19 adds that some of the disciples even hid themselves behind locked doors in fear of reprisal by the Jewish religious leaders. From these and other passages, we get the picture of a group of disenchanted and extremely frightened men. Even Peter, Jesus' most stalwart and bold disciple, denied Christ three times to protect his own life. But something happened to these terrified men that turned them into bold spokesmen and diligent workers for Christ, men willing to forsake everything, including their lives, to spread the good news about Him. Only the resurrection could adequately account for such a dramatic turnaround.

By the time of Pentecost, just a few weeks after Jesus' postresurrection appearances, the same cowardly, panic-stricken group of apostles were boldly and publicly preaching the risen Christ in the very city and before the very authorities that had crucified Him. They no longer feared death, and no amount of persecution could silence them.

The apostle Paul also experienced a profound life-changing event. Paul was probably the greatest enemy of the early church, putting believers into prison and executing them. Yet, while on a trip to Damascus to persecute the Christians living there, something happened to Paul that turned him into the greatest evangelist of the church. What so affected him? He saw the risen Christ (Acts 9).

It can be argued that people will gladly die for a cause so long as they believe it is right even if, in fact, it is wrong. But they will never die for a cause they know is false. It is ludicrous to believe that the apostles willingly forfeited the comforts of life, their jobs and family, and their financial security and instead accepted ridicule, persecution, imprisonment, torture, and in many cases horrible deaths all the while knowing Jesus' resurrection was a fabrication. No. They knew He was alive, risen from the dead, and it was that knowledge that propelled them to live for Him at all costs. What about the sudden birth of the Christian church on Pentecost (Pentecost is the day in which the Holy Spirit first came to indwell believers)? Scholars have been able to trace the origin of the Christian church back to around A.D. 32. Acts 2:41 records that about three thousand people were saved on the day of Pentecost. What caused the church to spring into existence so abruptly? What caused so many thousands of devout, highly religious Jews to join a new religious movement that was vehemently opposed by their religious leaders? They heard and trusted the good news of the resurrected Christ and became filled by His Spirit.

Sunday as the day of Christian worship is another tradition that can be traced back to the very beginning of the church. The first Christians were Jews. The Jewish Sabbath was, and still is, on Saturday. What led the early Jewish Christians to start worshiping on Sunday? In fact, why did the early Christians even adopt the name "Christian" (Acts 11:26)? Because Sunday is the day that Jesus the Christ—God's Messiah Son—was resurrected from the grave.

THE CHALLENGES

More than enough evidence has been presented to demonstrate Jesus' victory over death. However, we need to confront some common challenges to this evidence and event. None of these are very serious and, as you'll see, all are easily refuted.

JESUS WASN'T REALLY DEAD
WHEN HE WAS BURIED

One of the most common arguments to explain away the resurrection is the claim that Jesus was not dead when placed in the tomb. This is the so-called swoon theory or drug hypothesis. It claims that Jesus either feigned death, fainted on the cross, or was drugged so that He appeared dead. After burial, He revived, made His way out of the rock tomb, and appeared to His disciples. They mistakenly thought He had resurrected and built a whole movement around their error.

We need to first understand there is not a shred of evidence to support this theory. Nowhere in Roman or Jewish history does anyone argue or even imply that Jesus did not die on the cross. It took eighteen centuries after Christ's death before this idea found an advocate.

The fact is that the historical record refutes this theory at every turn.

Mark 15:44 relates that Pilate certified Christ's death before he turned His body over to Joseph of Arimathea for burial. Then Joseph and Nicodemus prepared Jesus' body for burial (John 19:39–40) by wrapping it in linen and spices (which likely weighed about one hundred pounds). Certainly they would not have gone through all this if they had had any indication that Jesus was still alive.

In John 19:31–34, it states that the Roman soldiers came to break the legs of the prisoners hanging on the crosses to hasten their death. But because Jesus was already dead, they did not break His legs. However, one of the soldiers did thrust a spear into Jesus' side. Verse 34 reports that "blood and water" flowed from His wound. According to modern medicine, this phenomenon most likely indicates a ruptured heart. There's little doubt, therefore, that Jesus was dead when lifted down from the cross.

The site of His burial raises another problem for this theory. Engineers have estimated that the large stone rolled in front of His tomb to seal it (Matt. 27:60) probably weighed one-and-a-half to two tons. It was positioned in a trench slopping downward so it could be rolled into place but not easily removed. In fact, it would have taken several men to roll it out of the way. When Mary Magdalene, Mary the mother of James, and Salome were on their way to the tomb to finish preparing Christ's body, they were concerned over who would remove the stone for them. They knew that their combined strength was not enough (Mark 16:2–3). And yet, when they got to the tomb, the stone had been moved from the entrance. Who moved the stone? It is inconceivable that Jesus, after spending several hours in a cold tomb, mortally wounded, dehydrated, and famished, would be capable of moving such a huge stone—even if He had been alive and in great health!

It's little wonder that this challenge to the resurrection has never won much support.

THE DISCIPLES STOLE JESUS' BODY

In Matthew 27:62–66, the Jewish authorities, remembering that Jesus predicted He would rise from the grave in three days, requested that Pilate place a guard around His tomb to prevent anyone from stealing His body and then claiming that He had risen as predicted. But after Jesus *did* rise from the grave, Matthew 28:11–15 reports that a conspiracy was formed. The Jewish authorities bribed the soldiers guarding the tomb, telling them to claim that Jesus' disciples came at night and stole His body while the guards slept.

The first thing to note is that the conspiracy was hatched because Jesus' tomb was in fact empty. If His body had still been there, nothing would have had to be fabricated. So here's implicit evidence that Jesus had arisen.

Second, and most obviously, how could the soldiers know who, if anyone, stole the body if they were asleep when the robbery took place?

A third problem surfaces from the expectations of Jesus' followers. To begin with, Mary Magdalene and the other women who first visited the tomb did not expect to find it empty. They would not have gone to the tomb to anoint Jesus for burial if they did. Nor did the disciples expect Jesus to rise from the grave. Indeed, when the women first reported to the disciples that the tomb was empty, the disciples rejected their story (Mark 16:11). Even after seeing the empty tomb, the disciples *still* did not realize that Jesus had risen (John 20:9). If the followers of Jesus failed to understand that Jesus would rise from the grave, why would they have stolen His body? Why would they devise a scheme to preach a resurrected Christ if they did not expect Jesus to be resurrected in the first place?

Furthermore, the biblical picture of the disciples between Jesus' arrest and post-resurrection appearances is not in harmony with the bold and daring men that would have been needed to pull off such an imaginative scheme as stealing Jesus' body and then perpetuating a resurrection hoax. The disciples abandoned Jesus even before His trial and were so frightened that some locked themselves in their rooms. In addition, the tomb was heavily guarded (Matthew 27:62–66), so a robbery attempt filled with danger would have been no match for the terrified disciples. And even if the guards had been asleep, the disciples could not possibly have moved a one- or two-ton stone without waking them.

Still another problem is found in Matthew 27:66, which states that a Roman government seal was placed on the stone over the tomb. If the disciples had stolen the body, they would have had to remove the stone, which would have broken the seal. This would have brought upon them the full force of Roman law and a harsh and swift punishment. If Pilate or other Roman authorities had really believed the disciples had stolen the body, they would have arrested and questioned them. But there is no record in Scripture or elsewhere that this ever happened.

Perhaps the best answer to the question of whether or not the disciples stole the body is to show that they had no motive to do so. Throughout their lives, the disciples gained neither worldly wealth nor fame nor honor. In fact, they were imprisoned, tortured, and all but one (John) executed. Had they stolen Jesus' body, they would have known Jesus had not risen from the dead. They would have endured harsh lives and ruthless deaths for nothing. It is preposterous to argue that the disciples went through their final years with no earthly rewards and possible spiritual damnation to preserve a fantastic lie. It takes an irrational faith to believe that, whereas the resurrection only requires a rational faith founded on fact after fact.

THE ROMANS STOLE JESUS' BODY

Again, there is no motive. In fact, the Romans had a strong motive *not* to steal the body because they had the responsibility of preserving the peace in Palestine. Stealing Jesus' body would have incurred the anger of the Jews by sanctioning the growth of a new religious movement in opposition to Judaism. Besides, even assuming the Romans were the thieves, they certainly would have produced the body as soon as the Christian movement imperiled the peace in Jerusalem.

THE JEWISH AUTHORITIES STOLE JESUS' BODY

It's just as unlikely that the Jewish religious leaders would have stolen Jesus' body. They were the ones who pushed for Jesus' crucifixion to stop His religious movement. Acts 4 relates that they did everything possible to crush Christianity. If they had stolen Jesus' body, it would have been to their full advantage to have produced it as soon as the disciples began to preach that Jesus had risen.

Moreover, the Jewish authorities remembered that Jesus had predicted He would rise in three days, and they requested that the tomb be guarded to prevent His body from being stolen so such a story could not arise (Matt. 27:63–64). This being the case, why would they turn around and steal the body themselves, then keep it hidden while Christianity grew in numbers because of the resurrection message? It doesn't make sense. That's exactly what the Jewish authorities wanted to avoid.

MAYBE JOSEPH OF ARIMATHEA REMOVED JESUS' BODY

There are several objections to this theory. First, there is no motive. Joseph was a follower of Jesus and would not have moved the body to keep the disciples from stealing it. Second, if he was not really a Christ-follower, he would have produced the body to stop the disciples as soon as they began to preach the resurrection of Christ. Third, if he removed the body for fear that someone else would steal it, the Roman authorities would have had to agree and would likely had known where he moved it and been able to produce the body at will. Fourth, as a friend of Jesus and the disciples, he would certainly report any location changes to the disciples. And, fifth, if the disciples knew Joseph had moved the body, they would not have preached the resurrection of Christ and died for a lie.

JESUS' TOMB WASN'T REALLY EMPTY

Within two months after the resurrection, the apostles began to preach the gospel message in Jerusalem. If Jesus was still in the tomb, it would have been a simple matter for the Jewish or Roman authorities to recover His body, publicly display it, and destroy the growing Christian movement. Moreover, Matthew 28:11–13 reports that the Jewish authorities bribed the soldiers to tell a false story, in order to account for the empty tomb. Thus we have hostile witnesses (people who would wish to refute the resurrection story) clearly acknowledging that the tomb did not house Jesus.

An interesting historical comment on the factuality of the resurrection comes, indirectly, from hostile witnesses. A critic can inadvertently admit to a fact that does not support his cause when he fails to present his own evidence against it. When this happens, it is a good indication that the fact is genuine. In the case of the resurrection, if the opponents of Christianity could have produced the body of Jesus or any other evidence that He did not rise from the grave, they would have done so. Yet there is not a shred of evidence from the contemporaries of Christ that attempts to disprove the historicity of the resurrection.

THE WOMEN WENT TO THE WRONG TOMB

According to this theory, during the dingy morning hours when the women returned to Jesus' tomb to complete the burial procedures, they simply made a mistake. They went to the wrong tomb, found it empty, and concluded Jesus had risen from the grave.

This is mere silly speculation. For one thing, Jesus was not buried in a public cemetery full of empty tombs but in a private burial ground. It is unlikely that His tomb would have been confused with another.

Second, after the women reported to Peter and John that the tomb was empty, the two disciples immediately dashed off to check it out for themselves, and all this took place in broad daylight (John 20:1–10). Did they make the same mistake? That's extremely improbable.

Third, John and Peter both saw the empty grave clothes that had been wrapped around Jesus and sealed with spices (John 20:4–6). That can't be accounted for on the wrong-tomb hypothesis.

Fourth, since a guard was placed at the tomb, the Romans and Jews obviously knew where the grave was located and would have produced the body once resurrection stories started to circulate.

And finally, if Jesus' tomb was not empty, one must still account for the numerous post-resurrection appearances of Christ over a forty-day period.

THE PEOPLE WHO SAW JESUS AFTER HIS RESURRECTION WERE HALLUCINATING

With a little reflection, this theory does not hold water. To begin with, hundreds of people saw the risen Christ over a forty-day period, over a wide geographic area, and under a variety of circumstances. Hallucinations are not contagious. Moreover, people who suffer hallucinations normally do so because they want to see something or expect to see something. The disciples were not psychologically prepared to hallucinate because they were not expecting Jesus to rise from the grave. Perhaps the best argument against hallucinations is the fact that on three separate occasions, Jesus was not even recognized (Luke 24:13–31; John 20:15; 21:4). How can you not recognize something you expected or wanted to see badly enough to hallucinate about it? Besides, if the post-resurrection sightings were the products of hallucinations, no one ever produced the body to prove it.

JESUS IS ALIVE!

The evidence is conclusive: Jesus Christ, three days after His death and burial, rose from the grave alive in bodily form, thereby demonstrating that He is God.

The Bible teaches that all believers will be raised like Christ and be clothed in a resurrected, glorified, immortal body (1 Cor. 15:40–50; see 1 John 3:2). Jesus is proof of that.

All that's left is for us to heed Paul's words: "if you confess with your mouth the Lord Jesus and believe in your heart that God has raised Him from the dead, you will be saved" (Rom. 10:9).

8

How Can One God Be Three?

Speaking through the prophet Isaiah, God said, "My thoughts are not your thoughts, / Nor are your ways My ways . . . / For as the heavens are higher than the earth, / So are My ways higher than your ways, / And My thoughts than your thoughts" (Isa. 55:8–9). God is infinite, man is finite, so there are mysteries about God that man cannot fully understand. One of these mysteries is the Trinity, the tri-personality of God. According to Christian orthodoxy, God is one God in essence, power, and authority, and also eternally exists as three distinct co-equal persons. These three persons are the Father, the Son (Jesus), and the Holy Spirit. This does not mean that Christians believe in three gods (polytheism). Rather, the doctrine of the Trinity is that there is only one God who exists in three distinct persons, and all three share the exact same divine nature or essence.

Understanding this fully is beyond human comprehension and has no human parallels, although various analogies have been offered. One of these analogies is the three physical states of water. Water is not only a liquid but also a solid (ice) and a gas (vapor), yet its chemical composition (substance) never changes in all three forms (two parts hydrogen and one part oxygen—H_2O). Although such analogies help us visualize the concept of the Trinity, they all fall short in some way. In the case of the water analogy, although the molecule H_2O can be liquid, solid, or gas, it is never all three at one time. The Trinity, on the other hand, is all three persons as one God.

The word *Trinity* is not used in Scripture, but it has been adopted by theologians to summarize the biblical concept of God. Difficult as it is to understand, the Bible explicitly teaches the doctrine of the Trinity, and it deserves to be explained as clearly as possible, especially to non-Christians who find the concept a stumbling-block to belief. So let's dig into this topic by addressing four key questions.

IS THE DOCTRINE OF
THE TRINITY IRRATIONAL?

The doctrine of the Trinity is certainly a mystery but that doesn't mean it's irrational. The concept cannot be known by human reason apart from divine revelation, and, as we'll soon see, the Bible definitely supports the idea of the Trinity. But for now, I want to demonstrate that the doctrine of the Trinity, although beyond human comprehension, is nevertheless rational. Our acceptance of it is congruous with how we respond to other data about the known world.

There are many things about the universe we don't understand today and yet accept at face value simply because of the preponderance of evidence supporting their existence. The scientific method demands that empirical evidence be accepted whether or not science understands why it exists or how it operates. The scientific method does not require that all data be explained before it is accepted.

Contemporary physics, for instance, has discovered an apparent paradox in the nature of light. Depending on what kind of test one applies (both of them "equally sound"), light appears as either undulatory (wave-like) or corpuscular (particle-like). This is a problem. Light particles have mass, while light waves do not. How can light have mass and not have it, apparently at the same time? Scientists can't yet explain this phenomenon, but neither do they reject one form of light in favor of the other, nor do they reject that light exists at all. Instead, they accept what they've found based on the evidence and press on.

Like physicists, we are no more able to explain the mechanics of the Trinity than they can explain the apparent paradox in the nature of light. In both cases, the evidence is clear that each exists and harbors mystery. So we must simply accept the facts and move on. Just because we cannot explain the Trinity, how it can exist, or how it operates does not mean that the doctrine must be rejected, so long as sufficient evidence exists for its reality. So let's now explore this evidence.

HOW DOES THE BIBLE PRESENT THE DOCTRINE OF THE TRINITY?

THE OLD TESTAMENT

Although the doctrine of the Trinity is fully revealed in the New Testament, its roots can be found in the Old Testament.

In several places, God refers to Himself in plural terms. For example, "Then God said, 'Let *Us* make man in *Our* image'" (Gen. 1:26; see 3:22; 11:7; Isa. 6:8).

The Messiah was prophesied in the Old Testament as being divine. Isaiah 9:6 states that the Messiah will be called "Mighty God," a term applied in the Old Testament specifically to Yahweh (see Mic. 5:2).

Isaiah 48:16 refers to all three members of the Godhead: "Come near to Me, listen to this: From the first I have not spoken in secret, from the time it took place, I was there. And now the Lord God [Father] has sent Me [Jesus], and His Spirit [the Holy Spirit]" (NASV).

The Old Testament also makes numerous references to the Holy Spirit in contexts conveying His deity (Gen. 1:2; Neh. 9:20; Ps. 139:7; Isa. 63:10–14).

THE NEW TESTAMENT

The New Testament provides the most extensive and clear material on the Trinity. Here are just a few of the texts that mention all three members of the Godhead and imply their co-equal status.

- Matthew 28:19, the baptismal formula: "Go therefore and make disciples of all the nations, baptizing them in the name [not 'names'] of the Father and of the Son and of the Holy Spirit."
- Matthew 3:16, at the baptism of Christ in the Jordan: "And after being baptized, Jesus went up immediately from the water; and behold, the heavens were opened, and He saw the Spirit [Holy Spirit] of God [Father] descending as a dove, and coming upon Him [Jesus]" (NASV).
- Luke 1:35, the prophetic announcement to Mary of Jesus' birth: "And the angel answered and said to her, 'The Holy Spirit will come upon you, and the power of the Highest [Father] will overshadow

you; therefore, also, that Holy One who is to be born will be called
the Son of God [Jesus].' "
- The trinitarian formula is also found in 1 Peter 1:2, 2 Corinthians
13:14, and 1 Corinthians 12:4–6.

DIGGING DEEPER

To explain the doctrine of the Trinity, I will take an inductive (scientific) approach. By this I mean I will accumulate general facts in Scripture that lead to a specific conclusion—that the nature of God is triune. The argument will go like this:

1. The Bible teaches that God is one (monotheism) and that He possesses certain attributes that only God can have.

2. Yet when we study the attributes of the Father, the Son, and the Holy Spirit, we discover that all three possess the identical attributes of deity.

3. Thus we can conclude that there is one God eternally existing as three distinct persons.

God Is One (Monotheism)

The Hebrew *Shema* of the Old Testament is "Hear, O Israel: The LORD our God, the LORD is one!" (Deut. 6:4; see Isa. 43:10; 44:6; 46:9). Some people have argued that this passage actually refutes the concept of the triune nature of God because it states that God is one. But the Hebrew word for "one" in this text is *echod*, which carries the meaning of unity in plurality. It is the same word used to describe Adam and Eve becoming "one flesh" (Gen. 2:24). Scripture is not affirming that Adam and Eve literally become one person upon marriage. Rather, they are distinct persons who unite in a permanent relationship.

The New Testament confirms the teaching of the Old: "You believe that God is one. You do well; the demons also believe, and shudder" (James 2:19, NASV; see 1 Tim. 2:5; 1 Cor. 8:4; Eph. 4:4–6).

God Has a Certain Nature

Both the Old and New Testaments list the attributes of God. We won't consider all of them here, but what follows are some of the clearest expressions of what constitutes deity.

- God is omnipresent (present everywhere at once): Psalm 139:7–10; Jeremiah 23:23–24.
- God is omniscient (possesses infinite knowledge): Psalms 139:1–4; 147:4–5; Hebrews 4:13; 1 John 3:20.
- God is omnipotent (all-powerful): Psalm 139:13–18; Jeremiah 32:17; Matthew 19:26.

The Father Is God

To the Jews, who do not accept the Trinity, God is Yahweh. In the Old Testament, *Yahweh* is to the Hebrews what *Father* is in the New Testament and to Christians. The attributes of God (Yahweh) listed above are the same for Yahweh and Father because both names apply to the one God. Although the concept of God as Father is not as explicit in the Old Testament as it is in the New, nevertheless, it has its roots in the Old (see Pss. 89:26; 68:5; 103:13; Prov. 3:12).

In the New Testament, the concept of the Father as a distinct person in the Godhead becomes clear (Mark 14:36; 1 Cor. 8:6; Gal. 1:1; Phil. 2:11; 1 Pet. 1:2; 2 Pet. 1:17). God is viewed as Father over creation (Acts 17:24–29), the nation of Israel (Rom. 9:4; see Exod. 4:22), the Lord Jesus Christ (Matt. 3:17), and all who believe in Jesus as Lord and Savior (Gal. 3:26).

The Son Is God

Like the Father, Jesus possesses the attributes of God. He is omnipresent (Matt. 18:20; 28:20). He is also omniscient: He knows people's thoughts (Matt. 12:25), their secrets (John 4:29), the future (Matt. 24:24–25), indeed all things (John 16:30; 21:17). His omnipotence is also taught. He has all power over creation (John 1:3; Col. 1:16), death (John 5:25–29; 6:39), nature (Mark 4:41; Matt. 21:19), demons (Mark 5:11–15), and diseases (Luke 4:38–41).

In addition to these characteristics, Jesus exhibits other attributes that the Bible acknowledges as belonging only to God. For example, He preexisted with the Father from all eternity (John 1:1–2), accepted worship (Matt. 14:33), forgave sins (Matt. 9:2), and was sinless (John 8:46).

The Holy Spirit Is God

The Holy Spirit is also omnipresent (Ps. 139:7–10), omniscient (1 Cor. 2:10), and omnipotent (Luke 1:35; Job 33:4).

Like Jesus, the Holy Spirit exhibits other divine attributes that the Bible ascribes to God. For instance, He was involved in creation (Gen. 1:2; Ps. 104:30), inspired the authorship of the Bible (2 Pet. 1:21), raised people from the dead (Rom. 8:11), and is called God (Acts 5:3–4).

The upshot of all this is that God is triune. In a formal argument, we can put it this way:

Major Premise:	Only God is omnipresent, omniscient, and omnipotent.
Minor Premise:	The Father, the Son, and the Holy Spirit are omnipresent, omniscient, and omnipotent.
Conclusion:	Therefore, God is triune as Father, Son, and Holy Spirit.

The Trinity

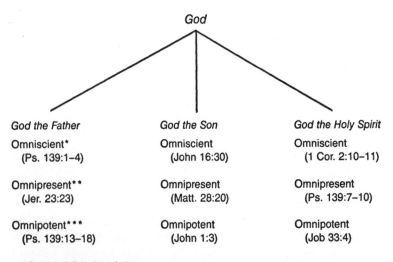

God

God the Father

Omniscient*
(Ps. 139:1–4)

Omnipresent**
(Jer. 23:23)

Omnipotent***
(Ps. 139:13–18)

God the Son

Omniscient
(John 16:30)

Omnipresent
(Matt. 28:20)

Omnipotent
(John 1:3)

God the Holy Spirit

Omniscient
(1 Cor. 2:10–11)

Omnipresent
(Ps. 139:7–10)

Omnipotent
(Job 33:4)

*God has infinite knowledge
**God is present everywhere at once
***God is all-powerful as in being the creator

HOW DOES JESUS TEACH THE DOCTRINE OF THE TRINITY?

In the Bible, Jesus claims to be God and then demonstrates this claim by displaying the attributes of God and by raising Himself from the dead. So what Jesus has to say about God must be true. And Jesus clearly teaches that God is triune.

Jesus Is Equal with the Father and Holy Spirit

In Matthew 28:19, Jesus tells His followers to "make disciples of all the nations, baptizing them in the name of the Father and of the Son and of the Holy Spirit." He uses the singular word *name* but associates it with three persons. The implication is that the one God is eternally three co-equal persons—Father, Son, and Holy Spirit.

Jesus Is One with the Father

In John 14:7 and 9, Jesus identifies Himself with the Father by saying to His disciples, "If you had known Me, you would have known My Father also; and from now on you know Him and have seen Him. . . . He who has seen Me has seen the Father" (see John 5:18). Jesus is not claiming to *be* the Father; rather, He is saying that He is one with the Father in essence.

Jesus Is One with the Holy Spirit

Continuing in John 14, Jesus tells His disciples that, after He is gone, He will send them "another Helper" who will be with them forever and will indwell them (vv. 16–17). The "Helper" is the Holy Spirit. The trinitarian implication lies with the word *another*. The apostle John, as he wrote this passage, could have chosen one of two Greek words for *another*. *Heteros* denotes "another of a different kind," while *allos* denotes "another of the same kind as myself." The word chosen by John was *allos*, clearly linking Jesus in substance with the Holy Spirit, just as He is linked in substance with the Father in verses 7 and 9. In other words, the coming Holy Spirit will be a different person than Jesus, but He will be the same with Him in divine essence just as Jesus and the Father are different persons but one in their essential nature. Thus, in this passage, Jesus teaches the doctrine of the Trinity.

So far we have seen that the authors of Scripture and Jesus Christ teach the triune nature of God. Therefore, the only way the doctrine of the Trinity can be rejected is if one refuses to accept the biblical evidence. Some groups, such as the Jehovah's Witnesses, do this by reinterpreting and altering Scripture. Others, such as the Unitarians (who claim that Jesus is just a man), arbitrarily and without any evidence deny anything supernatural or miraculous in the Bible. Both the Jehovah's Witnesses and the Unitarians are guilty of the very same thing of which they accuse Christians—irrationality. They refuse to accept the evidence for the Trinity regardless of how legitimate it is. This is unscientific and irrational. If one approaches Scripture without bias, he will clearly discover what the church has maintained for centuries: God is triune—one God in essence but eternally existing in three persons as Father, Son, and Holy Spirit.

A COMMON OBJECTION

Perhaps you've wondered or heard someone say, "If Jesus is one in essence with the Father, an equal member of the triune Godhead, why does He say, 'the Father is greater than I'" (John 14:28)? This question actually moves away from the doctrine of the Trinity and launches us into the doctrine of the incarnation, the process whereby Jesus, as the eternal Son of God, came to earth as man. Nevertheless, because this question is frequently raised as an objection, it needs to be answered.

Numerous passages in Scripture teach that Jesus, although fully God, is also fully man (John 1:14; Rom. 8:3; Col. 2:9; 1 Tim. 3:16). However, Philippians 2:5–8 states that, in the process of taking on humanity, Jesus *did not* give up any of His divine attributes. Rather, He gave up His divine glory (see John 17:5) and voluntarily chose to withhold or restrain the *full use* of His divine attributes. There are numerous instances in Scripture where Jesus, although in human form, exhibits the attributes of deity. If Jesus had surrendered any of His divine attributes when He came to earth, He would not have been fully God and thus could not have revealed the Father as He claimed to do (John 14:7, 9).

The key to understanding passages such as John 14:28 is that Jesus, like the Father and the Holy Spirit, has a particular position in the triune Godhead. Jesus is called the Son of God, not as an expression of physical birth, but as an expression of His position in relationship to the Father and Holy Spirit. This in no way distracts from His equality with the Father and the Holy Spirit or with His membership in the Godhead. As man, Jesus submits to the Father and acts in accordance to the Father's will (see John 5:19, 30; 6:38; 8:28). So when we read passages such as Mark 14:36 where Jesus submits to the Father's will, His submission has nothing to do with His divine essence, power, or authority, only with His position as the Incarnate Son.

Perhaps an illustration will help to explain this. Three people decide to pool their money equally and start a corporation. Each are equal owners of the corporation, but one owner becomes president, another vice-president, and the third secretary/treasurer. Each are completely equal so far as ownership, yet each has his own particular function to perform within the corporation. The president is the corporate head, and the vice-president and secretary/treasurer are submissive to his authority and carry out his bidding.

So when Jesus the God-man submits to the Father's will or states that the Father is greater than He or that certain facts are known only by the Father (e.g., Matt. 24:36), it does not mean that He is less than the other members of the Godhead but that in His incarnate state He did and knew only that which was according to the Father's will. The Father did not will that Jesus have certain knowledge while in human form. Because Jesus voluntarily restrained the full use of His divine attributes, He was submissive to the Father's will.

Why did Jesus choose to hold back from fully using His divine powers? For our sake. God willed that Jesus feel the full weight of man's sin and its consequences. Because Jesus was fully man, He could fulfill the requirements of an acceptable sacrifice for our sins. Only a man could die for the sins of mankind. Only a sinless man could be an acceptable sacrifice to God. And it is only because Jesus *is* an equal member of the triune Godhead, and thus fully God, that

He was able to raise Himself from the dead after dying on the cross and thereby guarantee our eternal life.

When all the evidence is accounted for and the verdict read, the Bible clearly teaches that the Father, the Son, and the Holy Spirit are three distinct, co-equal, co-eternal members of the Godhead, yet one in essence, power, and authority. All three are one God. Were this not the case, if the Trinity were not a reality, there would be no Christianity.

9

Why Should Christianity Be Accepted As the Only Way to God?

Just before Easter Sunday, I had the opportunity to share with a lady who claimed to have had a profound religious experience. She was once a Christian, but this other incident had totally transformed her life. She did not clearly state what her religious experience entailed, but it resulted in a firm belief that her personal encounter with deity was a genuine revelation. Moreover, she was convinced that Jesus was just a man who achieved "Christhood" through His own spiritual enlightenment (in a way, I suppose, similar to her own), and that Satan was a myth. She considered Jesus one of many prophets and the Bible one of many holy books. The writings of Buddha, Confucius, Muhammad, Moses, and others were all divine revelations that ultimately lead faithful searches to the same God.

As our conversation progressed, it became apparent that she had never considered Christianity in light of its historical evidences. Rather, its truth-claims rested solely on one's subjective opinions. Thus it merited no more or no less consideration than any other religion, allowing *her* to decide in her own mind its authenticity. She is not alone in this view.

Many non-Christians assume that all religions are paths to the same mountain top, that all religions lead to the Supreme Being and eternal bliss. The implication is that all religions are equal, similar in their teachings, and acceptable to God. It seems that most people who embrace this belief either have no affiliation with any kind of organized religion, or they belong to a religious group, such as the Unitarians and followers of the Bahai Faith, that accepts this belief as a central doctrine. The lady I was sharing with had become a Unitarian.

This belief, however, is born of ignorance. A little reflection shows how illogical it is. Not only do many religions believe that theirs is the only true revelation and the only path to salvation, but almost every major religion has a dramatically different view of the nature of God. How could they all be right? How could they all point to the same reality when they all perceive that reality so differently? It's simply logically impossible. Opposing views cannot all be right. In fact, only one can be right, and all the rest have to be wrong. Like arithmetic, there is only one correct answer to any figure, and all others are wrong, no matter how close to the right answer they may be.

Let me put this another way. Many people claim that all religions will ultimately be acceptable to God because they represent mankind's corporate attempt to find religious truth. They say that even if Christianity is God's only true revelation, He will still accept other religions because they represent sincere attempts to find Him.

As much as people may wish this to be true, it simply isn't. We'll soon see that religious beliefs and practices other than Christianity's are not an attempt to find God but are actually rebellion against Him. Non-Christian religions are unacceptable to God. I'll demonstrate this by giving some examples of exactly how the major world religions differ from Christianity, focusing on their views of the nature of God; showing why non-Christian religions represent willful rejections of God; and summarizing why God chose one particular plan for the redemption of man and no other.

THE GOD OF GODS, THE LORD OF LORDS

Christianity, like many other religions, claims to be God's only revelation of spiritual truth. And it maintains that Jesus is the only path to salvation. Jesus said, "I am the way, the truth, and the life. No one comes to the Father except through Me" (John 14:6). The New Testament writers agree: "there is salvation in no one else; for there is no other name under heaven that has been given among men, by which we must be saved" (Acts 4:12, NASV).

The Bible reveals that God is an infinite-personal Being who is perfect in truth and goodness. He is creator of the universe and thus stands apart from His creation (transcendent). However, God also upholds and maintains the universe and in that way is immanent in nature. God is not one in essence with nature (pantheism), but He is fully aware of and sovereign over all He created, and He reveals His existence and power through His creation (general revelation). God is also holy and can tolerate no sin. Indeed, He will punish wrongdoing, as decreed in Scripture.

Space allows for only a superficial look at the nature of God taught in the major non-Christian belief systems. But even this glance will demonstrate that their gods are incompatible with the God revealed in Scripture. The majority of the world's religions fall within the following divisions.[1]

EASTERN RELIGIONS

Eastern religions (such as Hinduism) and its Western offshoots (such as the New Age movement) differ in many ways, but most of them accept the same basic picture of God, which is *pantheistic*. This view denies a personal-creator God and identifies God as somehow being one in essence with nature. In other words, the universe and all that is in it is an extension of God itself, and this extension is frequently viewed as an illusion that needs to be transcended. What appears to be material may not really.exist.

In addition to a pantheistic concept of God, most Eastern religions entertain a pantheon of lesser gods, many represented by idols.

Pantheism clearly contradicts Christian theism. God cannot be both impersonal and personal, no creator and creator, all that is and different from creation, the greatest God and the only God. Either pantheism is true or Christianity is. Neither represent a view of God even remotely similar.

ANIMISM

Animism covers the religious expressions of the early American Indians, Australian aborigines, and many other preliterary cultures. Although most animistic religions possess a latent concept of a supreme God, generally, their religious beliefs focus on spirit beings that supposedly indwell both animate and inanimate objects such as stones, mountains, lakes, lightning, manufactured articles, trees, and animals. These spirits often have great power and cunning and exhibit the spectrum of human emotions, including hate, joy, anger, jealousy, fear, and love. Spirits influence every aspect of life (sickness, injury, marriage, childbirth, hunting, agriculture), so animists seek to appease the spirits by paying proper respect through prayer, offerings, sacrifices, and other appeals to the spirits' often capricious egos.

Obviously, the godlike creatures of animism and the creator-God of Christianity have next to nothing in common.

ISLAM

The Islamic concept of God is much closer to the Christian concept. In Islam, God is both personal (monotheism) and creator. However, the trinitarian aspect of God is denied in Islam and, therefore, Muslims reject Jesus as the Son of God. "Allah," as the Muslims call God, takes little interest in his creation. He is generally strict, aloof, capricious, and unpredictable, and he is responsible not only for good but also for evil. Allah sorely lacks the attributes of love, grace, forgiveness, and holiness so clearly revealed in the God of Christianity.

THE CULTS

A *cult* can be defined as a perversion of biblical Christianity. Most cults claim some affiliation with Christianity and even accept the Bible (with their own reinterpretations and modifications) as one of their holy books. However, all of the cults reject many of the central beliefs of the Christian faith, including the Trinity. Consequently, and without exception, all of the cults reject Jesus as the eternal Son of God, as one in essence, power, and authority with the Father and the Holy Spirit. The assorted views of God found in the cults run the gamut from nontrinitarian monotheism (Jehovah's Witnesses) to polytheism (belief in many gods, such as Mormonism) to pantheism (Christian Science). None of these views square with orthodox Christianity, and their various gods are far different from the God revealed in the Bible.

Because the nature of God differs fundamentally in the cults and the world's many religions, it is impossible to harmonize them and conclude they all mirror the same God. A religion's view of God will influence all of its subsequent doctrines. Consequently, the doctrines of sin, salvation, man, and other beliefs taught in these religions all conflict with Christianity. Either Christianity is true or some other religion, but only ignorance and irrationality could maintain they're all basically the same or all point to the same God. The Christian God—and Him alone—deserves and demands our worship. When people turn to other gods and worship them, the only true God declares that totally unacceptable, worthy of judgment (Exod. 20:3–6; Rom. 1:18–32).

RELIGIOUS REBELLION

ALL PEOPLE HAVE THE OPPORTUNITY TO KNOW GOD

The Bible teaches that God has revealed Himself to man in two specific ways. One is through *special* revelation, which is directed to specific peoples at specific times in history and includes very specific information about God (e.g., that salvation is through Jesus Christ alone). Special revelation is recorded in God's written Word (the Bible) and is most explicit in the person of Jesus Christ.

The other way God unveils Himself is through general revelation, which is that revelation that can be understood by all people at all times throughout history. It is a perpetual or continuous revelation, and it occurs in two primary ways: nature (Rom. 1:20; Ps. 19:1; Acts 14:16–17) and an intuitive (innate) moral consciousness God has placed in all human beings (Rom. 2:14–15).

General revelation in nature, according to Romans 1:20, reveals to everyone everywhere that God exists, that He is infinite and almighty, created and governs the universe, and judges evil. From this evidence, all people have the opportunity to know God.

General revelation through moral consciousness exhibits itself in a number of ways, but one profound way is in a fundamental, world-wide moral code that finds expression across cultural, religious, and historical barriers.[2] God is a moral Being who created a moral universe. Man, created in God's image, is instinctively aware of God's moral law. It is seen in every culture through prohibitions against such sins as murder, stealing, rape, lying, and betrayal. Like nature, this moral consciousness is designed to point people to God, the moral Lawgiver. When we respond positively to this intuitive moral code, we respond to its divine Author (Rom. 2:13–16).

Because God has revealed Himself to all people through nature and a moral consciousness, He expects all people, including those who have never heard of Jesus, to respond favorably to Him. He has revealed enough information about Himself so all people have the opportunity to seek Him. Non-Christians who have never heard of Jesus will be judged according to whether or not they respond to God's general revelation (Rom. 1:20). Thus people who have never heard of Jesus Christ are still accountable to the God of Scripture because He and the God of nature and morality are one and the same.

ALL PEOPLE HAVE THE OPPORTUNITY TO KNOW THE GOD OF SCRIPTURE

Since the personal-infinite-creator God we read about in the Bible is the same God revealed in nature and our moral consciousness, we can be sure that general revelation will not contradict special revelation. This is the key to understanding why other religions are not acceptable to God. If God has revealed Himself to all men equally through general revelation, and if people choose not to respond to this revelation and instead seek other gods, then they are guilty of rejecting the God of Scripture. Thus, other religions are forms of re-bellion against God. Let me explain how this happens.

The Bible teaches that God created the universe and revealed Himself to the first man, Adam. Adam knew God and had a close personal relationship with Him. Nevertheless, Adam rebelled against

God by willfully disobeying Him. This incurred God's judgment, and the first couple were banished from the Garden. Following Adam's footsteps, subsequent generations continued to rebel against God, resulting in the judgment of the worldwide flood (Gen. 6) and later in the dispersal of humanity at the Tower of Babel (Gen. 11).

Sometime after Babel, God began to build the nation of Israel, starting with Abraham, as the focus of His special revelation. Through Israel, God began to reveal to the world fuller truths about Himself and His plan for mankind's redemption. Prior to the Babel incident, the Bible does not relate that man, even in his rebellion against God, practiced idolatry, polytheism, or any other false religion. In other words, all knew of the one true God even if they rejected Him. It was only after the dispersal of humanity into various cultures and God beginning to focus His special revelation on the nation of Israel that we see the rise of false religions. Except for Israel, the nations of the world quickly turned away from their previous knowledge of God. They rejected God's general revelation of Himself and began worshiping idols and practicing polytheism and other deviant religions. Israel, alone among the world's nations, practiced monotheism and worshiped the one true God. So pantheism, polytheism, animism, and all the other false views of God grew out of human rebellion, not genuine searching.

This biblical teaching is substantiated by secular studies in comparative religions. In the nineteenth century, due to the influence of Darwinian evolution, it was thought that modern religions actually evolved from animistic roots into polytheism and later into monotheism (that is, belief in countless spirits evolved into the belief in specific gods which in turn evolved into the belief in one supreme God). If this is true, primitive societies would have no concept of a Supreme Being (monotheism). However, not only is there no evidence that animism evolved into polytheism and later into monotheism, but there is tremendous evidence supporting just the opposite. It appears that monotheism de-evolved into polytheism. Today, anthropologists and ethnologists have proven that most primitive animistic religions have a latent monotheistic belief, even though they also believe in other spiritual forces. This is a common element in the oldest cultures on earth: the Australians, Polynesians, Zulus, bushmen, Congo tribes, and Mongolians. All of these cultures worship a primal Father. Belief in an all-powerful supreme Being also predates polytheism and pantheism in Eastern religions. For example, the earliest reference to religion in China refers to a Supreme God called "Shang Ti." This belief goes back more than two thousand years before Buddhism, Taoism, or Confucianism arose in China. Similarly, an original concept of a supreme God is found in the early histories of Sumeria, Egypt, and other ancient civilizations.[3]

What were these religions like? Were they kind, loving, merciful, and pure as Christianity is? Not at all. Nineteenth-century Harvard law professor, Simon Greenleaf, gave an appropriate description of the depravity of humanity once the true God of Scripture was rejected:

> But the fact is lamentably true, that [man] soon became an idolater, a worshiper of moral abominations. The Scythians and Northmen adored the impersonations of heroic valor and bloodthirsty and cruel revenge. The mythology of Greece and of Rome, though it exhibited a few examples of virtue and goodness, abounded in others of gross licentiousness and vice. The gods of Egypt were reptiles, and beasts and birds. The religion of Central and Eastern Asia was polluted with lust and cruelty, and smeared with blood, rioting, in deadly triumph, over all the tender affections of the human heart and all the convictions of the human understanding. Western and Southern Africa and Polynesia are, to this day [the nineteenth century], the abodes of frightful idolatry, cannibalism, and cruelty; and the aborigines of both the Americas are examples of the depths of superstition to which the human mind may be debased. In every quarter of the world, however, there is a striking uniformity seen in all the features of paganism. The ruling principle of her religion is terror, and her deity is lewd and cruel. Whatever of purity the earlier forms of paganism may have possessed, it is evident from history that it was of brief duration. Every form, which history has preserved, grew rapidly and steadily worse and more corrupt, until the entire heathen world, before the coming of Christ, was infected with that loathsome leprosy of pollution, described with revolting vividness by St. Paul, in the beginning of his Epistle to the Romans.[4]

God made an adequate revelation of Himself to all people everywhere. He expects them to respond to this revelation by acknowledging Him and by seeking to obey their moral consciences. Yet most people reject this revelation and therefore reject God. Rather than worship Him, they create their own false religions and disobey their moral consciences. They worship creation instead of the creator. Thus other religions are not attempts to find God—instead, they represent rebellion against God.

ONLY ONE WAY

One final question needs to be answered. Why did God choose Christianity as the only means by which one can be saved? To a large degree, the answer should be clear. Only Christianity preserves an accurate picture of God as He is revealed in both general and special revelations. Nevertheless, let's probe a bit further.

According to the Bible, the presence of human sin is a direct result of Adam's fall. This was the historical event in which sin first entered humanity (Rom. 5:12). When God created the earth and life, He said that it was "very good" (Gen. 1:31). The earth was a place free from sin, evil, and human (and animal) suffering. It was also a place where man could have known and worshiped the one true God. Yet today the world contains sin, evil, human suffering, and false perceptions of God. And all of this originated with Adam's first act of disobedience.

Without going into all the details (see Gen. 1–3), it can be briefly said that when God created Adam, He gave him the freedom to choose to obey or disobey Him by not eating from a certain tree. This was a test for Adam to prove his obedience and love for God, and God warned him of the consequences of not acting wisely. Adam would be punished if he ate the forbidden fruit. Nevertheless, Adam chose to disobey, and, as a result, he became separated from God, sin entered the world, and numerous false religions eventually arose.

The Bible teaches that Adam was the corporate head of the human race—the representative of mankind. Just as the decisions made by the ruler of a nation affect all the people under that ruler, so Adam's decision to rebel against God affected all mankind. Furthermore,

when Adam sinned, he not only represented us, he acted in precisely
the same manner as any other man or woman would have in his
place. Like Adam, we too rebel against God and are equally guilty
and deserving of punishment.

Christian theology teaches that in his fallen state, man is totally
unable to reach out to God. The apostle Paul writes in Romans 8:7
that the mind of man is hostile toward God, and man does not subject
himself to God because he "is not even able to do so" (NASV; see Rom.
7:15–25). It is natural for fallen man to "suppress the truth" (Rom.
1:18) and "not see fit to acknowledge God any longer" (Rom. 1:28,
NASV). Thus for man to become reconciled with God, God Himself
must take the initial step to achieve reconciliation. I believe God *has*
taken this initial step by providing all people with an innate awareness of His existence (Rom. 1:18–2:16) that includes the ability to respond to or reject saving truth, whether it comes through general or
special revelation (Rom. 2:4; Titus 2:11). Explains the late Henry Clarence Thiessen of Dallas Theological Seminary, "Because man is without any ability or desire to change, God responded by prevenient
grace. This grace (sometimes considered a part of common or universal grace) restores to the sinner the ability to make a favorable response to God."[5]

However, the Bible also clearly teaches that the possibility of salvation is made available in only one way. Out of His immeasurable
love for man and His creation and of His own sovereign will, God
chose to make a fuller revelation of Himself. God came to earth as the
incarnate Son, Jesus Christ, to reconcile humanity to Himself.

The work of Christ here on earth is called the atonement. Literally,
the word means "to cover." It involves the removal or covering of
man's sins by the substitutionary sacrifice of Jesus Christ on the cross
(Rom. 5:8). Instead of guilty human beings making payment (redemption) for their own sins, Jesus—God Himself—did it for us (Mark
10:45; 1 Cor. 6:20). This opens the door to reconciliation between
God and man. Through Christ, man stands before God justified. That
is, on the basis of Christ's work, man is accounted righteous in God's
eyes (Rom. 3:23–24). Just as sin was charged to man's account
through Adam, so righteousness before God becomes ours when we
accept this work of Christ (Rom. 5:12–21).

We must realize that this forgiveness is not based on anything we can do. We could never do enough good works to earn God's favor. Salvation is a free gift from God based solely on our acceptance of Jesus Christ as Lord and Savior (John 3:16; Acts 4:12; Eph. 2:8–9; Tit. 3:5). To receive this free gift and the eternal benefits that go with it, we only have to invite Jesus into our lives, accepting Him and His work by faith (Rom. 10:9). The Christian message and hope are that simple.

So the reason Christianity claims to be the only path to salvation is because it is the one true revelation of God, and it is the only way God has ordained for mankind to become reconciled to Him. All other so-called paths lead away from the true God of Scripture and the work of Jesus on the cross. That Jesus actually had to die on the cross proves there is no other way to God. If there were, God would not have sacrificed His beloved Son.

In light of all this, we can clearly see how irrational it is for someone to say, "It doesn't matter what I believe so long as I am sincere." Sincerity is not the issue. One can be sincere and still be wrong. The facts are facts, whether one understands, accepts, or rejects them. Believing does not make a thing true anymore than disbelieving makes it false. Christians say that Jesus is the only way to God not because they invented the concept but because God Himself said it (John 14:6). Christ *is* the only way.

10

Do Christians Condemn People to Hell Who Have Never Heard of Jesus?

Non-Christians ask two questions more than any others. The first is, How can a good and loving God allow innocent people to suffer? This deals with the problem of evil, which I address in Chapter 13. The second question is, Does the poor, innocent native who has never heard of Jesus Christ go to hell when he dies? This question concerns the eternal fate of the heathen—people who do not acknowledge or have never heard of the God of the Bible. That's the issue we'll focus on here.

In the following pages, I will not attempt to set forth the undisputed biblical teaching on the fate of those who have never heard of Jesus. Some theological positions state categorically that there is no salvation for anyone who has not had a direct personal encounter with Jesus Christ. However, it is important from an apologetic perspective, as we attempt to answer this weighty and vexing question for non-Christians, that we point out there is another view equally supported by Scripture. This view provides for the possibility of salvation for people who have never had the opportunity to make a faith decision for Christ. Just as God called Abraham and Melchizedek out of paganism and into the true knowledge of the living God, so He can reveal Himself, as Clark Pinnock states, to those "who are chronologically A.D. but spiritually B.C."[1]

Christians believe that salvation is through Christ alone, but they also believe that not all people have an equal opportunity to hear Jesus' message of salvation and to receive Him as personal Savior. And, of course, we also have to deal with the countless millions of people who lived and died centuries before Christ. How could they have avoided hell?

I believe that the heathen do have the opportunity to receive salvation through Jesus Christ, *even if they never had the opportunity to hear His message.* I realize not all Christians accept this, but I believe it has biblical warrant. So we will move through it carefully and methodically, first by exploring four principles, then by addressing two objections.

WHAT HAPPENS TO THE HEATHEN IS UNCLEAR

Although I will present a strong biblical argument supporting the idea that the heathen have the opportunity to be saved even apart from ever meeting Jesus, the point still needs to be made that we do not know for certain how God will deal with these people. Only He has the complete answer. As C. S. Lewis remarks, "The truth is God hasn't told us what His arrangements about the other people are. We do know that no man can be saved except through Christ; we don't know that only those who know Him can be saved through Him." Then he adds this important thought:

> But in the meantime, if you are worried about the people outside, the most unreasonable thing you can do is to remain outside yourself. Christians are Christ's body, the organism through which He works. Every addition to that body enables Him [Jesus] to do more. If you want to help those outside you must add your own little cell to the body of Christ who *can* help them.[2]

In other words, if you really want to help the heathen, you first need to become a Christian yourself, and then you will be in a position to share the gospel message with them, thereby providing them a sure opportunity of salvation.

GOD WILL JUDGE RIGHTEOUSLY

Having established the fact that we do not know exactly what will happen to the heathen, we can rest assured that God will judge all human beings fairly. This is the clear teaching of Scripture (see Gen. 18:25; Ps. 145:17). Moreover, as Peter states, the Lord "is patient . . . not wishing for any to perish but for all to come to repentance" (2 Pet. 3:9, NASV). God wants everyone saved (1 Tim. 2:4; Ezek. 33:11), and what He does with those who never heard of Jesus Christ will be just. (This is not to say, however, that all people *will* be saved. The Bible is equally clear that all who reject Christ will be lost.)

For many Christians, the above two principles are an adequate answer to the question of what happens to the heathen. However, unbelievers tend to have a problem harmonizing the Christian portrayal of a good and loving God with a God who may refuse salvation to someone. Most non-Christians feel that a truly loving God should ultimately save all people. This brings us to the third principle.

GOD HAS PROVIDED A WAY OF SALVATION TO THE HEATHEN

At this point we need to reflect on the question, What happens to the poor, innocent natives who have never heard of Jesus Christ? Can they be saved? The answer is yes, they *can*. However, this is not the same as saying they *will* be saved or even it is *very likely* that they will be saved. Let me explain.

Jesus said, "It is not those who are healthy who need a physician, but those who are ill. . . . I did not come to call the righteous, but sinners" (Matt. 9:12–13, NASV). In other words, if a heathen (or anyone else for that matter) is innocent—free of sin—he does not have to worry about salvation; he is saved. God will not send innocent people to hell. The wrath of God is "against all ungodliness and unrighteousness of men, who suppress the truth in unrighteousness" (Rom. 1:18). God will punish the ungodly and unrighteous, not the sinless.

So the question becomes one of innocence. Can it be said that the heathen (or anyone else) are innocent in a biblical sense? No. It contradicts what the Bible reveals about man's sin nature. In Romans

3:23, Paul states that "all have sinned and fall short of the glory of God." There are no "innocent" people. The apostle John adds this sobering thought, "If we say that we have not sinned, we make Him [Jesus] a liar, and His word is not in us" (1 John 1:10).

The Bible teaches that sin is both a condition and an action. Man possesses an innate sin nature (condition) due to his rebellion against God, and it is because of his sin nature that he tends to perform sinful acts (action) (see Matt. 15:18–20; John 3:19; Rom. 7:18–23). Although some religions claim man is basically good and thus sin is either an illusion or ignorance, it is extremely difficult to deny rationally the presence of sin in man. People are far from perfect. We do not always behave in the manner we know we should. In fact, we frequently sin on purpose. A look at today's world, or for that matter at any era of human history, shows the presence of evil in *all* human beings. This fact is so self-evident that examples are unnecessary. So the bottom line is all humans, including Christians, are worthy of punishment and in need of a Savior.

The question, then, is not, What happens to people innocent of sin? But, What happens to those guilty of sin who have not had the opportunity to meet Jesus and ask and receive forgiveness for their sins?[3] The answer to this appears to be that those who have never heard the gospel message will be judged according to the information about God they do have (1 Tim. 1:13; Rom. 2:13–16; 5:15; Acts 17:30). God will judge according to what we know, not according to what we do not know. This implies, of course, that those of us who have heard the gospel message and reject it are far more deserving of punishment than those who have never heard of Jesus at all (Luke 12:47–48; Matt. 10:11–15; John 9:41).

Have Christians painted themselves into a paradoxical corner? On the one hand, God will not punish the heathen for not responding to Jesus if they have never heard of Him. On the other hand, the Bible makes it clear that a holy and righteous God will not tolerate sin. It will be punished. Christians are set free from this punishment because they have accepted Jesus as Savior. His sacrificial death on the cross paid the price for us. But what about the heathen? They too are sinners. Will they get off unpunished?

Although the heathen have never had the opportunity of hearing the gospel message and therefore of knowing Jesus Christ personally, they nevertheless have had the opportunity of knowing God. The heathen will be judged, not according to how they respond to Jesus, but how they respond to God the Father. Upon hearing the gospel message, people can choose or reject God the Son. Without that opportunity, however, people can still choose or reject God the Father with the knowledge they have.

If God's judgment of us is based on how much we know about Him and how we respond to what we know, then the question becomes, In what way has God revealed Himself to the heathen? Acts 14:17 states that God has given everyone a witness of Himself. This witness is general revelation through nature and our moral conscience. Hence, the heathen who have never heard of Jesus will be judged according to how they respond to this general revelation. Because God the Father and God the Son are one in essence, members in the triune Godhead, rejecting the Father is tantamount to rejecting the Son. Both Father and Son are one God.

THE HEATHEN ARE JUDGED ACCORDING TO THEIR RESPONSE TO GENERAL REVELATION

What follows is, to some degree, speculative. I think it's based on sound biblical teaching, but, as I admitted earlier, we do not know for certain just how God will ultimately deal with the heathen.

To understand how the heathen will be judged, we must understand something about the nature of sin. James 2:10 states that "whoever shall keep the whole law [God's requirements of man], and yet stumble in one point, he is guilty of all." Even one sin, regardless of how small it is, causes a person to fall under divine condemnation and require a savior. Why? Because God is not only love but also holy. A holy God cannot tolerate any sin, and He must punish it. Jesus, as God's only acceptable sacrifice, took the punishment in our place, thereby providing the only path to salvation. But His work must be appropriated individually by faith—it is not automatically given to all.

Now, this does not entail the idea that all sins are of equal gravity. In Matthew 23:23, Jesus mentions the "weightier matters of the law," and in John 19:11, He talks of a "greater sin" (see Luke 12:42–48; 1 Cor. 11:27–30; Matt. 12:31–32). The implication of these passages is that there are degrees of sin and probably degrees of punishment.

If it is true that some sins are greater than others and deserving greater punishment, we have a basis for assuming that sins done in ignorance are less blameworthy than sins done in the full knowledge of God's disapproval. If we apply this principle to the problem at hand, we can conclude that the heathen's failure to receive Jesus Christ as Lord and Savior, when they never had the opportunity of meeting Him, is deserving of less condemnation than those who have heard the gospel message and have rejected it. The following passages seem to support this conclusion.

Luke 12:47–48

This passage reflects a key biblical principle that to those who have been given much, much will be required. In theological terms, the parable explaining this concept plainly states that the person who knows God's will and fails to do it will receive greater punishment than the one who does not know God's will.

Romans 1:18–25

This passage is the clearest biblical presentation of general revelation in nature. It states that God considers the heathen "without excuse" if they do not accept His revelation in nature and respond to it. If God will punish the heathen for this, it seems logical that those who do respond to Him in light of general revelation will be less blameworthy than those who do not.

Romans 2:12–16

This text teaches that God's moral law is written on the hearts of all human beings, and they are judged according to how they respond to it because a proper response to the moral law is a proper response to the moral Lawgiver. On the other hand, rejecting this moral law is tantamount to rejecting God. Verses 12–13 state that those who do not respond appropriately to their moral conscience will certainly be punished whether or not they have heard of Jesus.

Acts 17:30–31; Romans 3:25

These passages seem to imply that, before the coming of Jesus, God was not judging heathen peoples for worshiping false gods out of ignorance because salvation through Christ alone had not yet been revealed. I am not saying these people were innocent of idolatry and would not be punished. They too will be judged through the work of Christ (Acts 17:31) because His judgment includes both past and present sins (Rom. 3:25). They were guilty, yes. But their guilt lay in the fact that they rejected the God of general revelation and willfully sought after false gods. Their punishment lies not in rejecting Jesus but rather in rejecting God the Father. They had an opportunity to receive salvation *prior* to the first advent of Christ.

TWO OBJECTIONS

Before concluding, we need to consider two common arguments against the position I've outlined. Both are attempts to usher the heathen into heaven independent of Jesus Christ.

The first argument goes like this: If the heathen are not given the chance of hearing the gospel message, they can't reject it, so then they stand a better chance of getting into heaven because they will be judged on the limited knowledge they have.

This sounds logical except for one crucial misconception. General revelation is only a general pointer to God. It may be satisfactory to tell us that God exists, that He is the creator of the universe, and that He judges man for his failure to acknowledge Him, but general revelation does not give a clear plan of salvation. The fact is, heathens without the gospel message have a much more difficult time responding favorably to God than those who receive a clear presentation of salvation through Jesus Christ. This is illustrated in Romans 1. Starting in verse 21, Paul writes that even though the heathen

knew God [through general revelation], they did not honor Him as God, or give thanks; but they became futile in their speculations, and their foolish heart was darkened. Professing to be wise, they became fools, and exchanged the glory of the incorruptible God for an image in the form of corruptible man and of birds and four-footed animals and crawling creatures. . . . For they exchanged the truth of God for a lie, and worshipped and served the creature [creation] rather than the Creator. (vv. 21–23, 25, NASV)

In short, although the heathen receive through general revelation a picture of God clear enough for them to acknowledge and seek Him, the sad fact is they usually reject God. In mankind's sinful state, in his rebellion against his creator, he continually attempts to suppress God's truth. So most heathen people turn from God and worship God's creation. Thus God instructs Christians to evangelize the heathen (Matt. 28:19). The apostle Paul puts it well in Romans 10:14–15: "How then shall they call on Him [Jesus] in whom they have not believed? And how shall they believe in Him of whom they have not heard? And how shall they hear without a preacher? And how shall they preach unless they are sent? As it is written, 'How beautiful are the feet of those who preach the gospel of peace, Who bring glad tidings of good things!'"

We may not know how God will ultimately deal with the heathen, but it is still our responsibility to bring them the word about Christ. In spite of the fact that the heathen may receive salvation through Christ if they respond to God the Father through general revelation, it is far more difficult for them to do so independent of a clear gospel presentation.

The second argument claims that although the heathen reject the Christian God, the fact they respond to general revelation at all, even if incorrectly, shows they are seeking God, and consequently God will honor their individual religious practices.

However, as we saw in the previous chapter, non-Christian religions are not attempts to find God but demonstrations of rebellion against Him. Instead of responding to general revelation in a positive fashion, most heathens voluntarily reject God and seek after false gods. Ephesians 4:17–19 says that people do this because of willful "ignorance" and "the blindness of their heart." Similarly, Romans 1:21–23 teaches that heathens "knew God" but "did not glorify Him as God" and willfully exchanged the glory of God for idols.

Therefore, it cannot be denied that the heathen are guilty of sin and deserve punishment. However, in His mercy, it appears that God will judge the heathen according to the degree of information about God available to them, the opportunities they had to acquire this knowledge, and how they chose to respond to this knowledge. All people have had the opportunity to know God either through general revelation or through the Christian message. Rejection of either of these revelations will result in damnation. People will be denied entrance into heaven, not because of what they have *not* heard, but because of what they *have* heard and rejected.

In light of this, it is clear that those who have had the opportunity to hear the gospel message and refused to accept it, or refused to hear it when offered, deserve hell even more than those who never heard it at all. The Bible makes it plain that those who have had the opportunity to hear the gospel message and turned their backs on it will not be saved (John 14:6; 1 John 5:11–12).

Finding God is not difficult. The prophet Jeremiah wrote, "you will seek Me [God] and find Me, when you search for Me with all your heart" (Jer. 29:13). And Jesus said, "Behold, I stand at the door and knock. If anyone hears My voice and opens the door, I will come in to him and dine with him, and he with Me" (Rev. 3:20). All we need to do is open the door.

11

Why Are the Bible and Science in Conflict?

If you believe the Bible cannot be harmonized with the findings of modern science, you're not alone. In fact, the belief that one cannot accept the Bible as factual because it conflicts with science is probably the number one reason most non-Christians reject the Bible. But this conflict is unnecessary. Science and the Bible do not contradict each other, so long as scientists stay within the realm of scientific investigation, and theologians do not attempt to lift scientific information out of Scripture that isn't there. Before we get into this, let's gain some perspective.

THE RISE OF MODERN SCIENCE

The conflict between science and the Bible arose fairly recently. Early scientists were in agreement with Christians that God created a rational universe and that man, being a rational creature, could discover how the universe functions. Nature was seen as the textbook of God's general revelation just as the Bible was seen as the textbook of His special revelation. Scientists held that the starting point of knowledge could be found in Scripture. In fact, the view that the Bible provides a general foundation of natural history on which scientific discoveries could rest was adhered to by all of science from its inception in the Middle Ages through the time of Isaac Newton.

Christianity was essential for the rise of modern science. It created an atmosphere that encouraged the investigation of nature. Unlike Eastern and tribal religions that identified deity with creation, Christianity desacralized nature by recognizing that the creator was *apart* from nature, not *a part* of nature. This removed all religious prohibitions to scientific investigation.[1]

SCIENTIFIC INACCURACIES?

A common misconception is that the Bible contains scientific fallacies and inaccuracies. Of course, orthodox Christians will never concede this is true. Either the Bible is God's Word, or it is not. If it is, it will be free from error in any form, spiritual, historical, or scientific. Christians believe that the Bible is a reliable document and trustworthy in every subject it treats. So it will not make statements that are unscientific or historically inaccurate.

Having said this, it must be pointed out that the Bible is *not* a scientific textbook. Science is in a constant state of change. New discoveries destroy or alter old theories and generate new ones. If the Bible was a science textbook, it would have quickly been out-of-date.

The central purpose of the Bible is not to teach science but to show man how to be reconciled with God and thus achieve eternal life through Jesus Christ. On the other hand, the Bible does not contain anything scientifically false. Whenever the authors of Scripture touch on a scientific matter, they present truth, not error.

Unfortunately, some theologians have drawn unwarranted scientific inferences from Scripture. For example, in the seventeenth century, Bishop Ussher concluded that the world was created in 4004 B.C. after he analyzed the genealogies in the Bible. Others have taken the biblical teaching that man is to have dominion over the earth and used it as an excuse to abuse nature. Other theologians have claimed that the Bible teaches the earth is the center of the universe. And, of course, non-Christian critics love to point to verses that seem to allude to a flat earth. But the fact is, the Bible nowhere teaches any of these things. They are the products of sincere but misguided theologians or critics who have inferred more from the Bible than what it teaches.

Actually, the Bible makes numerous scientific references that were far advanced for the science of its day. It contains none of the absurdities found in the sacred books of the East or in Greek mythology. For example, at the time of Job, Greek mythology taught that the world rested on the shoulders of Atlas, one of the great Titans, or Elder gods. Yet Job 26:7 says that God "hangs the earth on nothing" (literally, the earth rests in space without any visible means of support). Astronomers in antiquity counted the stars and estimated that they numbered about five thousand. But the prophet Jeremiah wrote, "the host of heaven [stars] cannot be numbered" just as the "sand of the sea [cannot be] measured" (Jer. 33:22). Isaiah 40:22 refers to the earth as a "circle." The Hebrew word used here is *chug,* which allows for the concept that the earth is a sphere. This is particularly interesting because people at that time generally believed that the earth was flat.

The Bible also describes numerous natural phenomena whose processes were probably unknown at the time. For example, Ecclesiastes 1:6 relates that the wind blows "toward the south, then turning toward the north, the wind continues swirling along; and on its circular courses the wind returns" (NASV), a clear description of the great circular movements of earth's winds. In the following verse, the author states that "all the rivers flow into the sea, yet the sea is not full. To the place where the rivers flow, there they flow again" (NASV). This, of course, is a picture of the earth's hydraulic system in which water evaporates from the oceans, rains on the earth, and then returns to the sea via rivers to repeat the cycle again.

Now some will argue that this is reading science back into the Bible, but that is not the point. These descriptions, whatever the authors meant, do not contradict known scientific facts even though they were recorded in the Bible centuries before modern science. And more importantly, many of these descriptions are in stark contrast with the fallacious beliefs recorded by contemporaries of the Bible's human authors. Only God could have imparted such accurate information to the biblical writers. As Kenny Barfield has said:

> The Bible is pregnant with gems of wisdom buried within its pages. Physicians are amazed by the rationality of its dictums [concerning sanitation, food, and sex laws]. Its commands for daily liv-

ing provide a rational basis for preventive medicine. Even unbelievers often heap accolades on its moral codes. Astronomers must admit to the accuracy of its simplistic, yet moving description of the heavens. Geologists have been stunned as they stumble across modern concepts hidden within its pages. The biblical writers demonstrate a careful, quiet avoidance of the faulty doctrines outlined by others who wrote in those times.[2]

The belief that the Bible is scientifically inaccurate often has its source in the fact that the Bible used pre-scientific and phenomenological language. This means that the Bible describes nature as it appears to be and uses the same language we use in everyday speech. For example, Ecclesiastes 1:5 refers to the sun as "rising and setting" (NASV). Isaiah 11:12 refers to "the four corners of the earth." Such statements are not scientific, but then neither are they unscientific. They are just expressions of the way ordinary people have always talked. Because the Bible is not a scientific textbook, it does not speak "scientifically" any more than television weatherforecasters do when they tell us what time the sun will "rise" and "set" the following day. We don't accuse them of being unscientific, and we shouldn't pass judgment on the Bible for speaking in the same manner.

EVOLUTION VS. CREATION

The conflict between science and Scripture almost always involves the issues of miracles or creationism. Does science discount miracles? Does science disprove the biblical view of creation? We will examine the evidence for miracles in the next chapter, but here we will focus on the debate between evolutionists and creationists over the origin of life. In today's climate, this latter issue has become one of the most hotly contested topics between Christians and non-Christians.

Generally, the debate between evolutionists and creationists centers on two related issues: Does evolution disprove the existence of God? Does evolution prove that the Bible is false—in particular, the biblical account of divine creation?

The first question was answered in Chapter 2. If by *evolution* one means *naturalistic* evolution, then its foundational assumption is atheism. According to this form of evolution, life originated and evolved by random natural processes of time and chance independent of a supernatural creator. Now we discovered that atheism is irrational and the evidence for God's existence extensive and conclusive. So even if some form of evolution is true, it does not disprove God's existence.

So now we can move ahead to the second issue: Does evolution disprove biblical creationism?

Now, it needs to be said in the very beginning that, despite the fact that naturalistic evolution is atheistic, many Christians are evolutionists. One *can* be an evolutionist and still be a Christian. Believing in evolution is not a factor that prevents one from receiving Jesus Christ as Lord and Savior. There are many devout and faithful Christians, including some well-trained and respected theologians, who believe in a form of evolution called *theistic* evolution.

Theistic evolutionists usually interpret the Genesis account of creation poetically rather than literally. They believe the biblical story of creation is meant to teach that the earth and life owes its existence to God, not to teach the method by which the earth and life came into existence. Generally, theistic evolutionists accept whatever prevailing evolutionary theory is in vogue, but they insist that God is the force behind natural processes. This allows God to employ evolution in the creation process, thereby preserving a harmony between theism and the theory of evolution.

There are also several creationist models popular among Christians, and we will look at two of them later. But the point for now is that there is no reason for anyone to allow evolution to interfere with his acceptance of the God of Scripture and the Lord Jesus Christ.

Granting all this, I want you to know that creationism, including a *literal* six-day-creation interpretation of Genesis, can be sustained theologically and scientifically. So although belief in evolution is not a reason to reject the Bible or Jesus Christ, nevertheless, accepting creationism does not automatically make the Christian religion unscientific or individual Christians anti-science. The fact is, not only is creationism a viable alternative to evolution, but, as we will see, the bulk of scientific evidence fits the creationist's model of origins better than the evolutionist's model does.

The real issue between evolution and creationism is not so much science as it is philosophy. An important part of this chapter is to help you understand why evolution is so widely accepted when so much scientific evidence refutes it. So let's get started.

THE PHILOSOPHY OF SCIENCE

Beginning in the eighteenth century and escalating in the nineteenth century, Christianity began to move from center stage as the dominant world view in Western culture. Meanwhile, secular humanism, empowered by the growth of modern science, supplanted Christianity as the dominant world view. Today, science has achieved in the minds of many divine status. Faith in science as the source of knowledge has become the god of post-Christian secular man. Thus, to a large degree, the issue of science versus the Bible is really a philosophical one. It is not just a matter of conflicting interpretations of facts but of conflicting faiths.

Modern science operates by a system of thought that often goes by the name of *naturalism* or *scientific materialism*. Naturalism is a philosophy. It teaches that the universe operates according to eternal, unchanging natural laws, and that nothing exists outside the material world. Reality is what we can see, hear, touch, taste, and smell. No supernatural reality exists. All of reality, at least potentially, can be understood by the human mind, and all phenomena have a natural explanation. This precludes the existence of God, miracles, angels, providence, immortality, heaven, sin, salvation, and answered prayer—at least as Christians understand them. All such things are incompatible with naturalism's world view.[3]

Atheistic evolution is part of the philosophy of naturalism. It begins with the philosophical presupposition that life came into existence accidentally through random processes over immense periods of time. It then sets out to find scientific evidence that supports this view. Evolution is a philosophy of the origin of life that ignores the biblical revelation of creation and the wealth of scientific evidence supporting it. Evolutionists are notorious for suppressing evidence that does not fit their hypothesis.

EVOLUTION—FACT OR MYTH?

Larry Laudan in his book, *Progress and Its Problems: Toward a Theory of Scientific Growth,*[4] observes that the history of science contains dozens of theories that have eventually been discarded as inadequate explanations of various phenomena. They were discarded or replaced by new ones. So we can probably rest assured that atheistic evolution will likewise one day be shown to be inadequate as the definite statement on the origin of life, especially as new evidences supporting creationism continue to emerge. Unfortunately, however, there are barriers to the widespread acceptance of creationism as a scientific model of origins that go beyond mere scientific verification. Let me explain why this is so.

Modern scientific theories revolve around *paradigms*. Paradigms are models or standards by which data is interpreted and predictions made. The success of any particular paradigm lies in the fact that it is more successful than competing paradigms in solving existing problems and in the promise of solving future ones. On the negative side, however, once a paradigm has become firmly established in an accepted world view, it is not easily surrendered. Instead, it tends to acquire a commitment far beyond what it had initially, even to the degree that scientists attempt to work hard to fit new data within a paradigm that has become inadequate.[5]

The danger of this is twofold. First, a tendency develops to exclude or ignore data that does not support the existing paradigm. Second, if the paradigm is propagating false information, its adherents are believing a lie.

The theory of evolution is an example of how a particular paradigm can influence a culture's overall world view, even when the paradigm is likely false. Evolution arose at a time in history (the nineteenth century) when science was becoming estranged from Christian theology. It not only explained data that was at that time not totally accounted for biblically, but it also provided a world view that precluded a creator God. This helped bring about a complete separation of science and religion that the secularists had been seeking. Today, evolution still fits best with the atheistic presuppositions of secular humanism.

The acceptance of well-entrenched paradigms such as evolution can be so intolerant and dogmatic that even when the evidence on which they depend is disqualified, they still tend to remain accepted models. Although a wealth of scientific data has accumulated to cast doubt on evolution, most scientists, adhering to the philosophy of naturalism, refuse to investigate alternative (i.e., creationist) concepts. Add to that the fact that science has been elevated to the status of absolute authority with regard to truth and you have an intolerable barrier to true investigation and knowledge. Science has decreed that the evolution paradigm explains the origin of life, and most people have unquestioningly bowed and accepted the decree as scientific fact. But is the decree justified? No, and here's why: The origin of life is more an historical matter than it is a scientific one.

The birth of the universe and origin of life were past, one-time events. No human being observed them, and no present processes approximate them. Now science can only verify data that can be repeated through observation and experimentation. Consequently, scientific investigation can never prove how the universe came into existence or if evolution was the means by which life developed. This is not to say that scientific investigation into the origin of the universe or of life is an invalid pursuit. But science cannot make dogmatic claims against biblical creationism. When scientists state emphatically that life arose accidentally through random processes over immense periods of time, they leave the realm of scientific facts demonstrable through observation and experimentation and move into speculation. And when they present only the evidence that best fits the evolutionary scenario, they imbibe presumptuous metaphysical (philosophical) claims that they have no scientific foundation to accept. At best, science loses its integrity and, at worst, embraces false and unsubstantiated views when scientists run amuck in these ways.

The same can be said about spiritual truths. Can science prove the nonexistence of God? Of course not. In fact, attempts to disprove God by a system that already philosophically denies God are absurd and illogical. Likewise, can science prove we are saved through Jesus Christ? Of course not. The truth is, scientific "facts" have never disproved one word of the Bible or one biblical claim. Nothing in science prevents us from believing that God created the universe and life, including man, and that He did so totally independent of evolutionary processes.

This brings us to the problem at hand: Does evolution stand the test of objective investigation? Both evolutionism and creationism are theories on the origin of life. Which theory is best supported by the evidence? If we look beyond the biased teachings of the evolutionary paradigm, we find that the creationist model is supported by more scientific evidence than the evolutionist model.

SCIENCE SPEAKS ABOUT CREATIONISM

Christians are logically justified and philosophically consistent to accept biblical creation *without* investigating scientific evidence. If the Bible is the Word of God, then what it teaches about creation must be true. God cannot lie. With this approach, the truth of biblical creationism depends on the Bible's reliability. Since the Bible is true, creationism must be a fact of science whether science recognizes it or not. There is no contradiction or faulty logic here because we have simply shifted the burden of proof away from science to Scripture. Nor is this circular reasoning because we are presenting evidence outside of Scripture to validate the Bible. The only difference is that the evidence one presents is historical evidence for the reliability of the Bible rather than scientific evidence. The Bible is God's divine Word; the Bible teaches creationism; therefore, creationism is true.

But to get a fair hearing for creationism in our society, we must rely on more than biblical reliability. We must submit scientific evidence to confirm the biblical view of creation. And that we can do. The creationist model for the origin and development of life is supported by a great deal of scientific evidence. In fact, the creationist model best explains the available scientific evidence on the origin of life. What follows are evidences *evolutionists* feel best support their theory. However, as you will see, these same evidences are much more believable and scientifically acceptable when viewed within the creationist model.

The Fossil Evidence

Historically, the most convincing evidence for evolution is the fossil record. Evolutionists claim that the fossil record displays a gradual evolution of animal and plant life from primitive forms to complex forms with transitional phases between major classes (e.g., between fish and amphibians, amphibians and reptiles, reptiles and birds, and so on).

But this scenario has no support. There is no evidence that complex life forms evolve from primitive life forms because no such transitional species between any of these groups of animals have ever been found in the tons of fossil-bearing rock recovered over the past one hundred thirty years. Textbook drawings of transitional species are simply artists' conceptions of what they *think* such animals would look like if they did exist. All the major groups of animals are distinct from one another throughout the fossil record, and their particular characteristics are fully formed and functional when they first appear. For example, when feathers and wings first show up, they are fully formed feathers and wings. No part-leg/part-wing or part-scale/part-feather fossils have ever been found. What use would a part-leg/part-wing have anyway? According to evolution, for any trait to be passed along, it must have survival value. Certainly a part-leg/part-wing would have no survival value to either a reptile or a bird. In fact, it would likely be a detriment.

On the other hand, the creationist model explains the absence of transitional species. The Bible teaches that God created living creatures "after their kind" (Gen. 1:24, NASV). This can be interpreted to mean that God created all the original kinds of animals with specific "gene pools" that contained all of the genetic potential needed for each type of animal to produce diverse varieties within its own kind. For example, the canine family probably arose from an original created kind. From the first dog, all the various wild and domestic dogs on earth developed. But this is not evolution in the sense that modern canines evolved from some pre-dog ancestor. Rather, the original created dog-kind developed, through adaption to diverse environmental conditions, into the numerous forms of dogs we see today. This process is called *microevolution,* which is not one species evolving from a more primitive species but a created kind fulfilling its full genetic potential within the limits of its original gene pool. Both extinct and modern canines have always been just dogs. In the fossil record, there has never been a half dog/half cat or half dog/half some other animal. There has always been just dogs.

Natural selection within created gene pools accounts for every change seen in every kind of animal on earth, extinct or modern. All the illustrations given by evolutionists to prove evolution are in reality no more than adaptions within specific gene pools. Science has never seen in nature or observed in a laboratory one species of animal evolve into another. When cockroaches become resistant to a pesticide, it does not represent the evolution of a new species of cockroach. Rather it illustrates natural selection within the cockroach gene pool, allowing insects already resistant to a particular pesticide because of their existing genetic makeup to become dominant within a population of cockroaches. But the new breed of resistant cockroaches are *still* cockroaches.

Mutations

A second important argument used to support evolution focuses on mutations. Evolutionists argue that the mechanism by which one species evolves into another is through genetic mutations. The idea goes something like this. Through a genetic foul-up, a species of animal is born with a new trait that aids its survival. For instance, an animal is born with a deformed ear that actually allows that animal to hear an approaching predator better than others of his species. Because this characteristic is beneficial, that particular animal survives to pass on the trait to its offspring, which in turn benefit from the same trait and pass it on to their offspring. Eventually, after millions of years and countless generations, the animals with the more efficient hearing dominate the species, and what was once a deformity is now part of the genetic makeup of all the animals within that particular species. Evolutionists teach that with vast amounts of time, thousands of these tiny mutations can eventually give rise to an entirely new species of animal. Thus accidental mutations plus long time spans plus natural selection ("survival of the fittest") result in the continual emergence of new species of animals.

The flaw in this theory is twofold. First, in practically every known case, a mutation is not beneficial but harmful to an animal and usually kills it. A deformity lessens the survival potential of an animal—it does not strengthen it. And even if there are "good" mutations, the tremendous number of bad mutations would overwhelm the fewer number of good ones. What one would expect to see, if mutations were passed along to future generations, is a tendency for a species to degenerate and eventually become extinct, not evolve upward to a new or better species.

The second flaw in the mutation theory is that the time needed for a primitive animal to evolve into a higher animal through random mutational changes is mathematically impossible. The problem lies in the fact that there must be a series of both related mutations and subsequent mutations that are complementary to one another. A new trait does not evolve in one generation. For a deer to evolve greater speed requires not only that it slowly, over countless generations, develops more powerful legs but that corresponding mutations in other areas of its body must also take place at the same time. To run faster, more efficient circulation, heart, lungs, and so on are needed. Creationist Dr. Gary Parker explains that the chances of getting three related mutations in a row is one in a billion trillion (10^{21}). To illustrate the odds of this, he states that "the ocean isn't big enough to hold enough bacteria to make it likely for you to find a bacterium with three simultaneous or sequential related mutations."[6] Moreover, the time that would be needed for enough mutations to occur to evolve even a simple organism is many billions of years longer than what evolutionists themselves believe the age of the earth to be.

A similar problem exists with regard to the probability of life accidentally coming into existence from nonlife through chemical processes in the earth's alleged primordial soup. With the discovery of the genetic code, we now know that the amount of information coded in the organization of a simple living cell is so vast that its accidental formation by random processes is beyond possibility. According to Sir Fred Hoyle, an eminent mathematician and astronomer, if the earth is 4.6 billion years old, as most evolutionists believe, the probability of a single living cell originating by random processes would be one chance in $10^{40,000}$ (ten with forty thousand zeros behind it). In other words, the probability is so small that it is not even considered as a viable option by most scientists familiar with information theory and probability studies. Today, thanks to "super computers," it is firmly established that chance, long time spans, and mutations cannot account for the origin of life nor confirm the evolution of even a simple organism. As Hoyle puts it, "The chance that higher life forms might have emerged in this way is comparable with the chance that a tornado sweeping through a junkyard might assemble a Boeing 747 from the materials therein."[7]

The Age of the Earth

The third ingredient vital to the evolution recipe is an old earth. Although the age of the earth is not a factor in the creationist model of origins (remember, even if the earth is 5 billion years old, it is still not old enough for even simple organisms to evolve), time is of the utmost importance on the evolution model.

Evolutionists generally agree that the age of the earth is between 4.5 and 5 billion years old. The most common dating methods used by science to substantiate this age are one of several radiometric systems.[8] These methods measure geologic time according to the rate of disintegration of radioactive elements. They are based on the assumption that decay processes have remained fairly stable throughout geologic history.

Today, much data is available that questions the accuracy of radiometric dating systems, and there are numerous other dating methods that suggest a young earth. In fact, over sixty chronometers date the earth as young (in geologic time, a young earth would be tens of thousands to hundreds of millions of years old rather than billions of years old). Dating methods that point to a geologically young earth include the decay of the earth's magnetic field, the accumulation of meteoritic dust on the earth's crust, the amount of helium in the atmosphere, the influx of sediment into the oceans via rivers, and the influx of specific chemicals into the oceans. In all of these cases, if the earth was billions of years old, the amount of decay or accumulation would be much greater than they are today.[9]

Further Evidence

Thermodynamics

The first and second laws of thermodynamics are foundational to all of science and have never been contradicted in observable nature. The first law, also called the "law of conservation of mass-energy," states that matter and energy are neither being created nor destroyed. In other words, matter and energy do not have within themselves the ability to create. This implies that they must have been created. The first law of thermodynamics points away from evolution to a creator.

The second law, also called the "law of increasing entropy," states that entropy (which is the measurement of disorganization) always increases in an isolated system (a system which does not have an external influence that can sustain or increase its available energy, such as the universe). Now, what does this mean? Simply put, it means that the natural course of anything is to degenerate. An old automobile in a junkyard eventually rusts away. An animal is born and eventually grows old and dies. A star burns out and vanishes. In short, the universe is running down. But if the universe is running down, it must have had a beginning. It is not eternal. This implies a creator. It also contradicts evolution which depicts life moving upward rather than slowly degenerating.

The Anthropic Principle

One of the most compelling evidences supporting creationism involves the anthropic principle, although it is sometimes used as an argument supporting evolution. The anthropic principle observes that the earth is fashioned so precisely that life as we know it could not exist if the earth were even minutely different. Evolutionists acknowledge this and then argue that, although the universe is incredibly complex and wonderfully ordered, we should not be surprised that life came into existence through random process. Why? Because the very fact that we exist demonstrates that evolution occurred. In other words, in an infinite universe, the diverse circumstances needed for life to occur were bound to fall into place sooner or later—even if only once—no matter how unlikely it may be.

The fundamental problem with this argument should be obvious. It is merely a philosophical statement that relies on circular reasoning. It assumes that evolution accounts for the origin of life and then states, because life exists, we have proof that evolution is true. To counter this, we can offer our own philosophical statement. Robert Newman does this well: "If such a being as the God of the Bible exists, then an apparently designed universe such as ours would be a likely result rather than such a surprise as we have in an accidental universe."[10]

Hence, we are right back to arguing which model, creation or evolution, best fits the available evidence. And here is where the creationists can use the anthropic principle to their advantage. The value of the anthropic principle, as a support for creation, lies in its recognition that life can exist only within very narrow margins. For example, if the earth was located closer or farther from the sun, life could not exist due to excessive heat or cold. If the chemical composition of the atmosphere varied only slightly, the air would be poisonous to life. If the sea-to-land-mass ratio, depth of the oceans, and the earth's cloud cover were different, the earth's ability to store and release heat would change dramatically. All such events could result in the absence of life on earth. Rather than all of these variables being the result of accidental processes (luck), it appears much more probable that the earth was specifically designed to sustain life. And if it was designed, there must be a Designer—God.

Actually, this concept can be carried a step further. According to the evolutionary scenario, when the earth was formed, it did not initially possess the right chemical balance for life to exist. A hardening ball of gases would hardly support life. For the earth to reach a stage in which it could support life, some form of *inorganic* (nonliving) evolution would have had to occur. This would be necessary in order to achieve the right combination of ingredients from which organic molecules could emerge. Even if we can envision organic evolution (the evolution of living plants and animals), it takes a colorful imagination to accept the premise that nonliving elements such as gases and minerals evolved to a point where they could support life. I'm convinced that evolutionists demand we believe in the absurd.

Applying Scientific Evidence

Evidence	Creationism	Evolutionism
No transitional fossils	Not expected because God created "kinds."	Needed for evolution to work but missing in the fossil record.
Mutations	Most mutations are "bad" and destroy organisms. The earth is not old enough for "good" mutations to account for evolution.	Without an abundance of good mutations, there is no way to account for evolutionary change.
Age of earth	Creation model fits with both an old and young earth.	Old earth is necessary for evolution.
Thermodynamics	Demonstrates the universe had a beginning (created) and is running down (will end).	Violates the evolutionary assumptions that the universe is eternal and uncaused.
Anthropic Principle	Explains the order and design in the universe as the product of an intelligent Creator. God created the earth specifically to sustain life.	Evolution requires that the ingredients necessary to support life are the product of random processes.

CAN EVOLUTION AND THE BIBLE BOTH BE CORRECT?

So far, my purpose has been to demonstrate that evolution does not fit the facts of science. In spite of the evidence supporting creationism, however, some readers will still find it difficult to set aside a lifetime of evolutionary indoctrination and become creationists. The question, then, is, Can creationism be harmonized with evolutionary concepts? Can the Genesis account of creation and evolutionism both be correct? Many theologians and scientists would answer the question yes. However, they all have one thing in common. They all reject atheistic evolution as well as theistic evolution and accept, instead, one of several creationist theories (creationism).

Various creationist models attempt to harmonize Genesis 1 and 2 with certain evolutionary concepts such as an old earth. However, all creationists agree that God is the creator *and* sustainer of the universe and that macroevolution (where one species eventually becomes another species) is unsupported by the scientific evidence. The following briefly describes the two most widely accepted creationist theories.

THE GAP THEORY

This position claims that a "gap" of perhaps five billion years occurred between Genesis 1:1 and Genesis 1:2. During this time, prehistoric life evolved and major geologic changes occurred. At some point in recent geologic time, a giant cataclysmic event took place that ushered in the extinction of prehistoric life and the beginning of the modern earth. Some theologians suggest that this cataclysmic event was the result of Satan rebelling against God. Actually, the biblical evidence for this view is scant.

PROGRESSIVE CREATIONISM

Progressive creationism (one example is the day-age theory) claims that the six days of creation are not literal twenty-four-hour days but may represent six geologic time periods of unspecific duration. During these "days," God intervened with specific creative acts. This view relies largely on two biblical observations.

First, the Hebrew word for "day" *(yom)* can refer to an indefinite period of time rather than to a twenty-four-hour day. In normal biblical interpretation (hermeneutics), questionable words are checked out in other passages in order to zero in on their exact meaning. It appears that in Genesis 2:4, the word *yom* covers the entire span of creation. *Yom* seems to have a similar meaning in Genesis 5:2 and other passages. Add to this 2 Peter 3:8, which says that "with the Lord one day is as a thousand years, and a thousand years as one day," and there are some good grounds to argue that the six days of creation may not be six literal days. (However, literal six-day creationists claim that Exodus 20:11 refutes this view.)

The second argument that appears to lend support to progressive creationism is even stronger. It points out that although Adam and Eve were both created on day six according to Genesis 1:27, in Genesis 2:4–25 a time interval elapsed between the creation of Adam and the creation of Eve. After Adam was created, he was placed in the Garden of Eden to tend and cultivate it, had time to name all the animals, became lonely—and all this happened before Eve was made. It seems impossible that all of this activity would take place in one twenty-four hour period.

Thus, many creationists conclude that the word *day* likely refers to a longer period of time than twenty-four-hours. Exactly how long is an open issue for discovery and debate.

The Origin of Life

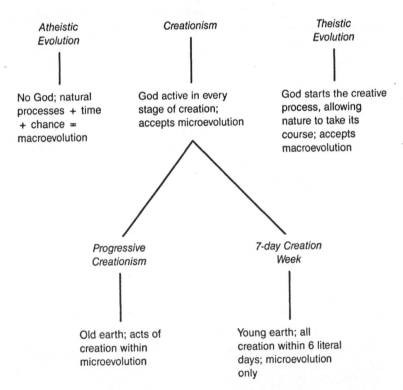

Atheistic Evolution

No God; natural processes + time + chance = macroevolution

Creationism

God active in every stage of creation; accepts microevolution

Theistic Evolution

God starts the creative process, allowing nature to take its course; accepts macroevolution

Progressive Creationism

Old earth; acts of creation within microevolution

7-day Creation Week

Young earth; all creation within 6 literal days; microevolution only

I want to reemphasize here that progressive creationism is not to be confused with theistic evolutionism. Even if the earth is five billion years old, there are still no transitional fossils to support the claim that primitive animals evolved into higher animals. And as explained above, the mechanics for achieving macroevolution through mutations are beyond scientific credibility. Nor does a five-billion-year-old earth significantly lower the odds of life emerging spontaneously from inorganic material. The way I see it, the primary goal of progressive creationism is to explain an old earth (the geologic ages) and thereby allow more time for the number of species to increase from among the original created kinds on a microevolutionary model. Whether one accepts a six-day creation week or one of the progressive creationism models, in the Christian view God is still the sovereign creator and sustainer of the universe.

Space prevents a more in-depth examination of the various creationist models, but I hope what has been offered here has confirmed that Scripture allows for a variety of interpretations of Genesis 1 and 2.

My own position? I think J. P. Moreland voices it well:

The exegetical problems [of Genesis 1 and 2] should cause us to allow the possibility that several different understandings of the text, within the framework of inerrancy, are genuine contenders. The day of creation is a difficult question, but on exegetical grounds alone, the literal twenty-four-hour-day view is better. However, since the different progressive creationist views are plausible exegetical options on hermeneutical grounds alone, then if science seems to point to a universe of several billions of years, it seems allowable to read Genesis in this light. It would be wrong to let science elevate an understanding of Genesis which is not antecedently plausible on hermeneutical grounds alone. But in this case, an old cosmos seems allowable. On the other hand, it does not seem possible to hold to a great antiquity for man. Even with gaps in the genealogies, it seems that Adam and Eve would be recent, surely within fifty thousand years, probably earlier. In any case, Christians should continue to promote various paradigms of Genesis 1 and 2 which do not do damage to the text. There are too many difficult exegetical issues for dogmatism and infighting among us.[11]

IN HARMONY

When all the evidence is in, one fact stands out. Believing in atheistic evolution demands an enormous amount of faith. In fact, in light of the scientific evidence, it takes much greater faith to believe in evolutionism than it does to believe in creationism. Evolution requires us to believe that out of chaos, time, and chance arose order, design, and harmony. It teaches that life came from nonlife, that human ethics and morality came from amorality, that human intelligence came from irrationality. By comparison, creationists look out upon the orderly universe, the design and harmony in nature, human morality and rationality, and see their source in an intelligent, moral, all-powerful, creative God. Which requires the most faith to believe?

Today, an increasing number of evolutionists are recognizing that evolution is no longer a viable theory of origins.[12] They recognize that time and chance, operating via mutation and natural selection, do not produce new species, let alone account for the origin of life. As one scientist puts it, people like Carl Sagan are simply "peddling the old mechanistic world view in relation to astronomy: the primordial soup that he starts all his expositions with, the non-existent mythical primordial soup. I think these people have no respect for facts at all. The facts are too disturbing."[13]

So it turns out that science and the Bible don't conflict. What's at odds are unscientific dogmas and uninformed interpretations of Scripture—positions everyone is better off without.

12

How Do We Know Miracles Really Happen?

Although Christianity is a historical religion, resting on a foundation of verifiable facts, it nevertheless recounts numerous supernatural events. For this reason, the answer to the question of whether Bible miracles are true alone determines the authenticity of the Christian faith. Why? Because the dual miracles of the incarnation and the resurrection of Jesus Christ encompass the entire fabric of Christianity. If these two unparalleled miracles did not occur, Christianity crumbles.

Both Jesus and the apostles recognized this. When the scribes and Pharisees asked Jesus for a "sign" of who He was, His response was, "no sign will be given . . . except the sign of the prophet Jonah. For as Jonah was three days and three nights in the belly of the great fish, so will the Son of Man be three days and three nights in the heart of the earth" (Matt. 12:39–40). In other words, the sign of Jesus' divine messiahship, His incarnation as the Son of God, was His miraculous resurrection (Rom. 1:4). The apostle Paul agrees: "if Christ has not been raised, your faith is worthless; you are still in your sins. Then those also who have fallen asleep in Christ have perished. If we have hoped in Christ in this life only, we are of all men most to be pitied" (1 Cor. 15:17–19, NASV).

Of the four evidences used by the authors of the New Testament to confirm the Christian message, miracles are the most convincing and important. (The other three are prophecy, natural theology, and inner

151

experience.) R. C. Sproul is right, miracles "and they alone ultimately prove that Christ is the Son of God and that the Bible is the Word of God. All other 'evidence' is corroborative."[1]

WHAT IS A MIRACLE?

A biblical miracle is a willful act of God, explainable only by His existence and power, and it has three specific ingredients: (1) it is perceivable by both believers and unbelievers; (2) it appears to either intervene or facilitate the normal sequence of natural laws through which God governs the universe; and (3) it is done for the purpose of executing a divine act, validating a religious truth, or illustrating a religious principle.

There are two kinds of Bible miracles: miracles in which God acts within natural laws, sometimes referred to as miracles of providence, and miracles in which God alters or interrupts natural laws, sometimes referred to as miracles of creation.

Miracles of providence occur when God interrupts the natural flow of history or nature but does so without actually violating natural laws. For example, 2 Kings 19:35 and Isaiah 37:36 record the account of the Lord destroying the 185,000 man army of Sennacherib, king of Assyria, after Hezekiah prayed for deliverance (2 Kings 19:20–35). By all qualifications, this was a miracle from God. Without divine intervention, Hezekiah would have been defeated, and Jerusalem would have fallen to the Assyrians.

This same account was reported by the early Greek historian, Herodotus. But he explained that the Assyrian army was infected by a sudden outbreak of a virulent plague caused by rodents. So although the event is miraculous in that it was a direct intervention of God, it nevertheless may have involved natural phenomenon functioning in a normal fashion but at just the appropriate time.

Similar examples are found in the destruction of Sodom and Gomorrah, which could have resulted from some catastrophic geological phenomenon (Gen. 19:24–25); the three-and-a-half-year drought that occurred in answer to the prayers of Elijah (James 5:17–18); the earthquake that opened the prison doors at Philippi (Acts 16:26); the tribute coin found in the fish's mouth (Matt. 17:24–27); the parting and closing of the Red Sea as Moses raised and lowered his hands (Exod. 14:15–31).

In all of these cases, the events themselves can be accounted for by natural phenomena. For example, finding a coin in a fish's mouth may be unique, but not a miracle. Fish have been known to swallow stranger things than coins. But for Jesus to say that at a certain time a certain fish will be caught that will have a coin in its mouth of the exact value needed to meet a particular financial need is much different. Likewise, with the parting of the Red Sea, the miracle was not the mighty wind—perhaps someday science can artificially generate winds of that power—but the fact that the wind parted the water at the very moment Moses raised his hand and ceased blowing, allowing the water to inundate the Egyptians, at the very moment Moses lowered his hand. In both instances, the miracle was not *how* the events occurred, but rather the *timing* of the events and their relationship to religious truth.[2]

Miracles of creation are acts of God in which unique and extraordinary events occur that temporarily set aside or transcend natural laws. Examples here include Jesus changing water into wine during the wedding at Cana (John 2:1–9), His feeding the five thousand from only five loaves of bread and two fish (Matt. 14:15–21), and His raising Lazarus from the dead (John 11:17–44).

Critics of these accounts have claimed that many events once thought to be miraculous, such as some healing miracles, can now be accomplished by modern medicine. Some have even argued that, in the future, science will likely be able to revive people who have died. The response to this is that miracles are not dependent on whether they can be explained or even duplicated. Like miracles of providence, the *timing* is the crucial issue. R. C. Sproul gives an appropriate response:

Suppose by the year 2000 scientists are able to revive dead bodies. This is not the same thing as saying that in A.D. 29 it was a natural phenomenon to revivify a dead body. . . . Because one could resurrect a body in A.D. 2000 by natural means does not imply that was the case two millennia earlier. Manifestly, raising a body from the dead, as Christ's body was raised, was something which could have been done—at that time in any case—only by the immediate exercise of divine power. Whatever scientists may be able to do in the future could hardly disprove a past miracle. . . . Science [does] not bring us any closer to the actual supernatural, miraculous character of the original events to which we refer.[3]

WHY ARE BIBLE MIRACLES NEEDED?

The fact that God used miracles as an instrument of revelation demonstrates they're a necessary ingredient of the Christian faith. Liberal theologians have attempted to remove biblical miracles from Christian theology, but in doing so they have sacrificed the supernatural power of Christianity. Jesus without miracles becomes a mere man; the Bible without miracles, only the words of men.

It appears in Scripture that God has two primary uses for miracles.

MIRACLES AUTHENTICATE GOD'S MESSENGERS

As you'll remember, special revelation is recorded in the Bible, and it contains very specific information about God not accessible from general revelation. For example, by special revelation we learn that salvation is through Jesus Christ. Although initially given to particular people at particular times in history, special revelation is nevertheless fitted for all. This means that the spiritual truths, divine promises, ethical principles, and instructions for an abundant life are available to all people.

The problem inherent in special revelation is how can God convince people who did not personally receive this revelation that it is genuine, that it really comes from Him. To do this, God must give evidence that His chosen messengers, those to whom special revelation was given and who recorded it in the Bible, have His authority. So special revelation depends on miracles to affirm that "the one who bears the revelation [proves] that he is actually from God."[4] Moses, for example, was chosen by God to deliver the Israelites from bondage in Egypt (Exod. 3:7–10). Pharaoh, understandably, wanted proof that Moses was really sent from God for that purpose (7:9). The miracles God performed through Moses authenticated to Pharaoh that Moses was divinely appointed to liberate the Hebrews (5:1). Likewise, the

New Testament apostles performed many miracles to confirm they were empowered as messengers of God's revelation (2 Cor. 12:12; Heb. 2:3–4). This was especially the case when they were planting the early churches (Acts 9:32–42).

MIRACLES AUTHENTICATE THAT JESUS IS THE DIVINE MESSIAH

Miracles played a major role throughout Jesus' earthly life: His miraculous conception in the virgin Mary (Luke 1:35), the miraculous signs and wonders He performed to confirm His deity and divine power (John 5:36; 11:41–42), and, most explicitly, His resurrection from the dead (Matt. 12:38–40).

Jesus performed hundreds of miracles—most of them never recorded in the Bible (John 21:25). The miracles that were recorded serve a very specific purpose. They always had a religious message and were never done arbitrarily for amusement or display. Jesus' miracles either met a serious human need that required, in first century Palestine, a miraculous intervention (as in the case of healing) or confirmed His own identity and authority as the Son of God (John 10:37–38). There were times Jesus refused to perform miracles because they did not fall in one of these two categories (see Luke 23:8–9).

ARGUMENTS AGAINST MIRACLES

Over the past three centuries, there have been numerous arguments against the possibility of miracles, especially biblical miracles. The majority of these arguments can be categorized into the following four broad areas.

MIRACLES DO NOT "FIT" IN THE MODERN WORLD

The common intellectual arguments against miracles are philosophical and scientific, and we'll work our way through those in a few moments. But the truth is, most people who reject miracles today do so because disbelief in them is inherent in modern society. People reject miracles, not because they have critically analyzed the evidence for and against them and consciously decided that miracles are impossible, but because our culture *assumes* the impossibility of miracles, and this assumption has become part of the essential character of our modern world view.

The prevailing faith in Western culture is secular humanism (the renouncement of religion and the elevation of man as the measure of all things). The philosophical foundation of secular humanism is naturalism. As explained in the previous chapter, naturalism is the belief that the universe is a closed system that functions according to eternal, unchanging natural laws and that nothing exists outside the material world. Reality is what we can experience with our five senses. There is no supernatural. There is no knowledge beyond what humans can ultimately discover and comprehend, and all phenomena has a natural explanation.

Because miracles depend on the existence of a God who is active in His creation and naturalism rejects such ideas, the belief in miracles has all but vanished among secular scholars and scientists—the philosophical trendsetters in Western society. In short, miracles have been defined out of existence. If we get behind all the red tape against miracles, the *real* reason miracles are rejected by most people today is because our prevailing world view assumes they are impossible. Of course, that's not an argument, only a bias.

THE PHILOSOPHICAL CASE
AGAINST MIRACLES

Whether one believes miracles are philosophically possible is largely determined by one's belief or disbelief in the supernatural. If God exists, miracles are possible. God, as most people perceive Him, is all-powerful, all-knowing, and the creator of the universe. Nothing is impossible for God so long as it is not out of character with His nature (e.g., God cannot do evil because, by His nature, He is good). Philosophically, the question of miracles is mute if one accepts the existence of God. Miracles are possible in a theistic world.

The classic philosophical argument against miracles was made by eighteenth-century philosopher David Hume in his *Enquiry Concerning Human Understanding*. Since then, other philosophical arguments have been presented, but most are simply restatements of

Hume's reasoning. So we'll focus our attention on his case against miracles.

According to Hume, the universe functions by unchanging natural laws. We know these laws are "firm and unalterable" because they are established by consistent human experience. No one has ever seen natural laws violated. This "uniform experience amounts to proof" that miracles cannot exist (e.g., that a dead man cannot rise from the grave). Why? Because the relative probability of a miracle occurring, in light of this uniform experience, is so low as to be virtually impossible. Therefore, if anyone claims to have observed a miracle, it is highly probable that he is mistaken because the evidence against an alleged miracle will always outweigh the evidence supporting it. In fact, it would be a *greater* miracle if his testimony were correct than if the miracle he claims to have observed was actually true. Thus, when someone claims to have seen a miracle, the wise man will conclude that the observer was mistaken and the miracle, in fact, never occurred.[5]

Now, what is wrong with this argument? The fallacies are numerous, and we will look at the five most obvious.

First, it does not take a trained philosopher to see that Hume's argument is circular. As C. S. Lewis observes, "We know the experience against [miracles] to be uniform only if we know that all the reports of them are false. And we can know all the reports to be false only if we know already that miracles have never occurred. In fact, we are arguing in a circle."[6]

Second, Hume's implication that the apparent uniformity of nature is due to unchangeable natural laws is a scientific assumption that has lost its mooring in light of current data in physics. It's virtually impossible today to sustain the premise that natural laws are set and unalterable. We will look at this more closely when we examine the scientific case against miracles.

Third, Hume assumes it's impossible to demonstrate the existence of a supernatural being. To Hume, every event must have a natural explanation. Beneath his whole argument is this presupposition. But presuppositions do not amount to fact, nor do they prove anything.

Fourth, Hume's argument presupposes that any historical evidence for the miraculous is erroneous. He brazenly claims that any-one who witnesses a miracle (such as a dead man come to life) must be mistaken in spite of the strength of the evidence. This flies in the face of standard and accepted canons of historical investigation. If Hume's approach to miracles were applied to other areas of historical inquiry, it would effectively destroy most of the historical facts we take for granted. In fact, in the nineteenth century a logician named Richard Whately took Hume's historical criteria for establishing an event as a miracle and applied it to the life of the French military leader Napoleon Bonaparte. With great satirical bite, Whately dem-onstrated that belief in Napoleon's existence was as ill-founded as belief in miracles. If, as Hume argued, miracles are unknowable, then so is the life of Napoleon Bonaparte.[7] One wonders if the evidence for Hume's existence would even be as great as the evidence for Napo-leon. Perhaps Hume never lived either!

Fifth, Hume's premise that uniform human experience is the criterion by which facts are ascertained is a philosophically weak ar-gument. C. S. Lewis makes the point that "experience, even if pro-longed for a million years, cannot tell us whether the thing is possible." Experience can tell us what *normally* happens in nature, but it cannot tell us with absolute certainty what *will* happen. Even if no one has seen a dead man rise from the grave, it is still not proof that it will not occur. A miracle does not deny that nature adheres to general principles or natural law, but, as Lewis says, such "norm or rule . . . can be suspended. A miracle is by definition an exception."[8]

There are many other problems with Hume's philosophical posi-tion, but we don't need to go into them here.[9] Hume's real problem with miracles appears to be more spiritual than philosophical. As the late Dr. Carnell observed, "Hume's canons are . . . arbitrarily chosen by a prejudiced mind as devices to discredit the Christian Scriptures, rather than seriously thought out rules for historians to follow when sifting and screening the records of the past."[10]

THE SCIENTIFIC CASE AGAINST MIRACLES

The conflict between Bible miracles and science centers on the latter's insistence that miracles, including the miracle of creation, are not in harmony with the "facts" of science because there is no such thing as a supernatural entity capable of influencing or altering natural law. We have already answered this challenge in Chapter 2 by proving the existence of God. And, as explained above, if God exists, then miracles are possible in spite of the claims of science. Nevertheless, an apologetic defense requires that we confront this argument on the scientists' own turf. There are four areas of *objective* evidence that deny the claim that miracles conflict with scientific fact.

The first area concerns the limits of scientific inquiry. As we saw in Chapter 11, science can only prove things that are verifiable through repeatable observation and experimentation. Science can't prove anything that happened in history. And Bible miracles are a matter of history, not of science. This means that the authenticity of a miraculous event requires historical investigation, not scientific.

> Laws of nature are a description of what *happens,* not a handbook of rules to tell us what *cannot happen.* "In choosing his laws of nature, therefore, the scientist should first consult history, and after deciding by historical evidence what has happened, should then choose his laws within the limits of historical actuality. The non-Christian thinker, intent on repudiating miracles, proceeds by a reverse method. He chooses his law without regard to historical limits, and then tries to rewrite history to fit his law. But surely this method is not only the reverse of Christian method, it is clearly the reverse of rational procedure as well."[11]

The second area deals with the nature of natural laws. These laws which science faithfully accepts are not as steadfast and reliable as many scientists like to claim. For almost three hundred years after Isaac Newton (1642–1727), the physical world was thought to operate much like a machine. It was seen as orderly, predictable, and adhering to absolute natural laws. But today, this paradigm of nature is rapidly changing. A new Ensteinian physics has emerged that is changing the old mechanical view of nature by revealing startling new information about the physical universe. The quantum theory has revealed, at least in the subatomic world, an *unpredictable* universe that is not responsive to alleged immutable natural laws. What science now holds is that natural laws describe the way nature generally behaves; they do not prescribe how nature must behave.

The third area of evidence challenges a common assumption in evolutionary science—namely, that the universe operates within a *closed system*. What this means is that no outside force (i.e., a supernatural force) exists which can add or subtract to existing natural laws or to the available energy that runs the universe. This assumption effectively rules out miracles, but it is also on trial, and its prosecutor is science itself.

The current big bang theory, widely accepted by science, claims that at some point in time the universe came into existence as a result of some tremendous explosion of an unknown cause. This could only happen if a force outside the universe, operating independent of known natural laws, fulfilled the role of this unknown cause. Likewise, the second law of thermodynamics, which reveals that the universe is running down, also demands the existence of a force that operates outside known natural laws. If the universe is running down, it must have had a beginning. And if the universe had a beginning, natural laws cannot account for it. Thus something outside natural law and therefore outside the known universe must have created it. This makes a closed system impossible.

Finally, C. S. Lewis makes an interesting observation on the relationship between natural laws and miracles that is worth mentioning. He points out that nature must normally behave according to regular patterns for us to know a miracle when it occurs. In other words, God had to create an orderly universe, or we would not recognize when He intervened miraculously in human history. Says Lewis:

Nothing can seem extraordinary until you have discovered what is ordinary. Belief in miracles, far from depending on an ignorance of the laws of nature, is only possible in so far as those laws are known. We have already seen that if you begin by ruling out the supernatural you will perceive no miracles. We must now add that you will equally perceive no miracles until you believe that nature works according to regular laws. If you have not yet noticed that the sun always rises in the East you will see nothing miraculous about its rising one morning in the West.[12]

Before we move on, let's consider the concept of natural law within a biblical framework. In light of the evidence we've reviewed, it's fair to say that any definition of natural law in harmony with biblical teachings would be the most accurate to reality. It would reflect the meaning given it by the very Being who created natural laws. Natural laws, then, can only be understood if they are seen as originating from the divine Mind. The Bible teaches that the triune God is the creator (Gen. 1:1; Job 33:4; Ps. 104:30) and sustainer of the universe (Col. 1:16–17; Heb. 1:3). As such, God is free and capable to act as He chooses within or without His created natural laws. So what scientists once thought were unchangeable natural laws are in reality simply a general description, taken from our limited human experiences and observations, of God's normal ways of controlling and sustaining the natural, ecological balances in the universe. Natural laws are *not* independent of God but represent God's will imposed upon His creation.

MIRACLES OCCUR IN OTHER RELIGIONS

The final argument against miracles draws its strength from the assumption that because many religions claim to have had miraculous incidents, and because of the fallacious character of these miracles, Christian miracles are somehow disqualified—guilty by association. Although it is beyond the scope of this book to examine the miracles of other religions individually, we can compare the evidences supporting Christian miracles with the lack of similar evidence in non-Christian religions. This will help to determine if the miraculous claims in other religions are unauthentic and establish that Christian miracles are unique.

Let me quickly add that I am not saying God has never worked miracles in the lives of non-Christians. On the contrary, there appears to be valid historical evidence that miracles have occurred involving people other than Christians.[13] The reason God chose to perform these miracles lies hidden in the mysteries of His sovereign will, but undoubtedly they play a part in His grand design to bring glory to Himself in the eyes of humanity. But one thing is certain: such miracles—and they are few and far between—are never used to validate the claims of any false prophet. Nor has it ever been demonstrated that God has used a miracle to confirm religious truth contradictory to Christianity.

There are three major areas of comparison between biblical miracles and the purported miracles in non-Christian religions.

The first evidence that needs to be examined in order to authenticate a religious miracle is the reliability of the document in which the alleged miracle is recorded. In Chapter 3, we saw that the Bible, alone among the world's many religious books, has been proven by the canons of historical and legal investigation to be divine revelation. By comparison, all other religious writings in the world, without exception, are unable to verify their truth-claims. Other religious documents are the words of men, not of God. They all fall under one of three categories: (1) collective philosophical conjectures, (2) the subjective inner thoughts and feelings of self-appointed gurus, or (3) undocumented and often incredulous experiences of so-called prophets. This being the case, the miraculous claims of non-Christian religions should be viewed with extreme skepticism.

The second evidence is a comparison of the kinds of miracles found in the Bible with those that supposedly occurred in non-Christian religions. For example, the miraculous stones (the "Urim" and "Thummin") used by Joseph Smith to decipher the "reformed Egyptian hieroglyphics" in which the Book of Mormon was supposed to have been originally written are clearly occultic. Yet no Christian miracles involve occultic elements.

Pagan miracle claims are even more outlandish and bizarre. They do not reveal a God in harmony with His creation. Rather they expose a capricious, unstable god (or gods) who defies his own nature and our ability to comprehend him. As C. S. Lewis points out, "The immoral, and sometimes almost idiotic interferences [miracles] attributed to gods in Pagan stories, even if they had a trace of historical evidence, could be accepted only on the condition of our accepting a wholly meaningless universe."[14]

On the other hand, if biblical miracles are real, they are precisely what one would expect if the God of the universe intervened in humanity in an historical, space-time context or altered the normal functions of nature for a specific purpose. Christian miracles are in harmony with the mind and actions of the God described in the Bible, and they always serve a specific purpose. Biblical miracles do not require a meaningless universe, nor do they demand a redefinition of reality. As the apostle Peter said, "We did not follow cunningly devised fables when we made known to you the power and coming of our Lord Jesus Christ, but were eyewitnesses of His majesty" (2 Pet. 1:16, NKJV).

The third evidence comes from a comparison of specific biblical miracles with their counterparts in non-Christian religions. You may be surprised to learn that some biblical miracles have parallels in pagan religions. But a close comparison shows a marked refinement and precision in the biblical accounts that are lacking in other traditions. For example, the worldwide flood recorded in Genesis 6–9 is found in many religious traditions worldwide. A catastrophe of such significance and scope is bound to turn up in other ancient religions. The fact that other religions embrace a flood tradition is profound support for the historicity of the event. Indeed, a lack of nonbiblical confirmation of such a spectacular phenomena would cast suspicion on its authenticity.

Evidence for Miracles

Argument Against Miracles	Assumption	Answer
Do not "fit" modern world	No such thing as miracles	Miracles can be investigated for truthfulness
Philosophical	God does not exist	Only works if no God; however overwhelming evidence God exists
Scientific	Miracles violate "facts" of science	Science can only confirm testable data; miracles are matter of history
False miracles found in other religions	Disqualifies Christian miracles—guilt by association	Biblical miracles are not fanciful, are in harmony with the nature of God, and sustained by historical evidence

On the other hand, we should not be surprised if non-Christian accounts of the flood contain many inaccuracies and are embellished with myths. Only the Judeo-Christian religion has God's special revelation, and thus only the Bible preserves an accurate historic account of the Noahic flood. All other accounts pervert this epic event. A comparison of the Genesis account of the flood and its closest parallel, the Babylonian Gilgamish Epic, shows a remarkable similarity—but also a remarkable dissimilarity—with regard to the latter's fanciful version and mythical elements.

This same dissimilarity is found in other biblical miracles where parallel accounts occur among pagan or cultic renditions.[15]

ARE MIRACLES PROVABLE?

We have finally arrived at the only valid criteria for determining the factuality of any miracle—historical evidence. We have ruled out the claim that miracles are philosophically impossible. If God exists, and the overwhelming preponderance of evidence insists that He does, then miracles are not only possible but highly probable. We have also ruled out the claims that miracles are scientifically impossible. Natural laws are not absolutes; they are descriptions of nature's general regularity. God is the Creator and Sustainer of the universe and can intervene in His own creation in any fashion He chooses and at any time He chooses (Ps. 115:3).

MIRACLES ARE A MATTER OF HISTORY

If miracles cannot be ruled out by a simple appeal to philosophy or science, then they can be ruled out only by a lack of historical evidence. There is no other criteria by which miracles can be falsified. On the other hand, this also means that history just might confirm miracles instead of falsifying them. So the outcome of historical investigation is the deciding factor with regard to the historicity of Bible miracles; and it only requires concrete historical evidence to prove that biblical miracles have occurred.

The Bible is a religious book, but it is also an historical book. In Christianity, you cannot separate historical facts from spiritual truths without destroying the gospel message; the Bible's spiritual subject matter is intrinsically and mutually bound to history. This is nowhere more evident than with the historic resurrection of Jesus Christ. A mythical resurrection is no resurrection at all.

History acknowledges that miracles are unique events. They are not the norm but rather defy the norm. However, this does not mean that miracles are antihistorical or nonhistorical. Moreover, because miracles are unique events does not mean that they must be approached differently than any other historical event. The same canons of investigation used to determine the authenticity of any historical happening can be used to determine the authenticity of miracles.

BIBLE MIRACLES ARE TRUE

How does an historian determine the authenticity of an alleged historical incident? There are three criteria by which a responsible historian works. I will apply these rules to the investigation of a miraculous event.

For one thing, an historian is unbiased in his approach. In the case of an alleged miracle, he does not allow his own presuppositions for or against miracles to influence his investigation. He holds to the conviction that in order to determine whether or not an event occurred depends on the evidence.

Furthermore, when examining an alleged miracle, the historian does not attempt to interpret it according to existing known phenomena. In other words, he does not try to make it fit with the natural laws we generally take for granted. He judges it according to its own merits.

And lastly, an historian seeks the best evidence available to support or disavow the alleged miracle. What kind of evidence is best? There is only one kind reliable enough to determine beyond reasonable doubt the historicity of any event: primary-source evidence (firsthand testimony). This entails recorded documentation by qualified and honest eyewitnesses to the event. If an observer does not disqualify himself by contradictions, inaccuracies, or obvious biases, his testimony is considered valid evidence. The most convincing and irrefutable historical incidents, miraculous or otherwise, rely on this kind of documentation.

If we apply these rules of historical investigation to the miracles surrounding Jesus, we can conclude beyond doubt that they occurred exactly as described in the Bible. The New Testament Gospels fulfill the requirements of primary-source evidence. They were written by eyewitnesses to the events they recorded (Matthew and John) or by people who personally knew and interviewed the eyewitnesses (Mark and Luke). No document from antiquity equals the Bible when it comes to the attestation of sound historical investigation.

In light of the historical evidence confirming the authenticity of Bible miracles, we can agree with the Psalmist when he wrote that, "The fool has said in his heart, 'There is no God'" (Ps. 53:1). The same applies to those who deny the possibility or historicity of miracles.

13

Why Is There Evil and Suffering in the World?

The problem of evil has been called the "Achilles heel" of Christianity. Simply put, it claims that the God of Christianity is inconsistent and incompatible with the world around us. Christians claim that God is an all-powerful, loving Being, yet evil and suffering are rampant in the world. How do these facts mesh? C. S. Lewis puts it this way: "If God were good, He would wish to make His creatures perfectly happy, and if God were almighty, He would be able to do what He wished. But the creatures are not happy. Therefore God lacks either goodness, or power or both."[1] In other words, either God wants to prevent evil but does not have the power to do it, or He has the power to do it but does not want to. In either case, He is not the kind of God described in the Bible.

This problem poses a powerful and passionate argument against Christianity, but it is also a very unambiguous and well-defined argument. The problem of evil can be reduced to the assumption that the Christian God is incompatible with the way the world is. So to demonstrate the fallacy of this claim, Christians only need to prove that God *is* compatible with the way the world is. In this chapter, I will show that Christianity not only explains the presence of evil and human suffering, but it explains it better than any other religion or philosophy. More than this, Christianity offers the only possible solution to the problem of evil. If this is true, then the God of Christianity not only exists, but He exists precisely as revealed in the Bible, and He is compatible with the world as it is.

Christians recognize that God does not always do what we would like Him to do or, in fact, what we think He ought to do (see Ps. 115:3). Christians also know that it is presumptuous and dangerous to claim that God ought to act in ways which seem good to us, and, if He does not, it will weaken our love and respect for Him. God has the ability to see the whole picture; we mostly see just our immediate needs. God is sovereign and infinite; we are limited and finite (Isa. 55:8–9). Humans will never fully understand why God chooses to act as He does in many situations or why He allows events to happen that seem inconsistent with His character. Nevertheless, although much of what God does is a mystery, we do have His assurance that what He does is ultimately in the best interest of those who believe in Him (Rom. 8:28). If we know God, we will learn to trust Him, even if we do not fully understand what He is doing. If we know God, we know that what He is doing is rational and is not contrary to His attributes of love and holiness.

That God is sovereign and never violates His attributes of love and holiness are truths readily grasped and accepted by Christians. However, for many non-Christians, the widespread facts of human suffering, disease, hunger, and oppression, fly in the face of the Christian claim that God is in control and loves us. To unbelievers, this seems to be a meaningless and unsubstantiated rationalization because they think Christians do not have an answer to the problem of evil.

This opinion should not surprise us. Without the Holy Spirit, non-Christians are unable to fully apprehend Christian truths (1 Cor. 2:12–14), let alone find comfort in them. Nevertheless, and in spite of this, Christians can offer a viable solution to the problem of evil. We'll do this by answering several puzzling questions.

HOW DID EVIL ENTER THE WORLD?

In order to respond to the problem of evil from a Christian perspective, we need to review a subject touched on in Chapter 9: the nature and origin of sin.

When God created the earth and life, He said that it was "very good" (Gen. 1:31). The world was a place free from sin, evil, and human (and animal) suffering. Yet, the world today contains all three. Why? Because of the fall of Adam.

When God created Adam, He gave him a free will to choose to obey or disobey Him by not eating from a certain tree. God also warned him of the consequences of disobedience (Gen. 2:16–17). Nevertheless, Adam disobeyed and became separated from God. Through Adam's rebellion, sin entered the world.

Now Adam was the corporate head of the human race (the Hebrew name *Adam* is a general term for *mankind;* Rom. 5:12–19). Just as the decisions made by the ruler of a nation affect all the people subject to him, so Adam's decision to rebel against God affected all mankind. Furthermore, when Adam sinned, he not only represented us, he acted in the same manner as any other man or woman would have in his place. Like Adam, we too rebel against God and are equally guilty and deserving of punishment.

The fall resulted in the birth of a sin nature in Adam. Because all people shared in Adam's guilt, this sin nature was passed on to all future generations. As a result, sin is pervasive in every man and woman (Rom. 5:12; 1 Cor. 15:22), and it is out of this sin nature that we do sinful acts (Mark 7:20–23). Thus, the presence of evil in the world today can be laid upon man, not God.

Now, the idea that all of mankind is guilty because of Adam's sin is offensive to many people. "Why should I be punished for something Adam did?" is a common complaint. However, whether or not we should be held guilty for Adam's sin should not cloud the fact that people today, like Adam, are sinners. We sin enough to be guilty on our own merits. The fact is, sin is real, and mankind corporately sins. The biblical account of the fall is simply the explanation of how man's tendency to sin came about. No other religion or philosophy offers a better explanation (more on this shortly). So whether one agrees with the biblical account that sin entered humanity through Adam's fall or not, the fact remains that sin is real and evil reigns.

The biblical doctrine of the fall of man gives us the answer to why evil exists in the world. God did not desire or will sin to exist; it exists because man rejected God and incurred His punishment. Let me summarize this crucial biblical doctrine by making a few important points.

- It should be clear from this that there are no innocent people. No one is sinless and free from guilt before a holy God (Rom. 3:23). Because of the fall, sin has been charged to all humankind (Rom. 5:12–21).
- Adam had a free choice to obey or disobey God. He knew the consequences of disobedience. Although evil already existed in the person of Satan (who had himself previously rebelled against God), it was Adam's free choice that allowed sin to affect mankind. When there is freedom to choose between good and evil, there is always the possibility that evil will be chosen. Adam chose sin. With this choice came punishment and human suffering.
- The evil we see in nature (e.g., earthquakes and hurricanes that sometimes kill thousands of people) is also the result of human sin. Nature, in and of itself, is not evil. But the land was cursed because of man's sin, and violent physical manifestations in nature are a result of the fall (Gen. 3:17–19).
- Evil is not discretionary—it does not choose its victims. Evil is like a bomb thrown into a crowded room to assassinate a political leader. A lot of "innocent" victims are inadvertently hurt. Evil is an irrational thing resulting from the fall.

WHY DOES GOD ALLOW EVIL TO REMAIN?

It is true that God *permitted* evil to enter the world and that He now allows the consequences of that evil to continue. God is sovereign and all-powerful and *could* destroy all evil immediately if He chose. The key to understanding why God allows the consequences of evil to continue is bound up with human freedom.

God created Adam (and all people) to worship, obey, and have fellowship with Him—to love Him. Genuine love is inseparable from free will. God could have created Adam, and all other people, to think and act like robots. By divine mandate, God could have caused Adam not only to obey Him but to love Him. Would this have been genuine love? Of course not. Love can't be programmed; it must be freely

The Origin and Consequences of Evil

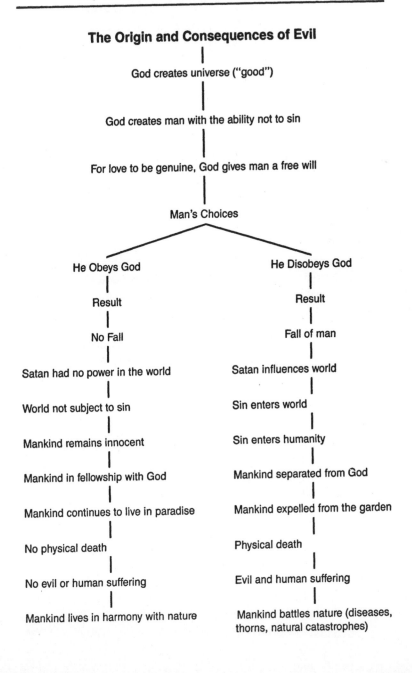

God creates universe ("good")

God creates man with the ability not to sin

For love to be genuine, God gives man a free will

Man's Choices

He Obeys God

Result

No Fall

Satan had no power in the world

World not subject to sin

Mankind remains innocent

Mankind in fellowship with God

Mankind continues to live in paradise

No physical death

No evil or human suffering

Mankind lives in harmony with nature

He Disobeys God

Result

Fall of man

Satan influences world

Sin enters world

Sin enters humanity

Mankind separated from God

Mankind expelled from the garden

Physical death

Evil and human suffering

Mankind battles nature (diseases, thorns, natural catastrophes) expressed. God wanted Adam to show his love by freely choosing obedience. That's why God gave Adam a free will. A free choice, however, leaves the possibility of a wrong choice. Adam made the wrong choice, thereby allowing sin to enter the world. As C. S. Lewis explains: "The sin, both of men and of angels, was rendered possible by the fact that God gave them free will: this surrendering of a portion of His omnipotence . . . because He saw that from a world of free creatures, even though they fell, He could work out . . . a deeper happiness and a fuller splendour than any world of automata would admit."[2]

For free will to be meaningful, there must be consequences when a wrong choice is made. God is holy and righteous, and He cannot tolerate sin in any form. When Adam chose disobedience, God had to respond with punishment. If God does not punish sin, sin would lose its moral character. Parents readily use this principle in raising children. If there are no consequences for a child's bad behavior, there is no reason for that child to stop the behavior. Mankind today is still in disobedience to God, and the consequences of Adam's fall still persist.

What I am saying here is this. Free will and the moral consequences of wrong choices *are* compatible with the Christian world view. As Geisler points out in his superb book, *The Roots of Evil:*

> It is important to remember that it may be necessary in a free world to allow evil to actually occur. It may be necessary for God to allow innocent suffering in order to give men full moral freedom. If the choice had been ours, we might have made the same decision. And it may be possible that all cases of individual and presently unjustified suffering are justifiable in view of the whole plan in the long run.[3]

Geisler goes on to say that God may have allowed evil in the world simply because "there is no better way for an all-loving, all-powerful God to defeat evil and produce a greater good than for Him to permit this present evil world."[4] He draws the analogy of a great football player enduring painful practice so he can excel in the sport.

In other words, "God freely chose to create a world He knew

would turn against Him and would bring upon itself and others untold human misery and woe . . ." because "no other alternative creation plan that God could have carried out would have been morally better than permitting this Morally Fallen World."[5]

This may sound confusing, so look at it this way. If the essential nature of God is love, and if in order for love to be genuine it must be freely given, then it is consistent with the Christian world view that the presence of evil is the sad but necessary consequence for achieving the best of all possible worlds—a world where mankind freely chooses to love and receive God and therefore secure a future eternal life in heaven.

Why God Allows Human Suffering

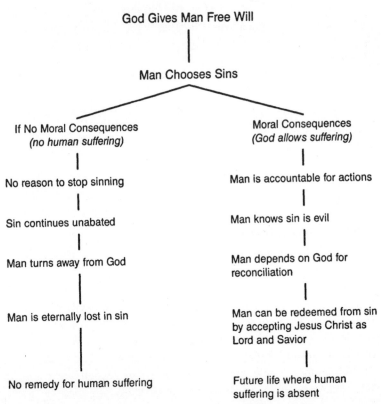

God Gives Man Free Will

Man Chooses Sins

If No Moral Consequences
(no human suffering)

No reason to stop sinning

Sin continues unabated

Man turns away from God

Man is eternally lost in sin

No remedy for human suffering

Moral Consequences
(God allows suffering)

Man is accountable for actions

Man knows sin is evil

Man depends on God for reconciliation

Man can be redeemed from sin by accepting Jesus Christ as Lord and Savior

Future life where human suffering is absent

DOES THE CHRISTIAN VIEW OF SIN BEST EXPLAIN THE PRESENCE OF EVIL?

Although some religious philosophers claim that sin is an illusion, it is nevertheless extremely difficult to rationally deny the reality of sin. People do not behave as they intuitively know they should. People throughout the world commit what every culture considers to be sinful acts (murder, lying, stealing, physical abuse, and so on). The Bible states that there is not a single human being, past or present, who is free from sin except for Jesus Christ (see Rom. 3:23; 1 Pet. 2:22). In fact, according to 1 John 1:8, if one thinks he is free from sin, he is deceiving himself. It is impossible to ignore the reality of corporate human evil. This fact is self-evident.

But the question remains: Does the Christian view of sin best explain the presence of evil? Yes. Christianity provides the answer most consistent with the world around us. This will become even more obvious after we peruse five other common explanations for evil and spot their inadequacies.

Evil Is an Illusion

To say that evil and human suffering are illusions (as many Eastern religions claim) does not solve the problem of evil because it ignores the problem rather than deals with it. A broken arm still hurts whether one denies it or not. And people still die from the diseases they don't believe exist.

Evil Is Independent of God

Some people believe that evil is a result of forces independent of God; it comes from a source equal to and not controlled by God. This view is called dualism, but it too fails to solve the problem of evil. As we've seen, God is all-powerful and the creator and sustainer of all. Nothing is outside of His control. So, in reality, dualism is an inadequate solution because it takes something out of His sovereign domain, which can't be done. Also, God would be incapable of ever solving the problem of evil and human suffering.

Evil Flows from Ignorance

To say that evil results from our ignorance of the right choices, as many of the New Age religions claim, is unsubstantiated by the facts. Throughout history, man has had many opportunities to make right choices based on adequate information and yet has willfully made wrong choices. For example, people know smoking causes cancer, fatty foods cause heart disease, pollution destroys our environment, and stockpiling nuclear weapons can result in the destruction of the earth. But this knowledge hasn't stopped us from engaging in these destructive behaviors.

Evil Is a Product of Evolution

Many secular humanists have maintained that sin is a product of evolution. But this is not consistent with the theory of evolution. If evolution is true, evil should have never evolved because it has no survival value. It should have been weeded out as early as the first animal organism or, at the least, no later than the appearance of social animals. Evil can only cause disharmony and pain among members of social orders, so it should have been eliminated long ago, assuming it ever grew out of the evolutionary process.

Evil Is a Relative Idea

Many atheists argue that evil is relative: cultures or individuals decide what's right and wrong; no universal standard exists. The problem is, not even atheists consistently live as if it's true. Let me explain.

Like Christians, atheists make moral decisions based on absolute statements of right and wrong. For example, atheists say murder, stealing, and rape are wrong. However, it is philosophically inconsistent for atheists to claim that ethics are relative and then make moral judgments that apply to other people and other cultures. Without a moral absolute as a universal standard for judging right and wrong, there is no basis for ethics. Indeed, without an absolute standard of right and wrong independent of man, it is impossible to even define what evil is in any universal sense. Hitler may have been right after all. On a relativistic ethic, there's no good reason to judge otherwise.

One by one, alternate explanations for evil can be eliminated. The only rational and adequate explanation left is the biblical one. Rather than searching for flaws in the Christian answer to the problem of evil, skeptics need to ask whether any other philosophical systems are valid. And as I've briefly shown, neither Eastern religions, the New Age movement, the cults, secular humanism, atheism, or evolutionism can account for the presence of evil in a way in harmony with the reality of human nature and the world as we observe it. Only Christianity provides a unified and complete (if not fully understood) answer to the problem of evil. People do sin, regardless of how hard they try not to. People sin in spite of knowing what they can do to avoid it. The consequences of evil are real, not illusions. Natural disasters and human suffering exist. Sin is not relative nor a product of evolution. Only God (as the Moral Absolute) can define *evil* and give meaning to the term. Without the Christian God and human freedom, evil is unexplainable.

WHAT HAS GOD DONE TO SOLVE THE PROBLEM OF EVIL?

GOD CONTROLS THE EFFECTS OF EVIL

Today, people continue to rebel against God. We curse Him, ignore Him, and flaunt our disobedience. Motivated by pride, greed, and selfishness, people destroy one another and willfully abuse and pollute God's earth. Truly, mankind is as deserving of punishment today as Adam was in his day. In fact, it's amazing God has not lost His patience and destroyed all of us. Rather than condemning God for allowing evil, we should be thankful that He withholds the punishment we deserve.

God has taken steps to prevent evil from running amok. He has implemented measures that prevent fallen man from literally destroying himself. God institutionalized governments to control lawlessness and promote social order, marriage to control sexual diseases, moral standards to guide the interrelationships of people, and the church to restrain evil by acting as a light of spiritual truth.

Most importantly, God prevents Satan from having full sway over the earth.

GOD HAS ALREADY SOLVED THE PROBLEM OF EVIL

The Bible teaches that God has already solved the problem of evil. As we saw, sin entered the world through Adam, and all men are condemned because all men are guilty of Adam's sin. But the Bible also teaches that Jesus' sacrificial death on the cross paid the penalty for that sin. All who accept Jesus as Lord and Savior are set free from the penalty of sin and will receive eternal life (Rom. 5:12–18). Furthermore, because of the work of Jesus, we do not have to be in bondage to sin. Through the power of God, we can break away from sin and live a more abundant life (6:4–11). And finally, the Bible teaches that at the end of this present world system, God will create a new earth where the consequences of sin will be put away forever. The new creation will be a place where "there shall be no more death, nor sorrow, nor crying. There shall be no more pain" (Rev. 21:4).

Here lies the ultimate answer to the problem of evil. No matter what one's world view is, whether a humanist, a pantheist, a cultist, a follower of the New Age, or a Christian, one fact is certain. No one gets through this life unscathed. No one escapes this world without experiencing pain, sorrow, sickness, and tears. God does not promise that if one becomes a Christian, he will necessarily have an easier life with less hardship and suffering. In fact, many Christians come to realize that God often uses suffering to draw us closer to Him in submission and dependence. But God does promise us two things.

First, eternal life. This is the great hope of Christianity. Our earthly life is temporary. We have a future life that will be free of pain and sorrow and one where no evil will exist. Christians are pilgrims on this earth. With this promise and assurance from God, we face the daily sorrows and hardships of life. We even experience real joy in spite of our suffering. No other religion in the world can promise this hope and then back it up by the power of God's Spirit.

Second, God dwells with us. God does not promise He'll remove our hardships or make our life more prosperous, but He does promise to lighten our load (Matt. 11:28–30). And Jesus promises to dwell with us, even in this earthly life (28:20). Christians have the joy of daily communion with Christ and the prospect of continual spiritual renewal and growth. We have a strength outside ourselves that helps us endure our suffering. No other religion in the world offers this.

The good news of Christianity is that Jesus died for our sins. Because of this, Christians enjoy a restored fellowship with God. Rather than blame God for the evil and pain we experience, we rejoice in what He has done to remedy the problem of evil through His Son, Jesus Christ.

14

Why Reject
Reincarnation?

In Chapter 1, I explained that one
of the purposes of apologetics is to defend Christianity against new
heresies and false religions. Christianity today is facing more philosophical and religious opposition than at any time since the first centuries of the church. A host of Christian cults have emerged over the
last 150 years that have become dominant religions in Western culture. The last few decades have also witnessed an unparalleled movement of Eastern religions into the United States. Many popular
groups, such as the New Age movement, Christian Science, Bahai,
and the Unity School of Christianity, maintain a pervasive Eastern
flavor.

One common denominator of many of these various religious
movements—and an area in which they have had tremendous influence in the West—is their belief in reincarnation as the guiding principle of salvation. Here we want to examine reincarnation, as well as
other fundamental doctrines of the New Age movement, and check
them out against Christianity.

REINCARNATION

Reincarnation is an ancient religious belief found in many pagan
religions. It teaches that through a series of deaths and rebirths, one
can eventually purge oneself of all sins and ultimately reach oneness,

or absorption, with the spiritual Absolute. There the human soul finds eternal peace.

Prior to the twentieth century, belief in reincarnation in the United States was confined to a few modest groups, such as the Unity School of Christianity and the Theosophical Society, that were practicing a form of quasi-Eastern religion. Today, however, many millions of people in Western countries (and hundreds of millions throughout the world) believe in reincarnation. Its teachings are being widely popularized by headline grabbers such as Jeanne Dixon and Shirley MacLaine. According to the late Dr. Walter Martin, 58 percent of Americans "either definitely believe in [reincarnation] or believe it to be a distinct possibility."[1]

Westerners usually associate reincarnation with Hinduism. However, the concept of reincarnation, as it is understood in the West, is not the same as that taught by Hindus. When Westerners think of reincarnation, they generally envision death and then rebirth into another human form. Hence the term *past lives.*

The Eastern concept of reincarnation is more properly called *transmigration.* Like reincarnation, the soul goes through cycles of birth, life, death, and then rebirth, but the rebirth of the soul is not necessarily in human form. Depending on the sins committed in an earlier life, a person may come back as something else, say as a rodent or an insect. This, of course, is appalling to most Westerners, so transmigration has been redefined as reincarnation in order to make it more appealing.

Transmigration of the soul has its roots in *karma:* the belief in retribution in later lives for sins committed in earlier lives. Because it is possible for a soul to wander through every form of life, all living things, even the lowest form, are respected and preserved. In famine-ridden India, the Hindus' reverence for all life, due to their belief in karma and the transmigration of souls, has resulted in a reluctance to kill cattle, rats, and even insects that consume thousands of tons of human food every year and carry numerous kinds of harmful diseases. People starve to death in the very streets where cows wander freely.

The danger of reincarnation to the church is twofold. First, reincarnationists claim that the Bible teaches reincarnation, thereby seducing many Christians into accepting unorthodox teachings and unbiblical interpretations of Scripture. Second, it opposes many of the cardinal doctrines of the Christian church, in particular the doctrines of the atonement, judgment, and resurrection.[2]

DOES THE BIBLE TEACH REINCARNATION?

Many reincarnationists claim that the Bible teaches reincarnation. They allege that the original authors of the New Testament actually sanctioned reincarnation but that later editors deleted this information. This is confirmed, they claim, because there are still "vestigial" passages in Scripture that openly teach reincarnation.[3] This position has two problems, at least.

First, textual critics have confirmed beyond any doubt that not only is the New Testament we have today 99.5 percent accurate to the original manuscripts, but that there is no evidence whatsoever that later copyists deleted or added to the Bible. There is simply no evidence to support the reincarnationist's view that portions of Scripture once favorable to their theology have been deleted.

Second, the "proof-texts" reincarnationists present as latent reincarnation passages are victims of poor exegesis; they do not stand up to even mildly critical scrutiny. We can see this by examining just three texts frequently cited by reincarnationists as their best evidence. If these three passages have been mistreated, we can safely assume that other passages have suffered the same fate.[4]

Matthew 11:7–14

In verse 14, Jesus said, "And if you care to accept it, he himself [John the Baptist] is Elijah, who was to come." Reincarnationists claim that John the Baptist is the reincarnation of Elijah. But several facts refute this.

We need to ask the logical question, Did John himself think he was the reincarnation of Elijah? The answer is found in John 1:21: "And they asked him [John the Baptist], 'What then? Are you Elijah?' And he said, 'I am not.'" In short, the very person whom the reincarnationists claim is reincarnated denies the fact himself. But the evidence does not stop here.

Elijah never actually died, which is critical to the reincarnation process. He was taken bodily ("translated"—2 Kings 2:1–11) into heaven. Reincarnation requires that one die before his soul reappears in another body.

Moreover, since Elijah appeared with Moses at Jesus' transfiguration (Matt. 17:1–3), he could not have been the reincarnation of John the Baptist. He was still Elijah.

So what did Jesus mean when He said that John the Baptist is Elijah? Jesus was referring to John's function as a prophet in the "spirit and power of Elijah" (Luke 1:17). This is in fulfillment of the Old Testament prediction of the coming of Elijah before the "great and terrible day of the Lord" (Mal. 4:5; see Matt. 17:10–12). Jesus was not saying that John the Baptist would be Elijah himself.

John 3:3

"Jesus answered and said to him, 'Truly, truly, I say to you, unless one is born again, he cannot see the kingdom of God.'" Reincarnationists claim that this verse refers to rebirth into another body. However, a reading of the whole passage in context gives the proper interpretation.

Nicodemus is puzzled because he thinks Jesus is referring to a physical rebirth (3:4). But Jesus resolves his confusion in the following two verses: "Truly, truly, I say to you, unless one is born of water and the Spirit, he cannot enter into the kingdom of God. That which is born of flesh is flesh, and that which is born of Spirit is spirit." In other words, flesh gives birth to flesh and spirit gives birth to spirit. Jesus makes it plain to Nicodemus that He is talking about a *spiritual* rebirth. Reincarnation, on the other hand, demands a *physical* rebirth.

Furthermore, in 1 Peter 1:23, Peter refers to the "born again" state as "imperishable." Born again into a physical body is not an imperishable rebirth; only a spiritual rebirth can be imperishable. So the biblical picture of being born again is incompatible with reincarnation.

John 9:1–2

"And as He passed by, He saw a man blind from birth. And His disciples asked Him, saying, 'Rabbi, who sinned, this man or his par-

ents, that he should be born blind?'" The connotation here to a reincarnationist is that the man was born blind because of sins in his
previous life (karma). However, if the entire passage is read, the reason for the man's blindness is explained. In verse three Jesus replies,
"It was neither that this man sinned, nor his parents [thus reincarnation is not even a consideration]; but it was in order that the works of
God might be displayed in him." In other words, the healing of the
man blind from birth glorified God and demonstrated His healing
power.

It is a common ploy of cultists to lift a passage out of context and
read their theology into it in order to use it as a support. With such an
improper technique of interpretation, one can make almost any
verse say almost anything. Proper biblical interpretation involves examining a passage within the context of adjacent passages, within
the context of related passages, and within the context of the theological fabric of Scripture as a whole. Almost always the proper interpretation of such proof-text verses are readily seen when read in context
with the entire passage. But reincarnationists bent on making the
Bible say what it doesn't ignore this procedure.

IS REINCARNATION COMPATIBLE WITH CHRISTIANITY?

The danger reincarnation poses to Christianity goes beyond a
handful of misinterpreted verses. It actually challenges several of the
cardinal doctrines of the Christian faith. Let's focus on three of them
so we can clearly see that Christianity and reincarnation are not bedfellows.

THE ATONEMENT

Theologically, *atonement* is the technical term for the work of
Christ in saving humanity. Literally, the word means "to cover," and it
conveys the idea that rebellious and sinful man is reconciled to God
by the sacrificial death of Christ on the cross (Col. 1:20). By dying in
the place of guilty man, Jesus paid for the sins of the world (1 John
2:2) so that believers stand forgiven and "righteous" before God
(2 Cor. 5:21). The key to the atonement is that the work of Christ

fulfills all of God's requirements for our salvation (Rom. 5:8–10). There is nothing we can do to earn salvation. It is a free gift from God (Eph. 2:8–9). All we have to do to receive this gift is to accept by faith Jesus as Lord and Savior (Rom. 10:9; 1 John 4:15).

Reincarnation, by contrast, claims that only through the continual cycle of death and rebirth is the soul ultimately purged of sin and deemed worthy of eternal peace through absorption with the eternal All. This doctrine eliminates the need for a personal savior and for the sacrificial work of Christ. It turns salvation into a form of "works righteousness" in which our deeds rather than the death of Christ atone for our sins (Titus 3:5).

It is impossible to harmonize reincarnation with the biblical doctrine of salvation.

THE JUDGMENT

The Bible teaches that, at the very moment of death, the soul immediately leaves the body (see Gen. 35:18). At that moment, believers are ushered into the presence of God (2 Cor. 5:8; Phil. 1:21–23) and unbelievers into hades (Luke 16:19–31). Hades is the abode of the unsaved between physical death and judgment. At the time of judgment, there will be a bodily resurrection of both the saved and the unsaved (John 5:29). The saved will spend eternity with the Lord in heaven (John 14:1–3). The unsaved will be cast into hell and be punished according to the degree of their sins and knowledge of God (Rev. 20:11–15; Luke 12:47–48). Matthew 25:31–46 describes hell as eternal and conscious separation from God (see 8:12; Rev. 20:15).

The theory of reincarnation, on the other hand, denies eternal separation from God and teaches that, through the endless cycles of death and rebirth, man's soul will eventually be purged of evil and united with the all-embracing One. There is no hell in reincarnation.

Reincarnation denigrates the holiness of God by removing absolute and final judgment. It tells people that they have countless chances to right their wrongs through countless new lives, which is false. Reincarnation is also a reproach to God's righteous justice because it punishes people in this life for sins they committed in past lives without allowing them to remember their past so they can avoid repeating their sins in the future. Finally, reincarnation removes any accountability on the part of man for choosing to reject Jesus Christ. If reincarnation were true, Jesus died for nothing.

THE RESURRECTION

The biblical doctrine of the resurrection teaches that man will die once (Heb. 9:27) and that at the resurrection his mortal body will be transformed into an immortal one (1 Cor. 15:42; see Rom. 6:9). This means that our resurrected body is a physical one, not a spiritual one. We know this because Jesus was resurrected in a physical body (Luke 24:39; John 20:27), and we are told that we will have a resurrected body similar to His (1 John 3:2; 1 Cor. 15:35–49).

Our resurrected body should not be confused with the state of our soul between physical death and the resurrection, as alluded to in 2 Corinthians 5:8. This "spiritual" (intermediate) body will last only until our physical resurrection. Our eternal body will be physical.

Reincarnation is entirely different than the Christian view of resurrection. Reincarnation entails the rebirth of the soul in a succession of many bodies. Whereas the resurrection is a one-time, final event, reincarnation is a continual process of birth, life, and death. While the Bible plainly speaks of one chance to receive salvation prior to the resurrection (Heb. 9:27), reincarnation speaks of countless chances to purge the mortal body of sin.

Reincarnation Is Not Christianity

Reincarnation	*Christianity*
Roots in Eastern religion	Roots in Judaism
Can have many physical lives	Only one physical life
At death, body reborn into another body	At death, only soul remains until resurrection
No resurrection	Resurrection
Can save self	Saved by grace
All eventually saved	Not all saved
Have many chances	Only one chance
No separation from God	Can be separated from God
No hell	Hell exists

IF REINCARNATION IS NOT FACTUAL, WHAT ACCOUNTS FOR IT?

It has been conclusively demonstrated throughout this book that the Bible is God's only written revelation to mankind. God has not revealed spiritual truth through any other religious book.

Now we can also conclude from what we've seen about reincarnation that it does not have God's sanction. It is totally incompatible with Christianity. So how can Christians account for the many well-documented stories of people recounting past-life experiences? There can be only two other explanations.

Psychological

The most common method of extracting past-life testimonies is under hypnosis. The human brain is the most complex and sophisticated object in the entire universe (outside of God, of course). Science has shown that the human brain is similar to a computer—any information stored within it is never lost. Past experiences, people we have met, sights we have seen, the information we have read in books, even long-forgotten events in our childhood—all such data are forever stored in our memory banks. So our subconscious mind is continually at work, absorbing, processing, and filing away this information, and through hypnosis it can often be recalled.

However, in the process of recalling this information, our mind can easily play tricks on us. It can make us think we are remembering something from a past life when in fact we are simply recalling something or someone we actually had contact with either directly (personally) or indirectly (through books, movies, hearing other people's accounts, etc.). We may enter a house we "just know" we have been in before, when in reality we were in a similar house years ago and just forgot about it. Or we may see a person we "just know" we knew from somewhere else, but in reality a similar person was described to us in a book. People have even been known to recall a language under hypnosis. But in all these cases, the apparent past-life experience is simply our subconscious memory releasing muddled information our mind had previously absorbed. This is a valid psychological explanation for many so-called past-life experiences, as Walter Martin relates: "The opinions of leading scientists, psychologists, psychiatrists and hypnotists are almost all [in agreement that it] is quite possible . . . to connect subconscious memories of 'forgotten' stories and facts with religious beliefs. Through hypnotic regression, it is possible to weave strange tales."[5]

Supernatural

Dr. Martin observes several basic characteristics that frequently emerge when people regress to "past lives" through hypnosis.

- People frequently speak in foreign languages they do not know.
- The religious content of what they relate—their theology— frequently refers to God, Jesus, and so on, but it never actually acknowledges the Christian concept of God or that Jesus is our resurrected Savior. Reincarnationists insist there are many paths to God, not just Christianity. They deny Satan, sin, and hell because God makes no requirements of us. And the Bible is not the inerrant Word of God.
- People usually don't identify themselves as the persons speaking. In other words, they seem aware that someone other than themselves is speaking.

Now what does all this mean? We know reincarnation is not a fact because it contradicts divine revelation. In fact, reincarnation is hostile to Christianity. If psychological explanations don't cover all cases, and if the events described in a past-life regression are actual facts that cannot be accounted for in a person's present life, then there has to be some other valid explanation for what appears to be a support for reincarnation.

That explanation is frightening but real: A supernatural person other than God, one who hates Jesus Christ and His church, must be feeding information to the person experiencing a so-called past-life regression. It seems like reincarnation, but it is really deception. This deceiver must be familiar with the past lives of countless people and capable of taking this information and tricking others into thinking that the experiences of a long-dead person actually apply to them in a former life. The only sinister supernatural person capable of doing this is Satan.

Let me inject another bit of evidence in support of this explanation. Another common way people "discover" they have lived before is through clairvoyance. They visit a medium who informs them that they have lived previously and then sets about to fill them in on their previous life. The Bible makes it plain that such occultic practices are right from Satan (Deut 18:11–12).

The Bible teaches that the temporary ruler of our fallen world is Satan (John 12:31; 1 John 5:19) and that his greatest desire is to thwart and distort God's plan of salvation through Christ (Matt. 4:1–11). Jesus calls Satan a murderer and states that whatever he says is a lie because "he speaks from his own nature; for he is a liar, and the father of lies" (John 8:44). Satan works primarily through deception (Gen. 3:1–7). He is able to perform what appears to be supernatural deeds (Exod. 7:11–12; Rev. 13:13). Counterfeiting a language, for example, is no problem for him. Furthermore, through his army of demons, he is able to influence the minds and actions of humans (Matt. 16:21–23). It is biblically certain that unbelievers, especially those who have submitted themselves to occultic practices, are vulnerable to satanic persuasion. Hypnosis and clairvoyance for the purpose of past-life regression is certainly an occultic practice. Consequently, many past-life experiences unexplainable by psychological phenomena are likely satanic deceptions.

The good news is, we can "resist the devil and he will flee from [us]" (James 4:7). The apostle John reminds us that "greater is He [Jesus] who is in [us] than he [Satan] who is in the world" (1 John 4:4) and that "the evil one does not touch him" who is born of God (1 John 5:18). We can identify Satan's deception and test the spirits to see if they are from God. And the test is simple: "Every spirit that confesses that Jesus Christ has come in the flesh is from God; and every spirit that does not confess Jesus is not from God; and this is the spirit of the antichrist" (1 John 4:1–3).

Reincarnationists deny that Jesus Christ is the incarnate Son of God, that He is God come in the flesh. Instead, they teach a religion of self-salvation through endless repetitions of death and rebirth. In spite of the hopelessness of this cyclic drama, reincarnationists try to paint a picture of a pleasant journey to spiritual fulfillment. But this too is part of Satan's deception. It is not at all in harmony with the true doctrine of reincarnation as taught in the Hindu archetype, transmigration. In no religion in the world have people suffered in such vast numbers or in such hopeless misery as the victims living under the dark cloud of the Hindu religion.

REINCARNATION AND THE NEW AGE MOVEMENT

For reincarnation to "work," it must fit within a religious framework that endorses an impersonal god who plays no role in man's salvation. In recent years, just such a "new" religion has invaded Western culture, and it may prove to be the most influential, seductive, and damaging religious movement ever to threaten the Christian church. It's the so-called New Age movement.

Reincarnation is only one doctrine—although perhaps the most pervasive—in this growing religious movement, so it is worth taking the time to become familiar with its companion teachings.

WHAT IS THE NEW AGE MOVEMENT?

Actually, the New Age movement is not new. It is simply the resurgence of ancient occultic practices mixed with Eastern pantheism (in particular, Hinduism) in a recipe tailored specifically to feed the spiritual hunger of Western secularized man. The New Age movement is secular humanism with a cosmic ingredient. It maintains the humanist motto that "man is the measure of all things" and the humanist goals of global peace, prosperity, and unity, but, to make humanism more spiritually palatable, it sugars it with "God."

However, *God*, as used in the New Age movement, is not the infinite-personal-creator God of the Judeo-Christian religion. Rather, their deity is a form of human potential. In man's search to find God, he discovers that all along God resided within himself. Man is God. Or to put it more accurately, man is one with the God-force that permeates all things and composes all things. Thus, secular humanism remains intact because man is still the standard. God is not a power over man but a divine potential within man that allows him to become one with God. The divine within man awaits to be released, and this will eventually happen on a worldwide scale (the goal of the New Age movement). When it does, a tremendous evolutionary transformation will occur within humanity that will usher in a new age of prosperity, peace, and world order. This will be the salvation of mankind, heaven on earth.

The New Age movement is very seductive and dangerous. Most people are unaware of its widespread infiltration into both Western society and into the Christian church, where it is changing traditional moral and spiritual values in a subversive and insidious fashion. As a result, some Christians unwittingly become involved in New Age practices. For example, many Christians read their horoscopes daily, "play around" with Ouija boards, have their palms read, visit fortune-tellers, or attend yoga classes. Although usually done in innocence, Christians engaging in these practices are tinkering with the occult. And the origin and power of the occult, in all its diversified forms, is Satan. The New Age movement encourages, through its philosophy and religious practices, satanic involvement. Most assuredly, where Christians fail to be on guard, Satan will make advancements into the church and into individual lives. We already saw how this can happen through the deception of reincarnation.

The New Age movement also promotes ungodly values that appeal to man's basic (and fallen) desires. It encourages covetousness and greed by promising prosperity and success. It arouses our pride by claiming we can be in complete control of our own destinies, even create our own realities. It promotes idolatry by encouraging us to seek after our own concept of God, thus avoiding accountability to the creator. Finally, it rationalizes moral infidelity by promoting a relative ethical system centered on man's personal desires and wants in opposition to God's standards.

HOW DO THE NEW AGE MOVEMENT AND CHRISTIANITY COMPARE?

God

The dominant world view of the New Age movement is pantheism, and it surfaces in Christian Science, Unity, Bahai, Transcendental

Meditation, Hare Krishna, the Church Universal and Triumphant, the Unification Church, and many other religious philosophies. Pantheism teaches that all of the universe is somehow part of God's essence. Rather than a personal Being, God is an impersonal Force (or Principle, Intellect, or Energy) that permeates the universe. Thus, God and nature are one because God cannot be separated from nature in pantheism. This impersonal It is not the creator of Christian theism. It and nature are one and the same. There's no distinction between man and It either. This is the reason New Agers can say man is divine.

Pantheism is thoroughly antithetical to the Christian view of God. The God of Scripture is not an intangible Force, one in essence with nature. The Bible reveals that God transcends nature as its creator and sustainer (Col. 1:16–17). He is a personal God. He is infinite and not to be identified with His creation. The apostle Paul warns that worshiping creation rather than the creator is exchanging "the truth of God for a lie" (Rom. 1:25). The God of Scripture is impossible to harmonize with the It of pantheism.

Man

Because man is part of God's essence, according to New Age theology, he too is divine. However, says the New Ager, the mass of humanity is ignorant of their divine potential. Thus the goal of the New Age movement is to awaken and release the divine essence in every human being. All knowledge and truth resides within man, not in a God outside and above man, and by awakening this divine potential, mankind will usher in a new age. Man will become God and the ruler of his own destiny.

The Bible, on the other hand, makes it plain that man is not divine. Although created in the image of God (Gen. 1:26), we are still *created* and only human. With regard to purely physical creation, man is no different than the rest of animal life (Eccles. 3:19–20). Nor does man exhibit a single attribute that distinguishes God as God (e.g., omniscience, omnipotence, omnipresence, sinlessness, holiness, eternality). More than once, the Bible condemns any action on the part of man or angels to seek or claim divine status (see Ezek. 28:1–10). Satan was cast out of heaven because he attempted to exalt himself as God (Isa. 14:13–15). Adam and Eve were banished from the Garden because they yielded to Satan's temptation that they could "be like God" (Gen. 3:5, 22–23). The New Age doctrine of man is antithetical to biblical revelation.

Sin

It follows that if man is divine, he must also be innately good. New Age philosophy totally rejects the biblical concept that sin is rebellion against God. To the New Ager, God is not a moral Being. In fact, what Christians call sin is actually amoral actions (neither moral nor immoral) that occur out of ignorance. Once one realizes his divine potential and gets in tune with God's essence, and thereby achieves right information, the so-called sin issue will vanish.

New Agers recognize no distinction between good and evil in an absolute sense. The concept of oneness—that all is God—prevents this. Sin must not exist in the sense we normally think of it. Rather, evil, like good, is all part of the cosmic balance. Because man is innately good, once he understands or becomes educated as to what is right and "moral," he will make the right decisions. However, since there is no absolute standard of right and wrong outside of man's own thoughts and feelings, ethics are relative. Man, not God, is the determining factor of what is right and wrong. Thus morality is subject to whatever individuals desire. Man is responsible only to himself and for himself.

This philosophy clearly denies biblical revelation and what we observe in the real world. The Bible teaches that sin not only concerns our actions but also our condition. Since the fall of Adam, man has a natural tendency to sin. It is out of this sin nature that people perform sinful acts, not only gross acts such as murder, but also sins we hardly realize we do. For example people steal pens and notepads from work. We tell white lies to save face. We fudge on our income taxes. Perhaps the best example of our innate sin nature is seen in children. Children must be taught to be good. By nature they lie, steal, cheat, and hit other children. So what the Bible reveals man confirms: we are corrupt in our very nature and, except for Jesus Christ, we all sin

(Rom. 3:23; 1 John 1:10). Once again, New Age philosophy is antithetical to the Bible, not to mention its incompatibility with the world we experience.

Jesus

One of the common threads of deception weaving through New Age ideologies is the practice of calling Jesus "divine." New Age religions separate Jesus the man from Jesus the Christ. As a man, Jesus possessed the same divine potential that all men do; although, in His case, He succeeded in perfecting and manifesting this divinity more than most. But the divine potential, the "Christ spirit" perfected in Jesus, was also perfected in Krishna, Buddha, and other religious teachers. Jesus was *a* Christ—He achieved the status of Christhood—but He was not *the* Christ. There is no *the* Christ. Thus, Jesus is not the incarnate Son of God who sacrificed Himself on the cross to bring forgiveness of sins and eternal life to all who accept Him. Instead, Jesus is just a man who, like some other great individuals, realized His divine potential and thereby became a "son of god" in the same manner anyone who fulfills his divine potential can become one with God's essence.

That Jesus is not just another guru of pantheism is clear from even a cursory examination of the Bible. Jesus taught that God is personal, not impersonal (Matt. 6:9). God can be known; He is not unknowable like the god of pantheism. Second, Jesus taught that God created (Matt. 19:4). As creator, God stands apart from creation; nature is not a part of God's essence. Third, Jesus taught that man is not divine but fallen (Mark 7:21–23) and in need of a Savior (John 14:6). Fourth, Jesus recognized a clear distinction between good and evil and taught that man is to obey Him (John 14:15). Fifth, and most importantly, Jesus claimed to be the Son of God, the holy Messiah, the Savior of the world, God in human flesh, not just a man who discovered his divine potential (John 10:30; 14:7, 9).

The Bible explicitly teaches that anyone who denies that Jesus is the Christ—the Son of God—is an antichrist (1 John 2:22) and that there are many antichrists in the world even today (1 John 2:18). The New Age movement denies this fact about Jesus.

Salvation

Because man is not sinful but innately good, he does not need to be saved. And because Jesus is not the only way to salvation, He is not the Savior. God can work through many religions.

Most New Agers believe in reincarnation and accept the doctrine of karma. If one experiences good karma in this life, he will release his divine potential and continue to move forward in future lives toward becoming one with the divine essence. Thus, salvation to a New Ager is not redemption through the work of Jesus but liberation from the illusions of this life and unity with the god-essence. Ultimately, everyone will be saved.

On the other hand, the Bible makes it clear that sin is real and that it is present in all human beings (Rom. 3:23). Scripture is equally clear that the only path to salvation is Jesus Christ (Acts 4:12; John 14:6). Moreover, the Bible teaches that there is a literal heaven, that Jesus will return a second time to receive His followers, and that believers will spend eternity in heaven with Him (John 14:1–3). This is the Bible's view of salvation. Salvation is not unity with the god-essence. And finally, as we already saw, the Bible condemns reincarnation by stating plainly that every man will die only once (Heb. 9:27) and that following death there will be the resurrection and judgment of both the saved and the lost (John 5:28–29).

Occult

A common element in New Age religion is involvement in the occult (the word *occult* carries the idea of secret or mysterious practices, often involving supernatural elements originating with Satan). The goal of New Age practitioners is to release the divine within. This entails developing a new, transforming awareness of oneself in relation to the god-force. To release this divine potential and to attain a new level of reality, altered states of consciousness are frequently sought through transcendental meditation, yoga, self-hypnotism, internal visualization, biofeedback, and other methods. Enlightenment is also sought through more direct occultic practices, such as the use of human mediums to contact the spirit world (often called *channel-*

lers) or divination (using crystal balls, palmistry, tarot card reading, astrology).

The Bible clearly condemns such practices and warns of the dangers of tapping into the spiritual (satanic) realm (Lev. 19:26, 31; Deut. 18:10–12). The only true and reliable source of spiritual truth is God's Word, the Bible. The only medium to understanding the Bible is the Holy Spirit (1 Cor. 2:10–14). And the only path to salvation is Jesus Christ.

Christianity Is Incompatible with New Age Beliefs

Teachings	Christianity	New Age
God	Personal Triune Creator	Impersonal Pantheistic A part of nature
Man	Human Sinner	Divine Innately good
Sin	Real Rebellion	Amoral or illusion Ignorance
Ethics	Absolute	Relative
Jesus	Human and divine Sinless Resurrected Savior Unique	Human only Good person Not resurrected We save ourselves We can all be "Christs"
Salvation	Only through Jesus	Reincarnation
Judgment	One chance	No judgment, many chances
Heaven	Abode of the saved	Absorption with the god-force
Hell	Abode of unsaved	Myth
Occult	Satan real Condemns occultic practices	Satan myth Encourages occultic practices

15

Is God an Environmentalist?

In 1967, historian Lynn White, Jr. published an article in *Science* entitled "The Historical Roots of Our Ecological Crisis." In this article White blamed Christianity for the ecologic crisis that dramatically came to public attention in the early 1960s. According to White, the Judeo-Christian religion is the reason Western man is so insensitive to his natural environment. The Bible teaches, claims White, that nature was created for man's personal use. Therefore, man is free to use nature as he chooses, with no regard for the welfare of the environment. Moreover, other religions, in particular primitive and Eastern religions, are more sensitive to the environment than Christianity and thus are a better source of environmental ethics.

White is not alone in blaming Christianity for the ecologic crisis. To this hour, Christianity is widely condemned in books, magazine articles, public lectures, and in other formats as the root cause of our environmental problems.

It's true that individual Christians have wrongly used biblical passages as a rationale to exploit the environment, just as some Christians were guilty of misusing (and misinterpreting) other passages to promote slavery. But the truth is, the Bible does not endorse the exploitation of the environment, and, in fact, it teaches a clear doctrine of ecological renewal and care. Before we get to the positive, however, we need to turn our attention to the environmental objections that have been raised against Christianity.

IS CHRISTIANITY TO BLAME?

Modern man's relationship with his physical environment is the same today as it was centuries before the Christian era. People throughout history, regardless of their culture or religious beliefs, have effected change on their environment for their own self-interests. To create better hunting grounds, tribes in North America, Africa, and Australia ravaged vast areas with fire centuries before the arrival of Christianity. Ancient hunters likely caused the extinction of the mammoth, mastodon, cave bear, and ground sloth. Deforestation in China occurred long before the influence of Christianized Europeans. Since antiquity, "slash-and-burn" cultivation practices have caused major erosion in many parts of the world. In classical times, overgrazing and the burning of brush and trees to create open grassland for stock devastated much of the Mediterranean world.

The earth is visibly more polluted today than in past epochs, not because of the influence of Christianity, but because modern technology allows one person with machinery to do the same damage as hundreds of people did with primitive tools and practices. And, of course, the impact on the earth today of over five billion people is immensely greater than the impact of only a half billion people estimated to have inhabited the earth in the seventeenth century. The point is, exploitation of the environment is not the product of Christianity, but the product of man. Man possesses an innate exploitative nature.

CAN NON-CHRISTIAN RELIGIONS OFFER HELP?

What the Bible teaches about ecology and environmental ethics will be examined shortly. But first we need to see that other religions do not offer a satisfactory theological foundation from which to develop an adequate environmental ethic and program.

Solutions to the ecologic crisis will result only when humanity incorporates and applies a *universal* environmental ethic on a worldwide scale. Why? Because the ecologic crisis is a worldwide problem. Since most ethics originate through religious channels, it is not surprising that various world religions are consulted to play a leadership role in formulating environmental ethics and solutions.

As we've seen, all ethics must rest on a moral absolute (i.e., God) that is *independent* of man. Otherwise, ethics become relative, subject to arbitrary modification according to man's self-interests. Under such a system, environmental ethics on a worldwide scale are impossible because one culture may decide that a certain action is acceptable while another may believe that the same action is ecologically immoral. For example, some Chinese think that killing African rhinos for their horns is perfectly acceptable, even though there are only a handful of African rhinos left. Other cultures, operating under a different set of environmental ethics, condemn this action. Who's to say who's right? Without a universal measuring stick, an unchanging moral absolute, any ethical system will fail to work on a worldwide basis. Time and again, history confirms that when man relies on his own scruples, he will ultimately seek first to fulfill his own needs. The question that needs to be answered, then, is not whether religion is the best source for environmental ethics, but which religion teaches environmental ethics from a moral absolute that provides adequate accountability.

The two religious perspectives considered more environmentally conscious than Christianity are animism (the religion of most primitive peoples) and Eastern religions (broadly speaking). These two views are thought to possess a reverence for nature not found in Christianity, so they are considered more suitable for developing an environmental ethic. Upon examination, however, both animism and Eastern religions disqualify themselves.

ANIMISM

In the 1960s, growing public awareness of the ecologic crisis caused many people to become interested in primitive cultures and their relationship with nature. In the United States, this interest focused on the American Indians. Indians were believed to possess a genuine feeling of kinship with plants and animals and a reverence for "Mother Earth" that related directly to their religious beliefs. With a few notable exceptions, American Indians did live in harmony with nature. They took from the land only what they needed and wasted little. But their ecological orientation was not motivated out of a spiritual reverence for other life forms. Rather, it was motivated out of a desire to manipulate the environment for their own welfare.

Early American Indians, like all other primitive peoples, practiced animism. They believed that both good and bad spirits indwell organic and inorganic nature (trees, animals, rocks, lakes, lightning, mountains, and so on). Because nature and the spirit world were inseparably bound together, the physical environment of the American Indian was not always friendly; it was often hostile and threatening. The American Indians' preoccupation with the spirit world had, as its goal, the comfort and safety of man, not the comfort or safety of nature. Their intent was to manipulate the spirit world so such things as good hunting, good weather, and tribal safety resulted. Reverence for nature was a side effect of their religion, an attempt to appease a hostile spirit world, not an absolute ethic taught from God. Their reverence, like all animists, was based on fear of the unknown and concern for tribal and individual well-being. Indians lived in harmony with the land to survive, but their so-called kinship with nature was not motivated by moral principles, as we might like to think.

If we turn to animism for guidance in environmental ethics, we receive a good model for individual conduct, by and large, but not a moral absolute that gives us accountability to a Being greater than ourselves.

EASTERN RELIGIONS

Eastern religions don't help us either. Because their view of God is generally pantheistic, God cannot have any power over nature. Only a God who transcends or is apart from nature (as the Christian God) can be the creator and controller of nature. And, of course, He cannot be expected to have any special interest in nature if He didn't create or control it. This alone disqualifies all Eastern religions as a source of environmental ethics. A God with no interest in or control over nature is not likely to promote environmental ethics.

The Eastern religion touted as the most ecologically sensitive is Buddhism. This is so for one major reason. The practicing Buddhist seeks to eliminate all physical needs. The appeal of such a philosophy, ecologically speaking, is that less human demands should result in less ecological abuse and less consumption of natural resources. Buddhists are taught that all sufferings come from cravings, and if there are no cravings, there is no suffering. Freedom from craving allows the practitioner to focus on following the "eightfold path" which leads to "nirvana," the highest spiritual level attainable. Whereas Western capitalism stresses consumption and the desire for material things, the Buddhist seeks to separate himself from material things.

The flaw in this philosophy, at least with regard to promoting religious-based environmental ethics, is that it is man-centered. The Buddhists' willingness to eliminate physical needs is not motivated out of a desire to conserve natural resources. It is simply a by-product of their goal to reach nirvana. Thus, Buddhism suffers from the same flaw as animism. If environmental ethics are a side effect of a religious philosophy and not a guiding doctrine, then ethics have no moral absolute to curtail man's natural tendency to exploit the environment. There is no accountability to God.

A second Eastern religion considered more ecologically sensitive than Christianity is Hinduism. This is largely due to their doctrine of *ahimsa* (the law of harmlessness toward all living things). Ahimsa has its roots in karma and the transmigration of souls. Hindus believe in the retribution in later lives for sins committed in earlier lives (karma). Because souls can wander through every form of life, all living creatures, even the simplest, are respected and preserved. Hence, many Hindus avoid harming any kind of animal life because that could affect their karma and therefore affect their future lives. The Hindus' reluctance to kill animals has allowed cows and rats to consume enormous amounts of human foods while many thousands of people starve to death.

Do you see the pattern? Hinduism, like animism and Buddhism, demonstrate reverence for other life forms but not out of an altruistic desire to save them for their own sakes. Rather, this reverence grows out of concern for their own futures. It's a by-product caused by self-interest, not a religious principle mandated by deity. To handle the

environment as we should, we need more than non-Christian religions can provide.

A CHRISTIAN VIEW OF ECOLOGY

Now that we know other religions can't give us what we so desper-
ately need, we need to explore Christianity to see if it can supply
what other religions lack: a theology that both teaches environmental ethics and holds man accountable to a moral absolute (God).

THE BIBLE SPEAKS

Throughout the Old Testament, God associates the welfare of Israel with the welfare of the land. He also instructs the Jewish people
on how to care for the land so it produces their food and yet retains its
viability (Lev. 19:25; 25:2–5). In fact, a common Old Testament theme
is that the fate of the land was directly affected by human actions.
When Israel broke God's covenant, the land suffered (Ps. 107:33–34;
Jer. 2:7; Hos. 4:1–3). The prophet Habakkuk reports that the Chalde-
ans' downfall was vindicated, in part, because they had cut down the
vast cedars of Lebanon, hunted its wild beasts, and violently misused
God's creation (Hab. 2:8, 17).

The Bible also teaches that God did not create nature just for man's
use. The earth and everything in it is God's (Ps. 24:1; Job 41:11). God
commanded all animal life to be fruitful and multiply, implying that
He wants all living things to survive and coexist in a balanced, natural environment (Gen. 1:22, 24). Scripture also teaches that nonhuman creatures are of value in themselves and are created, like man,
for a specific purpose (Job 40:15, 19). Throughout the Bible, God
demonstrates that He personally cares for nature and finds joy in it
(Ps. 104:10–14, 16–18, 21, 27). This is probably best illustrated by
how He prepared the natural environment to support animal life (see
Job 38, 39). God even purged the world of the effects of human sin
through a worldwide deluge. Then afterward, He made a covenant
with man that included all animal life. He promised Noah that as long
as the earth remained, He would never again destroy life and would
continue to preserve the regularity of nature (Gen. 9:8–11).

CHRISTIAN THEOLOGY SPEAKS

The Doctrine of Creation

Just as God created and sustains the universe, so He established natural laws by which nature operates and maintains its ecological balance. He takes an active interest in what He created; He cares for His creation. And creation is intrinsically good because He brought it into being (Gen. 1:31; Rom. 14:14).

The Doctrine of Man

The key to understanding man's relationship with the rest of creation is to understand that he has a dual position in creation. On the one hand, with regard to purely physical creation, man is equal with the rest of animal life in that he depends on his physical environment for survival. In this sense, man possesses a true kinship relationship with other life forms. On the other hand, man is created in God's image and, as such, transcends nature and is preeminent over it (see Luke 12:6–7). This gives him the ability and responsibility to take an active stewardship role over nature.

The Doctrine of the Fall

Man has a natural tendency to exploit nature. That he has done so throughout history, including the centuries prior to Christianity, we've already demonstrated. This universal exploitative nature occurred because of the fall (Gen. 3).

After Adam's creation, God placed him in the Garden of Eden and told him to "tend and keep it" (Gen. 2:15). The Garden was free of weeds, predators, and natural disasters. Adam's job was to be the steward over God's perfect natural environment. But, unfortunately, Adam rebelled against God, so he, along with his wife Eve, were expelled from the Garden. From that point on, man battled with nature to survive, and nature fought back with tooth and claw, thorns and thistles, and natural disasters.

According to Genesis 3:17–19, the fall resulted in an animosity between man and nature that did not previously exist. It marks the birth of man's intrinsic exploitative nature. The harmonious relationship that God intended between man and nature was destroyed. The Bible does not say, however, that man's caretaker role over nature was lost when Adam and Eve were expelled from the Garden. The fall did not remove any of man's accountability to God. Likewise, it did not remove his responsibilities as God's steward over nature.

The Doctrines of Dominion and Stewardship

Let me take a moment to summarize what we've covered. God is the creator, and He loves and cares for nature independently, but not above, His love and care for man. Man is in the unique position, among all created things, of being one with nature in the created realm, yet he transcends nature due to being created in the image of God. For this reason, man was given stewardship responsibilities over nature. However, due to the fall, enmity developed between man and nature, and man began to exploit his physical environment to survive. This exploitative tendency became ingrained in all mankind, and its effects became more pronounced as the human population grew and technology developed. Nevertheless, man is still accountable for his divinely given stewardship role over nature.

It needs to be understood that the natural environment in which God placed Adam and instructed him to be caretaker was a paradise that required no exploitation for Adam to survive. So whatever the words *subdue* and *dominion* mean in Genesis 1:28, they definitely do not convey environmental exploitation. The Bible never grants us a license to abuse and manipulate nature. Instead, it promotes stewardship. This concept is best illustrated in the parable of the talents (Matt. 25:14–30). The biblical definition of stewardship is caring for someone else's property with the goal of improving that property. Thus dominion, with regard to the environment, means caring for nature (God's property) as God's chosen steward. God commands us to care for nature, and we do not own what we care for. So we are not free to use nature contrary to His wishes. And from all that we have seen, God wishes nature to be protected, to be taken care of.

Moving Toward Environmental Ethics

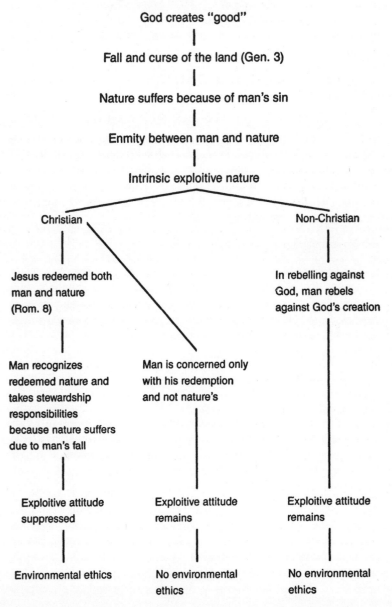

God creates "good"

Fall and curse of the land (Gen. 3)

Nature suffers because of man's sin

Enmity between man and nature

Intrinsic exploitive nature

Christian — **Non-Christian**

Jesus redeemed both man and nature (Rom. 8)

In rebelling against God, man rebels against God's creation

Man recognizes redeemed nature and takes stewardship responsibilities because nature suffers due to man's fall

Man is concerned only with his redemption and not nature's

Exploitive attitude suppressed

Exploitive attitude remains

Exploitive attitude remains

Environmental ethics

No environmental ethics

No environmental ethics

CHRISTIAN ENVIRONMENTAL ETHICS

Now that a doctrine of ecology is established, we can see a specific environmental ethic flow from Christianity. Here are some of its key tenets.

ANIMALS AND NATURAL OBJECTS HAVE RIGHTS

God created nature "very good" and provided His creatures with a healthy, balanced environment to meet all of their physical needs. Nonhuman life is of value to God, and man is instructed by the creator to care for and protect nature. Thus, wildlife and natural objects—including rivers, air, mountains, and so on—have rights. This is in harmony with those passages of Scripture that teach creation has value independently of man.

ENVIRONMENTAL ABUSE IS SIN

The Bible defines sin as "lawlessness" (1 John 3:4) and "unrighteousness" (5:17). When man destroys a unique natural habitat, pollutes a river or lake, or causes the extinction of an endangered species, he is disobeying God's instructions to act as a steward over nature. In refusing this task and abusing the environment, man rebels against God and engages in sin.

CHRISTIAN ENVIRONMENTAL ETHICS MUST CONTROL INDUSTRIAL AND TECHNICAL DEVELOPMENT

Throughout history, economic profit and technical efficiency have been the main considerations in the development of new technology. Social, moral, and environmental considerations have been secondary to economic rewards. Ethical restraints must be imposed on technology to prevent it from exploiting the environment for profit without concern for the environment. The solution to our ecologic crisis lies in the ability of present cultures to accept universal ethical principles with regard to the environment. Only the Bible presents ethical standards based on a Moral Absolute outside of man. This ethic must be implemented if environmental degradation resulting from unrestrained industrial development is to be controlled. We need environmental stewardship as a basis for our care of creation, and only Christianity can supply the ethical framework for this to happen.

CHRISTIAN ETHICS CAN BE APPLIED TO THE ENVIRONMENT

Developing environmental ethics is no more complicated than extending traditional Christian ethics to the natural realm. For example, if the human sin of greed is removed from our relationship with nature, as we are told to remove it from our relationship with people, we will operate our factories and mine our resources for profit, but not at the expense of social and environmental degradation. If the human sins of covetousness and pride are removed from our relationship with nature, we will purchase smaller cars and houses and fewer energy consuming gadgets and conveniences. If mankind extends the Golden Rule (Matt. 7:12) to include natural objects—that is, if we treat nature in the same manner as we want nature to treat us—we will not pollute our environment, destroy wildlife habitats, exterminate animal species, and we will be more willing to recycle nonrenewable resources. In short, the cardinal Christian principle of unconditional love, putting others before ourselves and giving without expecting to receive, can effectively and efficiently guide our ethical relationship with the natural environment.

No other religion or humanist philosophy in the world contains so precise and explicit ethical standards as the Bible. As long as man makes stewardship decisions within biblical moral principles, thereby caring for the whole household of creation, he will be performing his job as steward.

16

Why Don't Christians Practice What They Preach?

In the Sermon on the Mountain, Jesus said, "Let your light so shine before men, that they may see your good works and glorify your Father in heaven" (Matt. 5:16). God wants Christians to obey Him and to live according to the ethical standards described in the Bible. This is no secret, even among non-Christians. Unfortunately, no Christian consistently measures up to this standard. In one way or another, and at one time or another, every Christian fails God's standards. When unbelievers see this, regardless of the degree of the sin, they often respond with a critical admonishment that goes something like this: "I thought you were a Christian!" Or, "You call yourself a Christian?" Or, and even more contemptuous, "You Christians are a bunch of hypocrites!" Obviously, non-Christians expect Christians to practice what they preach. But does this justify the charge of hypocrisy? Even more importantly, is it a valid reason for an unbeliever to reject Christianity? I think the answer to both questions is no. Now let me show you why.

SINNERS OR HYPOCRITES?

THE LESSER CHARGE

There's no doubt that Christians go wrong, make mistakes, sin, even deliberately. The Bible affirms this at every turn. In fact, it teaches that *all* people are guilty of sin—Christians and non-Christians alike. And if anyone denies this, he is a liar (Rom. 3:23; 1 John 1:10). Indeed, the purpose of Jesus' coming, and the heart of His present ministry, is to save lost sinners. Jesus came to heal the sick, not the healthy (Matt. 9:12–13). For this reason, Christians are the first to admit they are sinners. That's how they came to Christ, accepting His invitation to all sinners to come to Him. Christianity even encourages its members to confess their sins "to one another" (James 5:16).

Does this make Christians hypocrites? No. Why? Because a hypocrite is a person who purposely and secretly claims to be something he is not. Christians who are honest and open about their sinfulness, therefore, are not hypocrites.

The heart of the problem, it seems, is that the non-Christian has the attitude that if a Christian sins, he is automatically a hypocrite. There are hypocrites in the church—this is true. Some people claim to be believers in Jesus Christ but secretly are not. Others vow to live according to Christian principles, but, when away from other Christians, don't. The confusion lies in thinking that *sinner* and *hypocrite* are synonymous. If one is a hypocrite, he is certainly a sinner. But being a sinner does not automatically mean that one is a hypocrite. All people are sinners, and thus all Christians are sinners. But not all Christians are hypocrites. In fact, because Christians so readily recognize the presence of sin in *all* people, and therefore emphasize the confession and repentance of sins among themselves, it is likely that fewer hypocrites exist within the Christian church than in any other organization, religious or secular.

The truth of Christianity is not dependent on the actions of individual Christians. We do not falsify science and say that all scientists are hypocrites because of an occasional quack. Nor do we condemn the field of medicine because some doctors perform abortions or in other ways break the Hippocratic oath. Likewise, the Christian church is not full of hypocrites simply because Christians sin.

THE MORE SERIOUS CHARGE

A much more serious objection is the claim that Christianity is hypocritical and thus fraudulent because the church's actions in history have contradicted its professed standards of love, forgiveness, and morality. The Christian church has been involved in some very brutal acts against non-believers, false religions, and even fellow Christians. Witches have been burned at the stake in the name of Christianity. Slavery has been defended. Science has been censured. Religious minorities have been persecuted. During the Middle Ages, holy wars and inquisitions resulted in the deaths of countless thousands of people. Even our present ecologic crisis has been blamed on Christian principles. Many people, judging Christianity according to the black pages of its history, have concluded that little or no good has ever come from the Christian faith. They consider Christianity a fraudulent religion and refuse to investigate its truth-claims.

This is a serious charge that deserves a serious answer. What I said above about the truth of Christianity not being dependent on the actions of its professed adherents is a starting answer, but we need to offer a fuller response.

A Borrowed Standard

First, the ethical standards critics use to judge Christianity have their source in Christianity. The critic claims that some Christians, over the ages, have engaged in horrendous atrocities, thus the Christian religion is hypocritical. But the moral absolute (ethical standard) by which the critic determines what an atrocity is turns out to be the Christian ethic. Why was murdering so-called witches wrong? God forbids murder. Why was torturing heretics during the inquisition wrong? God forbids torture. Why is abusing the environment wrong? Because God created nature "very good" and appointed man as steward over it. And so it goes. Non-Christians cannot stand in judgment over the actions of Christians without using the ethical standards described in the Bible as their source of reference. This can only mean that biblical ethics are considered the absolute standard of human morality by the very critics who reject Christianity. This reinforces the premise that Christianity is not the source of hypocrisy but people are.

Let me carry this thought a step further. Without Christianity, there would be no adequate moral foundation on which to make ethical decisions. Apart from God, one cannot judge what is right or wrong, know if what is wrong today will be wrong tomorrow, or know if what is wrong for me is also wrong for you.

All religions in the world, except Christianity, are founded on either the personal philosophies of men, without any objective verification, or are founded on historical claims that cannot be validated by archaeology or by other historical means of investigation. Only Christianity is based on historical events supported by objective, verifiable evidence. Because of this, only Christianity can legitimately offer objective truths as a basis for absolute moral decisions. Without a moral absolute independent of human thoughts and feelings, ethical systems are no more than arbitrary opinions and subject to man's whims.

Secular humanism, the New Age movement, and other religious philosophies claim that morality is relative, that morality lies within man, not God, and is determined by whatever culture one happens to reside in or by whatever beliefs one happens to agree with. Morality is simply a projection of man's own subjective feelings. There is no outside standard (such as the Bible) by which to judge good or bad.

If this philosophy is followed, persecuting minorities or murdering babies, the aged, and the infirm are perfectly acceptable acts, providing one's own belief system embraces it. In other words, carried to its logical conclusion, the philosophy that ethics are relative can result in moral anarchy because evil in one culture may be correct behavior in another. This is exactly what happened in Germany during World War II. Hitler's decision to slaughter millions of Jews was philosophically consistent with the Nazi belief system. To them, the Jews were subhuman creatures and the cause of many of man's misfortunes. Where there is no authority except man himself, there is no sin except in the eyes of the beholder. To the Germans, murdering the Jews was not a sin but a necessary and beneficial act. This kind of moral relativity is taught by many of the world's philosophies, and it allows for no ethical standard outside of man to condemn such horrendous acts.

To sum up, without a moral standard mandated by God and recorded in the Bible, there would be no universal standard of behavior applicable to all men and every culture whereby one can judge and condemn evil. With regard to the issue of hypocrisy, regardless of what individual Christians do or what the Christian church has been guilty of in past history, Christianity as the voice of God's moral will is in no way falsified. On the contrary, this is proven by the fact that the Bible is the very standard by which the Christian church has purged itself of evil and by which non-Christians themselves judge the actions of others.

Still another way to demonstrate Christianity is not hypocritical and thus fraudulent, in spite of the actions of some Christians, is to look at the positive influence Christianity has had on the world. Critics are quick to point out Christian involvement in holy wars and witch burnings, but they conveniently overlook the much greater good Christianity has contributed to mankind.

More than any other religion in the world, Christianity has contributed to human welfare, the arts, and social reform. Some of the finest paintings and sculptures in existence have been inspired by biblical characters and scenes. Many hospitals, and most colleges, orphanages, and charity organizations were begun and operated by Christians. The Christian church promoted child welfare programs until they became government policy. Today, hundreds of Christian relief agencies exist worldwide, and Christians are among the first to respond to disasters and famines wherever they occur. Christian ethics eventually undermined the structure of slavery. Before Jesus, women were the chattel of men. Jesus set the stage for women's emancipation. Many of the brutal practices in the Roman world, such as contests between gladiators and infanticide, were abolished after Christianity became the dominant religion. The political concept of checks and balances, so important to democratic government, is based on the biblical principle of wisdom being found in a "multitude of counselors" (Prov. 11:14; 15:22).

By contrast, one can look far and wide and fail to find comparable achievements growing out of any other religion in the world. Human misery at the hands of Hinduism, for example, is well known. Rather than concerning themselves with "esoteric" matters, the Christian church ministers to people. And let me add this. If one were to take a "body count" of destroyed lives as a result of misguided Christians, it would come nowhere close to the extermination resulting from other philosophical systems. The torture and murder that occurred in the twentieth century alone under the atheistic political systems of Nazi Germany and Soviet Marxism is many millions more than the number of people wrongly killed in the name of Christianity throughout the entire history of the church. As Dr. Robert Morey states, "Over one hundred and fifty million people in the last forty years have been killed by atheistic governments."[1]

THE BIBLE AND THE PROBLEM OF HYPOCRISY

There are hypocrites in the Christian church. Jesus clearly foretold this and spoke of a day when true believers will be identified and separated from the unfaithful (see Matt. 7:21–23; 13:24–30) and when all hypocrisy will be revealed (Luke 12:1–3). Jesus strongly condemns hypocrisy, especially among religious leaders who present a false sense of piety but are hypocritical to their calling (Matt. 23:15, 27).

Paul also addressed this issue. In 1 Timothy 4:1–2, Paul warns that in "later times" some people will fall away from Christianity due to the "hypocrisy of liars" (NASV). Elsewhere, in 1 Corinthians 5:11, Paul warns Christians not to associate with a professing believer who is living a life of open and direct sin (i.e., hypocrisy). In other words, Christians need to identify unrepentant hypocrites and remove them from ministering in the church. It is sad that when the church does this, so many critics take it as an opportunity to highlight the hypocrisy rather than to congratulate the church for trying to maintain its integrity. Recent events in televised evangelism illustrate this.

In his dealings with hypocrisy, Jesus did not show the gentleness He normally exhibited when confronting sinners. He was harsh and abrupt. Jesus knew that the evil of hypocrisy would discredit His work and cause countless people to turn from the church in disillusionment and disappointment. Hypocrisy is one of the most potent weapons in Satan's arsenal used to weaken the Christian testimony. A non-Christian, hearing the words and observing the actions of a hypocritical Christian, is quick to judge all of Christianity by his actions. It is tragic to think that there are many people alive today who will likely enter a Christless eternity because of the hypocrisy they observed in Christians.

Yet it must also be remembered that hypocrisy is not the product of Christianity. It is the product of sinful people. And like all other sins, the Bible condemns it. It is true that some Christians are hypocrites, but it is unfair and illogical to condemn Christianity for their ungodly actions. The truth of Christianity does not rest on the actions of its adherents. Rather, it rests on the reality of Jesus Christ and the fact that He rose from the dead to demonstrate His deity (Rom. 1:4) and confirm His promise of eternal life for those who receive Him as Lord and Savior (Rom. 10:9).

Why Do We Need a Religious Crutch?

This has been a book on Christian evidences. We have seen that Christianity is the only religion in the world that is able to validate its truth-claims with concrete, objective evidences that can be checked out. All other religions are unable to substantiate their spiritual claims in this fashion—they lack the textual, archaeological, and other historical testimonies that verify Christianity.

This is not to say, however, that the truth of Christianity rests solely on external evidences. There is a "subjective" side to Christianity that can be every bit as compelling as objective evidences. Christianity touches hearts and souls, not just minds. So it's fitting that our final apologetic task is to challenge a criticism that touches on our subjective, emotive side. I am referring here to the common statement made by unbelievers that "Christianity (and all religions in general) is a crutch for weak people."

THE HIDDEN ASSUMPTIONS

When someone accuses Christianity of being a crutch for weak people, he echoes Karl Marx's well-known dictum: "Religion is the opiate of the masses." When these, or any other, critical statements against Christianity are made, the first step in preparing a defense is to clearly understand what is being said. In particular, are there any underlying premises or assumptions? Often an evaluation of the assumptions discloses the fallacious nature of an argument and removes it as an effective objection against Christianity. Both of the above statements contain three questionable and fallacious assumptions.

The first one is that the mass of humanity is unable to cope with the realities of life—its hardships, sicknesses, disappointments, frustrations, afflictions, and deaths. People need the psychological security of Christianity or some other religion to assure them that life offers more than what they encounter in the here and now. They need to believe in a future state in which the present suffering will be gone. They need to believe in a time of universal bliss that will last forever.

Here's the second assumption: Because of the human psychological need for assurance in the face of the unknowable, and unexplainable, and painful, man created religion as a remedial measure, as an opiate for comfort and encouragement. When primitive man began to ask himself why things happened as they did, who he was, and where he was going after death, he concocted religion. Religion, then, evolved right along with man's evolving intellectual probing, social interactions, and awareness of his psychological needs.

The third assumption is this: There are a few individuals who are alert enough to perceive that people accept Christianity in order to meet these psychological needs but who themselves are fearless enough to face life without a religious crutch. Moreover, because these intrepid individuals are not addicted to religion, they are free to live life autonomously and free from the repressive rules and constraints of religion, including Christianity.

There are three sensible responses to these three assumptions, and together they demonstrate that Christianity is not a crutch for weak people (in the sense that the critic means it) and that the truth of Christianity is affirmed not only by objective evidences but by subjective experiences that reveal Jesus Christ meeting human needs at their deepest level.

THREE RESPONSES

RELIGION IS NOT A PRODUCT OF EVOLUTION

The theory that religion is a product of evolution began in the nineteenth century with the rise of Darwinian evolution and a new academic discipline called comparative religious studies. According to this theory, contemporary religions evolved from animistic roots. Animism was thought to be the key to the primitive mind and the earliest evolutionary stage of all religions. Polytheism evolved out of animism as the various spirits became viewed as individual gods. Monotheism eventually evolved out of polytheism as one of the many gods became supreme. Thus monotheism was considered the most sophisticated and advanced form of worship.

This theory was postulated most convincingly by English scholar Sir Edward Burnett Tylor in his epoch-making book *Primitive Cultures* (1871). Tylor and other intellectuals in the mid-nineteenth century, seduced by Darwin's theory of biological evolution, attempted to apply evolution to religion. Although Tylor's theory had great influence and was initially accepted by numerous students of religion, almost without alteration, it was nevertheless attacked by many of his successors.

Today the theory has fallen on hard times among many scholars because anthropologists and ethnologists have proven beyond doubt that religion is intrinsic to the oldest cultures. But if religion evolved, there should be a time when religion was absent from human cultures. And yet no such evidence has ever been found. Even Neanderthal man exhibited evidence of religious beliefs. Moreover, if monotheism evolved from animism, then primitive religions should be void of monotheism. But again, this is not the case. Not only is there no evidence that animism evolved into polytheism and later into monotheism, but there is tremendous evidence supporting just the opposite. It appears that monotheism de-evolved into polytheism and pantheism. Belief in a supreme God is a widespread characteristic of animistic religions.

Today, the various evolutionary theories on the origin of religion have largely been discredited. The assumption that religion evolved as a crutch in order to comfort fearful man and to explain the great mysteries of life is without verifiable evidence.

This becomes even more obvious when we consider the "kind" of God that Christianity supposedly evolved. The God revealed in the Bible is more than just a loving God. He is also a powerful God who knows our every thought and intention (1 Chron. 28:9) and from whom we can never hide (Ps. 139:7–12). He is a God who wants our obedience (Josh. 22:5; Luke 8:21; John 14:15) and whose wrath and judgment are totally beyond the control of man (Rom. 2:5; Eph. 5:3–6; Rev. 6:12–17). Certainly, if one were to invent a god, he would create a more manageable and less threatening one—one more easily appeased and controlled—as is the case with idol worshipers. Or one would invent a god who takes little interest in the affairs of man, such as the pantheistic god of Eastern religions.

EVEN COURAGEOUS PEOPLE NEED RELIGION

The notion that nonreligious people are courageous and don't need religion has two underlying premises: (1) Nonreligious people do not need a "crutch" to get by in life, and (2) Christians are weak people who need a crutch. Both assumptions are false.

The claim that nonreligious people don't need a crutch to get through life simply fails to measure up to what we see in the real world. There are crutches other than religion: drugs, alcohol, cigarettes, overeating, material possessions, abnormal sexual appetites, money, power . . . the list goes on and on. Many atheists use their disbelief in God as a crutch to enable them to lead a lifestyle they intuitively know is not in accord with God's moral law (Rom. 2:14–16; 7:22–23). Only the most naive person (or one in psychological denial) will claim he is totally autonomous and has no need of a crutch. The fact is, all of us need a crutch. The only real issue is what kind of crutch will we lean on?

There is reason for this. As we have seen in previous chapters, modern Western society operates according to the secular humanist world view. The object of faith to a secular humanist is himself. Yet a simple review of history demonstrates that man has never been able to attain the goals to which he aspires: a well-fed, crime-free, peaceful world without racial prejudices or inequality. Moreover, in spite of centuries of philosophical and religious experimentation, and in spite of modern science and widespread literacy, man has yet to answer the great questions plaguing him: Who am I? Why am I here? Where am I going when I die? A greater power than man is needed to create the utopian world we dream about, and a greater intelligence than man is needed to answer the ageless questions on the meaning of life.

The other assumption—that Christians are weak because they rely on God—is one of the most absurd excuses ever concocted to justify rejecting Christianity. Nowhere in the annals of history can one find more courage in the face of adversity, more perseverance in the face of affliction, and more boldness in the face of persecution than what faithful Christians have displayed. According to Jesus, the greatest expression of love is that one "lay down one's life for his friends" (John 15:13), and He set the example by dying on the cross for all mankind. From the time of His death to the present, countless hundreds of thousands of Christians have courageously faced persecution, torture, and death for their faith. The apostle Paul wrote of his own suffering for Jesus:

> Five times I received from the Jews thirty-nine lashes. Three times I was beaten with rods, once I was stoned, three times I was shipwrecked, a night and a day I have spent in the deep. I have been on frequent journeys, in dangers from rivers, dangers from robbers, dangers from my countrymen, dangers from the Gentiles, dangers in the city, dangers in the wilderness, dangers on the sea, dangers among false brethren; I have been in labor and hardship, through many sleepless nights, in hunger and thirst, often without food, in cold and exposure. . . . (2 Cor. 11:24–27, NASV)

Christians are not weak people. In modern society, where the Christian world view is ridiculed and rejected in movies, books, television, newspapers, and universities, where individual Christians are mocked for their faith and rejected by friends and coworkers when they try to talk about their Lord, it is far, far easier to be an unbeliever. Those who claim Christians are weak have never tried to live an active Christian life.

The Real Reason

The relationship between God and man is one of dependence. God is creator, and we are created. This means that we depend on God for our very existence. God had a purpose for creating us. He desired to have fellowship with us and for us in turn to have fellowship with Him and to worship Him (hence revelation). This relationship was designed to be everlasting, so God created us to have eternal peace and eternal life with Him. This means that we must depend on Him for our continued welfare—our physical, mental, and spiritual happiness. Unfortunately, humanity became separated from God through willful rebellion, and a Savior was needed to reconcile us to God. God Himself, through His Son Jesus, became our advocate for that purpose (1 John 2:1).

Now in man's rebellion against God, he often seeks to suppress his dependence on God (Rom. 1:18). He does this in two ways: total rejection of God's existence (atheism) or rejection of the Savior (non-Christian religions). Nevertheless, and in spite of this attempted suppression, man's knowledge of the one true God and his dependence on Him is never totally repressed. People know intuitively that God exists and that they need Him (Rom. 1:19–20). In his typical unassuming fashion, C. S. Lewis said it this way:

> God made us: invented us as a man invents an engine. A car is made to run on petrol, and it won't run properly on anything else. Now God designed the human machine to run on Himself. He Himself is the fuel our spirits were designed to burn, or the food our spirits were designed to feed on. There isn't any other. That's why it's just no good asking God to make us happy in our own way without bothering about religion. God can't give us happiness and peace apart from Himself, because it isn't there. There's no such thing.[1]

Why some people wish to repress the truth of God's existence and therefore feel justified in mocking Christianity as a crutch for weak people is a topic that can fill an entire book. But the essential reason can be summarized as follows.

If God exists as revealed in the Bible, He is the sovereign, all-powerful, all-knowing creator of the universe. This means that mankind is not autonomous and that he is not the measure of all things as the secular world maintains. If we are not autonomous, then we are accountable to someone else, namely God. Fallen man, in his rebellion, does not want to be accountable to God (Rom. 8:7; Eph. 4:17–19). So he struggles to maintain a false sense of autonomy, and he perceives those whom God has touched with truth as weaklings, as people needing a religious crutch in order to cope with life. The tragic paradox in this scenario is that the very things the unbeliever strives so hard to achieve in his autonomy—his total inner fulfillment and peace of mind—is his for the asking through the "crutch" of Jesus Christ. Apart from that "crutch," though, the unbeliever will never obtain his deepest desires.

ONLY JESUS CHRIST MEETS HUMAN NEEDS AT THEIR DEEPEST LEVEL

We now come to the most serious of the three assumptions noted above: Christians need the "psychological" assurance of Christianity in order to cope with life.

What *Crutch* and *Weak* Mean to a Christian

Now I can make a statement that would have sounded contradictory earlier: *Christianity is a crutch for weak people!* Obviously, my definitions of *crutch* and *weak* are different from the critic's. Nowhere in Scripture is a Christian's faith seen as a crutch in the sense of an escape from the reality of a fallen, suffering world (John 17:15). Likewise, nowhere are Christians portrayed as weaklings. On the other hand, throughout Scripture our faith is seen as a supporting pillar, an anchor, a means to healing broken and damaged lives. Likewise, throughout Scripture, believers are seen as depending on and drawing strength from the person who created and sustains them (2 Cor. 12:9–10) and who offers them life more abundantly (John 10:10). It's in these senses that Christianity is a crutch and Christians are weak. We gladly accept the power of God to us through His Son Jesus Christ (John 14:16).

Why We Need a Crutch

There are three basic needs all people seek to fulfill in order to have peace of mind. First, physical needs: food, shelter, rest, warmth, and so on. Second, emotional or psychological needs: love, acceptance, self-esteem, and many others. These two needs are tangible and easy to identify, and they are fulfilled by either our physical environment or other people. We need food and shelter to live; we get this from our environment. We need love, acceptance, and a feeling of worth to function happily in human society; we get this from human relationships.

Being human also means that we seek to satisfy a third basic need: spiritual fulfillment—peace of mind with regard to a belief in a supernatural Being who can answer life's most perplexing questions in a relevant and believable way that is consistent with reality. The quest for spiritual peace of mind is a worldwide phenomena and a characteristic of mankind as far back as history and archaeology allow us to investigate. As mentioned earlier, all peoples in every culture exhibit a belief in supernatural beings and seek to live in harmony with them. Cultures that have attempted to suppress this instinctive drive have invariably met with failure. The religious fervor in atheistic communist countries, now that religious freedom is returning, is an open acknowledgment that no society can totally suppress humankind's spiritual need.

C. S. Lewis and others have argued effectively that every natural desire the family of man exhibits is a manifestation of a real and necessary human need. In the physical realm, we crave food because we are hungry; we crave warmth when we become cold; we crave sexual fulfillment because we are created to enjoy intimate physical relationships. Likewise, in the psychological realm, we desire love because we were created to be loved, self-esteem because we were created of value. In the same manner, we crave spiritual fulfillment because God has placed this desire in us. As fourth-century theologian Augustine said, "Thou [God] hast made us for Thyself, and our heart is restless until it rests in Thee."

It is logical to assume that if man possesses a natural desire for something in which the world offers no fulfillment, there is something outside the world that will fulfill it. In short, we will have no longings that are unfulfillable, including spiritual longings.

It is crucial at this point to see something very clearly. Of the three innate drives we seek to fulfill, the spiritual drive is the most vital for peace of mind. Let me explain. Physical health does not necessarily lead to peace of mind. The suicide rate among handicapped people is far below the national average. Many handicapped people experience a genuine peace of mind as a result of spiritual fulfillment. Likewise, neither money nor material possessions guarantee peace of mind. Many spirit-filled poor people are vastly more content and happier than many rich people. Nor does emotional fulfillment necessarily lead to peace of mind. The suicide rate among mental-health workers (psychologists, therapists, etc.) is as high as it is in any other profession (some say higher). One would expect that those most knowledgeable in the means of attaining emotional good health would be the ones most likely to achieve it, but that's not necessarily true. As another example, many thousands of prisoners, isolated from normal social interactions, and after years of living angry, violent, and bitter lives, have come to possess a profound peace of mind and deep spiritual fulfillment by experiencing God's love and forgiveness.

What's my point? This: Whereas fulfilling spiritual needs can result in peace of mind in spite of unfulfilled physical or psychological needs, the opposite is not true. Fulfilling physical or psychological needs does not lead to peace of mind without spiritual fulfillment. Regardless of how satisfying one's life is with regard to good health, material prosperity, and emotional contentment, there exists a longing for something that this earth or human relationships cannot provide: spiritual peace of mind. And only God through Jesus Christ can satisfy that longing.

Two Objections

Before moving on, I want to address two objections that may have surfaced in your mind.

1. "I'm not a religious person, and I don't go to church. I have peace of mind without religion, so obviously religion is unnecessary in order to have peace of mind."

I'm not saying no peace of mind can result from good health or emotional stability. Obviously, fulfilling either of these two needs will result in a certain amount of satisfaction or else they would not be real human drives. But this is a much different kind of peace of mind than what one attains through spiritual fulfillment. Peace of mind that relies on good health, financial security, or emotional stability is tenuous and will vanish if these things are threatened. On the other hand, peace of mind founded on spiritual fulfillment will never die because its stability rests on the eternal power of God, not on human strength, success, or earthly objects.

2. "I agree that spiritual peace of mind supersedes all other human drives. But Christianity is not the only religion that offers spiritual fulfillment. Millions of people around the world worship other gods and follow other religions, and they too experience what you call 'peace of mind.'"

This objection contains a degree of truth. Spiritual fulfillment can be achieved in non-Christian religions. But the error here is that other religions are fakes. In other words, as pointed out numerous times throughout this book, they are perversions of religious truth. They are not genuine revelations from God. If Christianity is the only true religion, then Christianity alone will offer eternal peace of mind. False religions can only offer a false sense of security because they do not have the correct answers to life's bewildering questions, especially to What happens to me when I die?

To see this played out in real life, one needs only to examine religious conversions. Many millions of practitioners of false religions have converted to Christianity. They all acknowledge that Christianity is the only true religion and that what they thought previously was spiritual peace of mind turned out to be spiritual deception. On the other hand, it is very uncommon to see Christians convert to non-Christian religions. It is much more natural to walk from darkness to light than it is to walk from light to darkness (John 8:12). The few non-Christian religions that do boast a constituent of former Christians (such as Mormonism and Jehovah's Witnesses) all use the Bible as a "holy book" and parallel many of their teachings with Christian doctrine, thereby employing a subtle and deceptive way of enticing Christians into accepting their heretical beliefs.

How Spiritual Fulfillment Works

Christianity offers spiritual fulfillment in two ways.

The Philosophical Approach

I earlier defined spiritual fulfillment as "peace of mind with regard to a belief in a supernatural Being who can answer life's most perplexing questions in a relevant and believable way that is consistent with reality." Thus, in the Christian world view, *spiritual fulfillment* is gaining answers to precisely the same questions that the non-Christian world cannot answer:

- Who am I? What is my status in relation to the rest of life and the cosmos?
- Where did I come from? What is the origin of my existence?
- Why am I here? What purpose do I have for my existence?
- What happens to me when I die? Is there life after death, and how do I obtain it?

All of these questions are unanswerable by science or philosophy because they involve issues beyond the scientist's or philosopher's ability to respond. They are unanswerable by non-Christian religions because they do not have divine revelation. These questions can only be answered by an all-powerful, all-knowing Intelligence who stands above and apart from humanity and yet who loves His creatures so much that He invites them to share in a loving personal relationship with Him. This describes only the God of Scripture. Since God created man, He knows exactly what man needs to achieve eternal and complete happiness.

Christianity is true precisely because it offers answers to life's great mysteries that are in total harmony and consistency with the world as it exists. Unlike other religions, the Christian world view is coherent and believable; it is not mystical, esoteric, or far-fetched.

The Practical Approach

Christianity is also true because it meets human needs at their deepest level in a pragmatic way. Being a Christian is not always easy, but it promises something no other religion in the world can offer: it replaces the old, beaten self with a new spirit-filled self. Christianity has been the world's most successful religion not only because it is the true revelation of God but because it makes changes in the inner man. While other religions have rules and regulations to follow, Christianity has a risen Savior that promises a born-again life (John 3:3) if we trust in Him. Jesus assures us that He "came that [we] might have life, and might have it abundantly" (John 10:10, NASV; see Phil. 4:5–7, 19).

Jesus is our crutch because we cannot attain eternal peace and life without Him. Only God has the answers to the questions of life, and only through Jesus Christ can we experience spiritual peace of mind. Prominent theologian J. I. Packer put it like this: "Once you become aware that the main business that you are here for is to know God, most of life's problems fall into place of their own accord."[2]

Is Christianity a crutch for weak people? Yes, in the same sense that gasoline is a crutch for an automobile. As Lewis said, Christians "run" on Jesus Christ—not because they are weaklings, but because God's power becomes our power through acknowledging our dependence on Him. The apostle Paul says it best:

And He has said to me, "My grace is sufficient for you, for power is perfected in weakness." Most gladly, therefore, I will rather boast about my weaknesses, that the power of Christ may dwell in me. Therefore I am well content with weaknesses, with insults, with distresses, with persecutions, with difficulties, for Christ's sake; for when I am weak, then I am strong. (2 Cor. 12:9–10, NASV)

Notes

Chapter One

[1]John Warwick Montgomery, *LAW AND GOSPEL: A STUDY FOR INTE-GRATING FAITH AND PRACTICE* (Merrifield, VA: Christian Legal Society, 1986), 34.

[2]For a brief but fascinating history of Christian apologetics, complete with selected readings from the major apologists, see *CLASSICAL READINGS IN CHRISTIAN APOLOGETICS: A.D. 100–1800,* ed. L. Russ Bush (Grand Rapids, MI: Zondervan, 1983).

[3]Edward John Carnell, *AN INTRODUCTION TO CHRISTIAN APOLO-GETICS* (Grand Rapids, MI: William B. Eerdmans, 1952), 7.

[4]For some examples, see Saint Augustine's *CONFESSIONS,* trans. R. S. Pine-Coffin (New York, NY: Penguin Books, 1979); C. S. Lewis's *SURPRISED BY JOY* (New York, NY: Harcourt Brace Jovanovich, 1955); and *THE INTEL-LECTUALS SPEAK OUT ABOUT GOD,* ed. Roy Abraham Varghese (Chicago, IL: Regnery Gateway, 1984).

[5]R. C. Sproul, John Gerstner, and Arthur Lindsley, *CLASSICAL APOLO-GETICS* (Grand Rapids, MI: Zondervan, 1984), 16.

[6]Clark H. Pinnock, *SET FORTH YOUR CASE* (Nutley, NJ: Craig, 1968), 88.

[7]John Warwick Montgomery, *FAITH FOUNDED ON FACT: ESSAYS IN EVI-DENTIAL APOLOGETICS* (Nashville, TN: Thomas Nelson, 1978), 123.

[8]Carnell, ibid.

Chapter Two

[1]George H. Smith, *ATHEISM: THE CASE AGAINST GOD* (Buffalo, NY: Prometheus, 1979), 16.

[2]Steve Hallman, "Christianity and Humanism: A Study in Contrasts," *AFA JOURNAL* (March 1991), 11.

[3]Robert Jastrow, *GOD AND THE ASTRONOMERS* (New York, NY: W. W. Norton & Company, 1978), 116.

[4]More is said on general and special revelation in chaps. 9 and 10.

[5]Most books giving arguments for God's existence tend to be very techni-cal, for academic specialists only. But here I will cite five books, each geared

for nonspecialists, and each well worth your time. They are listed in their order of difficulty, from the easiest to comprehend to the ones requiring more reflection: William Lane Craig, *THE EXISTENCE OF GOD AND THE BEGINNING OF THE UNIVERSE* (San Bernardino, CA: Here's Life, 1979); Norman Geisler and Ron Brooks, *WHEN SKEPTICS ASK* (Wheaton, IL: Victor, 1990); C. S. Lewis, *MERE CHRISTIANITY* (New York, NY: Macmillan, 1952); D. Elton Trueblood, *PHILOSOPHY OF RELIGION*, reprint ed. (Grand Rapids, MI: Baker, 1973); J. P. Moreland and Kai Nielson, *DOES GOD EXIST? THE GREAT DEBATE* (Nashville, TN: Thomas Nelson, 1990).

[6]C. S. Lewis demonstrates this fact in his book *THE ABOLITION OF MAN* (New York, NY: Macmillan, 1947).

Chapter Three

[1]Gleason L. Archer, Jr., *A SURVEY OF OLD TESTAMENT INTRODUCTION* (Chicago, IL: Moody, 1974), 25.

[2]For these and additional archaeological evidences for the historical reliability of the Bible, see Josh McDowell, *EVIDENCE THAT DEMANDS A VERDICT* (San Bernardino, CA: Here's Life, 1979), 65–73; Clifford A. Wilson, *ROCKS, RELICS AND BIBLICAL RELIABILITY* (Grand Rapids, MI: Zondervan, 1977); Edwin Yamauchi, *THE STONES AND THE SCRIPTURES* (Grand Rapids, MI: Baker, 1972); K. A. Kitchen, *THE BIBLE IN ITS WORLD* (Downers Grove, IL: InterVarsity, 1977).

[3]Nelson Glueck, *RIVERS IN THE DESERT* (Philadelphia, PA: Jewish Publications Society of America, 1969), 31.

[4]For these figures and those that follow, refer to F. F. Bruce, *THE NEW TESTAMENT DOCUMENTS: ARE THEY RELIABLE?* (Downers Grove, IL: InterVarsity, 1984), and McDowell, *EVIDENCE THAT DEMANDS A VERDICT,* ibid.

[5]Josh McDowell, "Evidence for the Historical Accuracy of the New Testament," in *THE INTELLECTUALS SPEAK OUT ABOUT GOD*, ibid., 273–274.

[6]John A. T. Robinson, *REDATING THE NEW TESTAMENT* (Philadelphia, PA: Westminster, 1976).

[7]Sir Frederick Kenyon, *THE BIBLE AND ARCHAEOLOGY,* as quoted in McDowell, *EVIDENCE THAT DEMANDS A VERDICT,* 41.

[8]John Warwick Montgomery, *THE LAW ABOVE THE LAW* (Minneapolis, MN: Bethany, 1975), 87–88.

[9]For further verification of this, see Harold Lindsell's *THE BATTLE FOR THE BIBLE* (Grand Rapids, MI: Zondervan, 1976), chap. 9; Gleason L. Archer's *ENCYCLOPEDIA OF BIBLE DIFFICULTIES* (Grand Rapids, MI: Zondervan, 1982).

[10]Montgomery, *THE LAW ABOVE THE LAW,* 87.

[11]Ibid., 88.

[12]Ibid., 88–89.

[13]J. P. Moreland, *SCALING THE SECULAR CITY: A DEFENSE OF CHRISTIANITY* (Grand Rapids, MI: Baker, 1991), 138.

[14]The following information comes from John Warwick Montgomery's *HISTORY AND CHRISTIANITY* (San Bernardino, CA: Here's Life, 1965), 32–34.

[15]Also see F. F. Bruce, *THE NEW TESTAMENT DOCUMENTS: ARE THEY RELIABLE?* ibid.

[16]McDowell, *EVIDENCE THAT DEMANDS A VERDICT,* 81–85.

[17]Bruce, *THE NEW TESTAMENT DOCUMENTS,* 106–108.

[18]McDowell, *EVIDENCE THAT DEMANDS A VERDICT,* 82.

[19]Bruce, *THE NEW TESTAMENT DOCUMENTS,* 119.

[20]McDowell, *EVIDENCE THAT DEMANDS A VERDICT,* 83.

[21]Ibid.

[22]Bruce, *THE NEW TESTAMENT,* 119.

[23]Josh McDowell, *A READY DEFENSE,* compiled by Bill Wilson (San Bernardino, CA: Here's Life, 1990), 24.

Chapter Four

[1]Clark H. Pinnock, *SET FORTH YOUR CASE* (Nutley, NJ: The Craig Press, 1968), 71.

Chapter Five

[1]"The Time Is at Hand," in *STUDIES IN THE SCRIPTURES,* Series II (Brooklyn, NY: Watchtower Bible and Tract Society, 1909), 99.

[2]Quoted in Walter Martin's *THE NEW CULTS* (Ventura, CA: Regal, 1980), 147.

[3]John H. Gerstner, *REASONS FOR FAITH,* reprint ed. (Grand Rapids, MI: Baker, 1967), 115.

[4]Norman Geisler, *CHRISTIAN APOLOGETICS* (Grand Rapids, MI: Baker, 1987), 374.

[5]Norman Geisler and William Nix, *A GENERAL INTRODUCTION TO THE BIBLE* (Chicago, IL: Moody Press, 1968), 138–145.

Chapter Six

[1]Some excellent books on Jesus' historicity are Gary R. Habermas's *THE VERDICT OF HISTORY* (Nashville, TN: Thomas Nelson, 1988); F. F. Bruce's *JESUS AND CHRISTIAN ORIGINS OUTSIDE THE NEW TESTAMENT* (Grand Rapids, MI: William B. Eerdmans, 1974); E. M. Blaiklock's *JESUS CHRIST: MAN OR MYTH?* (Nashville, TN: Thomas Nelson, 1974).

[2]Peter Stoner and Robert Newman, *SCIENCE SPEAKS* (Chicago, IL: Moody Press, 1976), 106–107.

[3]C. S. Lewis, *THE CASE FOR CHRISTIANITY* (New York, NY: Macmillan, no date), 45.

Chapter Seven

[1]The following information and quotes are from John Warwick Montgomery's *LAW AND GOSPEL*, 34–35.

Chapter Nine

[1]For more information on the different concepts of God, I would recommend these resources: Norman L. Geisler and William D. Watkins, *WORLDS APART: A HANDBOOK ON WORLD VIEWS*, 2nd ed. (Grand Rapids, MI: Baker, 1989); Josh McDowell and Don Stewart, *HANDBOOK OF TODAY'S RELIGIONS* (San Bernardino, CA: Here's Life, 1983); James W. Sire, *THE UNIVERSE NEXT DOOR: A BASIC WORLD VIEW CATALOG*, 2nd ed. (Downers Grove, IL: InterVarsity, 1988).

[2]C. S. Lewis's *MERE CHRISTIANITY*, and his *THE ABOLITION OF MAN*.

[3]Henry Morris, *THE GOD WHO IS REAL* (Grand Rapids, MI: Baker, 1988), 51.

[4]Simon Greenleaf, "The Testimony of the Evangelists," quoted in Montgomery, *THE LAW ABOVE THE LAW*, 95.

[5]Henry Clarence Thiessen, *LECTURES IN SYSTEMATIC THEOLOGY*, rev. ed. (Grand Rapids, MI: William B. Eerdmans, 1983), 106.

Chapter Ten

[1]Clark H. Pinnock, *REASON ENOUGH* (Downers Grove, IL: InterVarsity, 1980), 10.

[2]Lewis, *THE CASE FOR CHRISTIANITY*, 55.

[3]R. C. Sproul, *REASONS TO BELIEVE* (Grand Rapids, MI: Zondervan, 1982), chap. 3.

Chapter Eleven

[1]Two books that present an insightful look at the historic relationship between the Bible and science are James C. Livingston, *MODERN CHRISTIAN THOUGHT FROM THE ENLIGHTENMENT TO VATICAN II* (New York, NY: Macmillan, 1971) and Bernard Ramm, *THE CHRISTIAN VIEW OF SCIENCE AND SCRIPTURE* (Grand Rapids, MI: William B. Eerdmans, 1987).

[2]Kenny Barfield, *WHY THE BIBLE IS NUMBER 1* (Grand Rapids, MI: Baker, 1988), 185.

[3]Ronald H. Nash, *FAITH AND REASON: SEARCHING FOR A RATIONAL FAITH* (Grand Rapids, MI: Zondervan, 1988), 47–48.

[4]Larry Laudan, *PROGRESS AND ITS PROBLEMS: TOWARD A THEORY OF SCIENTIFIC GROWTH* (Berkeley, CA: University of California Press, 1977).

[5]Thomas S. Kuhn, *THE STRUCTURE OF SCIENTIFIC REVOLUTIONS*, 2nd ed. (Chicago, IL: University of Chicago Press, 1970), 64–65, 77, 79, 127–128.

For a good discussion of Kuhn's argument, see Phillip E. Johnson's *DARWIN ON TRIAL* (Downers Grove, IL: InterVarsity, 1991), 118–122.

[6]Henry M. Morris and Gary E. Parker, *WHAT IS CREATION SCIENCE?* (San Diego, CA: Creation Life, 1982), 63.

[7]Sir Fred Hoyle, "Hoyle on Evolution," *NATURE*, 294 (November 1981), 105, quoted in Luther D. Sunderland, *DARWIN'S ENIGMA; FOSSILS AND OTHER PROBLEMS* (Santee, CA: Master Books, 1984), 58–59.

[8]For an excellent analysis in favor of these and other old-earth dating methods, see Robert C. Newman and Herman J. Eckelmann, Jr., *GENESIS ONE AND THE ORIGIN OF THE EARTH* (Hatfield, PA: Interdisciplinary Biblical Research Institute, 1991).

[9]Morris and Parker, *WHAT IS CREATION SCIENCE?* 254–257.

[10]Robert C. Newman, "Inanimate Design As a Problem for Nontheistic Worldviews," in *EVIDENCE FOR FAITH*, ed. John Warwick Montgomery (Dallas, TX: Probe Books, 1991), 69.

[11]J. P. Moreland, *SCALING THE SECULAR CITY*, 219–220. Henry Morris's *BIBLICAL COSMOLOGY AND MODERN SCIENCE* (Phillipsburg, NJ: Presbyterian and Reformed, 1982), 58–68, offers a fuller discussion of the major literal, six-day creationist understandings of the opening chapters of Genesis.

[12]See, for example, Luther D. Sutherland's *DARWIN'S ENIGMA* (Santee, CA: Master Books, 1984).

[13]Chandra Wickramasinghe, "Science and the Divine Origin Of Life," in *THE INTELLECTUALS SPEAK OUT ABOUT GOD*, 35.

Chapter Twelve

[1]R. C. Sproul, John Gerstner, and Arthur Lindsley, *CLASSICAL APOLOGETICS*, 161.

[2]Ibid., 284.

[3]Ibid., 283, 285.

[4]Carnell, *AN INTRODUCTION TO CHRISTIAN APOLOGETICS*, 268.

[5]David Hume, *AN ENQUIRY CONCERNING HUMAN UNDERSTANDING* (La Salle, NY: Open Court, 1955), 120–145.

[6]C. S. Lewis, *MIRACLES* (New York, NY: Macmillan, 1978), 102.

[7]Richard Whately, "Historic Doubts Relative to Napoleon Bonaparte," in *ESSAYS IN PHILOSOPHY*, ed. Houston Peterson (New York, NY: Pocket Books, 1959), 143–171.

[8]Lewis, ibid., 46.

[9]Nash, *FAITH AND REASON*, chap. 16.

[10]Carnell, *AN INTRODUCTION TO CHRISTIAN APOLOGETICS*, 267.

[11]Ibid., 258.

[12]Lewis, *MIRACLES*, 47.

[13]Ibid., 132–133.

[14]Ibid., 133.

[15]Josh McDowell and Bill Wilson, *HE WALKED AMONG US* (San Bernardino, CA: Here's Life, 1988), chap. 13.

Chapter Thirteen
[1]C. S. Lewis, *THE PROBLEM OF PAIN* (New York, NY: Macmillan, 1962), 26.
[2]Lewis, *MIRACLES,* 121–122.
[3]Norman L. Geisler, *THE ROOTS OF EVIL,* 2nd ed. (Richardson, TX: Probe Books, 1978), 36.
[4]Ibid., 45.
[5]Ibid., 51–52.

Chapter Fourteen
[1]Walter R. Martin, "Reincarnation and the Bible," *CHRISTIAN RESEARCH NEWSLETTER* (August–September, 1990), 5.
[2]Walter R. Martin, *THE KINGDOM OF THE CULTS* (Minneapolis, MI: Bethany House, 1981), 289–291.
[3]Joseph P. Gudel, Robert M. Bowman, Jr., and Dan R. Schlesinger, "Reincarnation—Did the Church Suppress It?" *CHRISTIAN RESEARCH JOURNAL* (Summer 1987), 9.
[4]Unless noted otherwise, the remaining scriptural citations in this chapter are from the NASV.
[5]Martin, *THE KINGDOM OF THE CULTS,* 293.

Chapter Sixteen
[1]Robert A. Morey, *THE NEW ATHEISM AND THE EROSION OF FREEDOM* (Minneapolis, MN: Bethany, 1986), 148–149.

Chapter Seventeen
[1]Lewis, *THE CASE FOR CHRISTIANITY,* 43.
[2]J. I. Packer, *KNOWING GOD* (Downers Grove, IL: InterVarsity, 1973), 29.